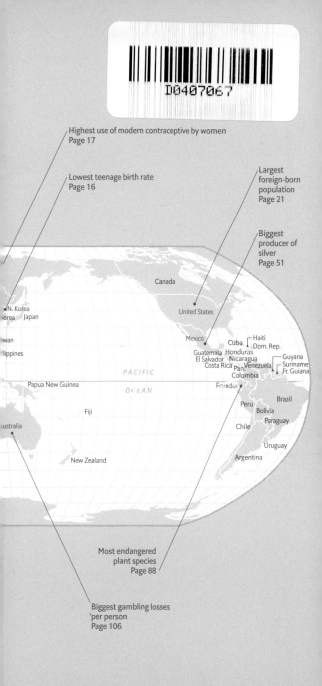

Highest use of modern contraceptive by women
Page 17

Lowest teenage birth rate
Page 16

Largest foreign-born population
Page 21

Biggest producer of silver
Page 51

Canada

N. Korea
orea Japan

wan

lippines

United States

Mexico

Cuba ┌ Haiti
└ Dom. Rep.
Guatemala Honduras
El Salvador Nicaragua
Costa Rica Pan Venezuela
Colombia

┌ Guyana
└ Suriname
└ Fr. Guiana

Papua New Guinea

PACIFIC

Ecuador

OCEAN

Fiji

Peru

Brazil

Bolivia

Paraguay

ustralia

Chile

New Zealand

Uruguay

Argentina

Most endangered plant species
Page 88

Biggest gambling losses 'per person
Page 106

The
Economist

POCKET
WORLD IN
FIGURES

2019 Edition

Published by
Profile Books Ltd
3 Holford Yard
Bevin Way
London WC1X 9HD

Published under exclusive licence from
The Economist by Profile Books, 2018

Material researched by

Andrea Burgess, Lisa Davies, Graham Douglas, Mark Doyle,
Ian Emery, Conrad Heine, Carol Howard, David McKelvey,
Georgina McKelvey, Guy Scriven, Christopher Wilson, Pip Wroe

The greatest care has been taken in compiling this book. However,
no responsibility can be accepted by the publishers or compilers
for the accuracy of the information presented.

Typeset in Econ Sans Condensed by MacGuru Ltd

Printed and bound in Italy by L.E.G.O. Spa

A CIP catalogue record for this book is available
from the British Library

ISBN 978 1 78816 114 5

Contents

CONTENTS

Health and welfare

Culture and entertainment

Introduction

This 2019 edition of *The Economist Pocket World in Figures* presents and analyses data about the world in two sections:

The **world rankings** consider and rank the performance of 185 countries against a range of indicators in five sections: geography and demographics, business and economics, politics and society, health and welfare, and culture and entertainment. The countries included are those which had (in 2016) a population of at least 1m or a GDP of at least $3bn; they are listed on pages 250–53. New rankings this year include topics as diverse as the average growth in refugee populations, the most congested cities, which species are the most endangered, cancer deaths, foreign-born populations, countries that imprison journalists, the most expensive places to go to the cinema and countries with the most millionaires. Some of the rankings data are shown as charts and graphs.

The **country profiles** look in detail at 64 major countries, listed on page 109, plus profiles of the euro area and the world.

Test your *Pocket World in Figures* knowledge with our **World Rankings Quiz** on pages 242–7. Answers can be found in the corresponding world rankings section.

Notes

The extent and quality of the statistics available vary from country to country. Every care has been taken to specify the broad definitions on which the data are based and to indicate cases where data quality or technical difficulties are such that interpretation of the figures is likely to be seriously affected. Nevertheless, figures from individual countries may differ from standard international statistical definitions. The term "country" can also refer to territories or economic entities.

Definitions of the statistics shown are given on the relevant page or in the glossary on pages 248–9. Figures may not add exactly to totals, or percentages to 100, because of rounding or, in the case of GDP, statistical adjustment. Sums of money have generally been converted to US dollars at the official exchange rate ruling at the time to which the figures refer.

Some country definitions
Macedonia is officially known as the Former Yugoslav Republic of Macedonia. Data for Cyprus normally refer to Greek Cyprus only. Data for China do not include Hong Kong or Macau. For countries such as Morocco they exclude disputed areas. Congo-Kinshasa refers to the Democratic Republic of Congo, formerly known as Zaire. Congo-Brazzaville refers to the other Congo. Euro area data normally refer to the 19 members that had adopted the euro as at December 31 2017: Austria, Belgium, Cyprus, Estonia, Finland, France, Germany, Greece, Ireland, Italy, Latvia, Lithuania, Luxembourg, Malta, Netherlands, Portugal, Slovakia, Slovenia and Spain. Euro area (16) refers to the 16 countries in the euro area that are members of the OECD. Data referring to the European Union include the United Kingdom, which in June 2016 voted in a referendum to leave the EU. Negotiations over the country's departure are due to run until 2019. For more information about the EU, euro area and OECD see the glossary on pages 248–9.

Statistical basis
The all-important factor in a book of this kind is to be able to make reliable comparisons between countries. Although this is never quite possible for the reasons stated above, the best route, which this book takes, is to compare data for the same year or period and to use

actual, not estimated, figures wherever possible. In some cases, only OECD members are considered. Where a country's data are excessively out of date, they are excluded. The research for this edition was carried out in 2018 using the latest available sources that present data on an internationally comparable basis.

Data in the country profiles, unless otherwise indicated, refer to the year ending December 31 2016. Life expectancy, crude birth, death and fertility rates are based on 2015–20 estimated averages; energy data are for 2014 and 2015 and religion data for 2010; marriage and divorce, employment, health and education, consumer goods and services data refer to the latest year for which figures are available.

Other definitions

Data shown in country profiles may not always be consistent with those shown in the world rankings because the definitions or years covered can differ.

Statistics for principal exports and principal imports are normally based on customs statistics. These are generally compiled on different definitions to the visible exports and imports figures shown in the balance of payments section.

Energy-consumption data are not always reliable, particularly for the major oil-producing countries; consumption per person data may therefore be higher than in reality. Energy exports can exceed production and imports can exceed consumption if transit operations distort trade data or oil is imported for refining and re-exported.

Abbreviations and conventions
(see also glossary on pages 248–9)

bn	billion (one thousand million)	km	kilometre
		m	million
EU	European Union	PPP	purchasing power parity
GDP	gross domestic product	TOE	tonnes of oil equivalent
GNI	gross national income	trn	trillion (one thousand billion)
ha	hectare		
kg	kilogram	...	not available

World rankings

Countries: natural facts

Countries: the largest[a]
'000 sq km

1	Russia	17,098		36	Turkey	785
2	Canada	9,985		37	Chile	756
3	United States	9,832		38	Zambia	753
4	China	9,563		39	Myanmar	677
5	Brazil	8,516		40	Afghanistan	653
6	Australia	7,741		41	South Sudan	644
7	India	3,287		42	Somalia	638
8	Argentina	2,780		43	Central African Rep.	623
9	Kazakhstan	2,725		44	Ukraine	604
10	Algeria	2,382		45	Madagascar	587
11	Congo-Kinshasa	2,345		46	Botswana	582
12	Saudi Arabia	2,150		47	Kenya	580
13	Mexico	1,964		48	France	549
14	Indonesia	1,911		49	Yemen	528
15	Sudan	1,879		50	Thailand	513
16	Libya	1,760		51	Spain	506
17	Iran	1,745		52	Turkmenistan	488
18	Mongolia	1,564		53	Cameroon	475
19	Peru	1,285		54	Papua New Guinea	463
20	Chad	1,284		55	Morocco	447
21	Niger	1,267			Sweden	447
22	Angola	1,247			Uzbekistan	447
23	Mali	1,240		58	Iraq	435
24	South Africa	1,219		59	Paraguay	407
25	Colombia	1,142		60	Zimbabwe	391
26	Ethiopia	1,104		61	Norway	385
27	Bolivia	1,099		62	Japan	378
28	Mauritania	1,031		63	Germany	357
29	Egypt	1,001		64	Congo-Brazzaville	342
30	Tanzania	947		65	Finland	338
31	Nigeria	924		66	Malaysia	331
32	Venezuela	912			Vietnam	331
33	Namibia	824		68	Ivory Coast	322
34	Mozambique	799		69	Poland	313
35	Pakistan	796		70	Oman	310

Largest exclusive economic zones[b]
Million sq km

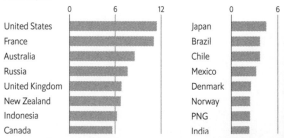

a Includes freshwater.   b Area extending 200 nautical miles (370km) from the coast.

Mountains: the highest[a]

		Location	Height (m)
1	Everest	China–Nepal	8,848
2	K2 (Godwin Austen)	China–Pakistan	8,611
3	Kangchenjunga	India–Nepal	8,586
4	Lhotse	China–Nepal	8,516
5	Makalu	China–Nepal	8,463
6	Cho Oyu	China–Nepal	8,201
7	Dhaulagiri	Nepal	8,167
8	Manaslu	Nepal	0,103
9	Nanga Parbat	Pakistan	8,126
10	Annapurna I	Nepal	8,091

Rivers: the longest

		Location	Length (km)
1	Nile	Africa	6,695
2	Amazon	South America	6,516
3	Yangtze (Chang Jiang)	Asia	6,380
4	Mississippi–Missouri system	North America	5,959
5	Ob'–Irtysh	Asia	5,568
6	Yenisey–Angara–Selanga	Asia	5,550
7	Yellow (Huang He)	Asia	5,464
8	Congo	Africa	4,667

Deserts: the largest non-polar

		Location	Area ('000 sq km)
1	Sahara	Northern Africa	8,600
2	Arabian	South-western Asia	2,300
3	Gobi	Mongolia/China	1,300
4	Patagonian	Argentina	673
5	Syrian	Middle East	520
6	Great Basin	South-western United States	490
7	Great Victoria	Western & Southern Australia	419
8	Great Sandy	Western Australia	395

Lakes: the largest

		Location	Area ('000 sq km)
1	Caspian Sea	Central Asia	371
2	Superior	Canada/United States	82
3	Victoria	East Africa	69
4	Huron	Canada/United States	60
5	Michigan	United States	58
6	Tanganyika	East Africa	33
7	Baikal	Russia	31
	Great Bear	Canada	31
9	Malawi	East Africa	30

a Includes separate peaks which are part of the same massif.
Notes: Estimates of the lengths of rivers vary widely depending on, eg, the path to take through a delta. The definition of a desert is normally a mean annual precipitation value equal to 250ml or less.

Population: size and growth

Largest populations
m, 2016

1	China	1,403.5	37	Iraq	37.2
2	India	1,324.2	38	Canada	36.3
3	United States	322.2	39	Morocco	35.3
4	Indonesia	261.1	40	Afghanistan	34.7
5	Brazil	207.7	41	Saudi Arabia	32.3
6	Pakistan	193.2	42	Peru	31.8
7	Nigeria	186.0	43	Venezuela	31.6
8	Bangladesh	163.0	44	Uzbekistan	31.4
9	Russia	144.0	45	Malaysia	31.2
10	Japan	127.7	46	Nepal	29.0
11	Mexico	127.5	47	Angola	28.8
12	Philippines	103.3		Mozambique	28.8
13	Ethiopia	102.4	49	Ghana	28.2
14	Egypt	95.7	50	Yemen	27.6
15	Vietnam	94.6	51	North Korea	25.4
16	Germany	81.9	52	Madagascar	24.9
17	Iran	80.3	53	Australia	24.1
18	Turkey	79.5	54	Ivory Coast	23.7
19	Congo-Kinshasa	78.7	55	Taiwan	23.6
20	Thailand	68.9	56	Cameroon	23.4
21	United Kingdom	65.8	57	Sri Lanka	20.8
22	France	64.7	58	Niger	20.7
23	Italy	59.4	59	Romania	19.8
24	South Africa	56.0	60	Burkina Faso	18.6
25	Tanzania	55.6	61	Syria	18.4
26	Myanmar	52.9	62	Malawi	18.1
27	South Korea	50.8	63	Kazakhstan	18.0
28	Colombia	48.7		Mali	18.0
29	Kenya	48.5	65	Chile	17.9
30	Spain	46.3	66	Netherlands	17.0
31	Ukraine	44.4	67	Guatemala	16.6
32	Argentina	43.8		Zambia	16.6
33	Uganda	41.5	69	Ecuador	16.4
34	Algeria	40.6	70	Zimbabwe	16.2
35	Sudan	39.6	71	Cambodia	15.8
36	Poland	38.2	72	Senegal	15.4

Largest populations
m, 2030

1	India	1,513.0	11	Ethiopia	139.6
2	China	1,441.2	12	Philippines	125.4
3	United States	354.7	13	Japan	121.6
4	Indonesia	295.6	14	Congo-Kinshasa	120.4
5	Nigeria	264.1	15	Egypt	119.7
6	Pakistan	244.2	16	Vietnam	106.3
7	Brazil	225.5	17	Iran	88.9
8	Bangladesh	185.6	18	Turkey	88.4
9	Mexico	147.5	19	Tanzania	83.7
10	Russia	140.5	20	Germany	82.2

Note: Populations include migrant workers.

Fastest-growing populations
Average annual % increase in population, 2015–20

1	Bahrain	4.3		Congo-Brazzaville	2.6
2	Oman	4.1		Guinea	2.6
3	Niger	3.8		Nigeria	2.6
4	Equatorial Guinea	3.6	29	French Guiana	2.5
5	Angola	3.3		Ivory Coast	2.5
6	Burundi	3.2		Kenya	2.5
	Congo-Kinshasa	3.2		Liberia	2.5
	Uganda	3.2		Togo	2.5
9	Tanzania	3.1	34	Afghanistan	2.4
10	Chad	3.0		Ethiopia	2.4
	Gambia, The	3.0		Guinea-Bissau	2.4
	Mali	3.0		Qatar	2.4
	Zambia	3.0		Rwanda	2.4
14	Burkina Faso	2.9		Sudan	2.4
	Malawi	2.9	40	Eritrea	2.3
	Mozambique	2.9		Yemen	2.3
	Somalia	2.9		Zimbabwe	2.3
18	Iraq	2.8	43	Gabon	2.2
	Senegal	2.8		Ghana	2.2
20	Benin	2.7		Jordan	2.2
	Madagascar	2.7	46	Namibia	2.1
	Mauritania	2.7		Sierra Leone	2.1
	South Sudan	2.7		Tajikistan	2.1
	West Bank & Gaza	2.7		Timor-Leste	2.1
25	Cameroon	2.6	50	Papua New Guinea	2.0

Slowest-growing populations
Average annual % increase in population, 2015–20

1	Latvia	-1.0		Montenegro	0.0
2	Bulgaria	-0.7		Russia	0.0
3	Croatia	-0.6		Slovakia	0.0
	Lithuania	-0.6		Spain	0.0
5	Bermuda	-0.5		Virgin Islands (US)	0.0
	Romania	-0.5	29	Albania	0.1
	Ukraine	-0.5		Cuba	0.1
8	Portugal	-0.4		Czech Republic	0.1
9	Georgia	-0.3		Macedonia	0.1
	Hungary	-0.3		Slovenia	0.1
	Serbia	-0.3	34	Armenia	0.2
12	Andorra	-0.2		Austria	0.2
	Belarus	-0.2		Barbados	0.2
	Bosnia & Herz.	-0.2		Germany	0.2
	Estonia	-0.2		Mauritius	0.2
	Greece	-0.2		Monaco	0.2
	Japan	-0.2		Syria	0.2
	Moldova	-0.2		Thailand	0.2
	Poland	-0.2	42	Jamaica	0.3
20	Guadeloupe	-0.1		Malta	0.3
	Italy	-0.1		Netherlands	0.3
	Puerto Rico	-0.1		Taiwan	0.3
23	Martinique	0.0		Trinidad & Tobago	0.3

Population: matters of breeding and sex

Crude birth rates

Births per 1,000 population, 2015–20

Highest			Lowest		
1	Niger	47.7	1	Monaco	7.0
2	Somalia	42.9	2	Portugal	7.5
3	Chad	42.6	3	Greece	7.9
4	Mali	41.8	4	Andorra	8.0
5	Burundi	41.5	5	Japan	8.1
6	Congo-Kinshasa	41.4	6	Italy	8.2
	Uganda	41.4	7	Spain	8.5
8	Angola	41.1	8	Singapore	8.7
9	Gambia, The	38.7	9	Germany	8.9
10	Mozambique	38.4		South Korea	8.9
11	Burkina Faso	38.2	11	Croatia	9.0
12	Nigeria	38.1		Hungary	9.0
13	Zambia	37.7		Taiwan	9.0
14	Tanzania	37.5	14	Poland	9.1
15	Benin	36.4	15	Bosnia & Herz.	9.2
	Ivory Coast	36.4		United Arab Emirates	9.2
	Malawi	36.4	17	Bulgaria	9.3
18	Guinea-Bissau	35.6		Channel Islands	9.3
19	Cameroon	35.5	19	Romania	9.5
20	South Sudan	35.4	20	Austria	9.7

Teenage births

Births per 1,000 women aged 15–19 years, 2015–20

Highest		Lowest	
Niger		North Korea	
Mali		South Korea	
Chad		Macau	
Equatorial Guinea		Hong Kong	
Angola		Taiwan	
Malawi		Switzerland	
Guinea		Singapore	
Mozambique		Netherlands	
Ivory Coast		Denmark	
Liberia		Japan	
Congo-Kinshasa		Slovenia	
Tanzania		Liechtenstein	
Sierra Leone		Cyprus	
Congo-Brazzaville		Belgium	
Madagascar		Luxembourg	
Nigeria		Sweden	
Uganda		Norway	

Fertility rates

Average number of children per woman, 2015–20

Highest			Lowest		
1	Niger	7.2	1	Moldova	1.2
2	Somalia	6.1		Portugal	1.2
3	Congo-Kinshasa	6.0		Taiwan	1.2
4	Mali	5.9	4	Cyprus	1.3
5	Chad	5.8		Greece	1.3
6	Angola	5.6		Hong Kong	1.3
	Burundi	5.6		Poland	1.3
8	Uganda	5.5		Singapore	1.3
9	Nigeria	5.4		South Korea	1.3
10	Gambia, The	5.3	10	Andorra	1.4
	Timor-Leste	5.3		Bosnia & Herz.	1.4
12	Burkina Faso	5.2		Hungary	1.4
13	Mozambique	5.1		Macau	1.4
14	Benin	4.9		Mauritius	1.4
	Tanzania	4.9		Spain	1.4
	Zambia	4.9	16	Austria	1.5
17	Central African Rep.	4.8		Channel Islands	1.5
	Ivory Coast	4.8		Croatia	1.5
19	Guinea	4.7		Germany	1.5
	Senegal	4.7		Italy	1.5
	South Sudan	4.7		Japan	1.5
22	Cameroon	4.6		Malta	1.5
	Congo-Brazzaville	4.6		Monaco	1.5
	Equatorial Guinea	4.6		Puerto Rico	1.5
	Mauritania	4.6		Romania	1.5
26	Guinea-Bissau	4.5		Slovakia	1.5
	Liberia	4.5		Thailand	1.5
	Malawi	4.5			

Women[a] who use modern methods of contraception

2016 or latest, %

Highest			Lowest		
1	China	84.0	1	South Sudan	1.7
	United Kingdom	84.0	2	Guinea	4.6
3	Norway	82.2	3	Chad	5.0
4	Argentina	78.2	4	Eritrea	7.0
5	Brazil	77.7	5	Congo-Kinshasa	7.5
6	Czech Republic	77.6	6	Gambia, The	8.1
7	Nicaragua	77.4	7	Zambia	8.9
8	France	77.3	8	Equatorial Guinea	9.5
9	Thailand	76.9	9	Albania	10.6
10	North Korea	76.5	10	Mozambique	11.3
11	Finland	75.4	11	Sudan	11.7
12	Uruguay	74.8	12	Bosnia & Herz.	12.0
13	Costa Rica	74.7	13	Central African Rep.	12.1
14	Colombia	72.9	14	Angola	12.5
15	Virgin Islands (US)	72.6		Benin	12.5
16	New Zealand	72.3		Ivory Coast	12.5

a Married or partnered women aged 15–49; excludes traditional methods of contraception, such as the rhythm method.

Population: age

Median age[a]

Lowest, 2016			Highest, 2016		
1	Niger	14.9	1	Monaco	51.0
2	Uganda	15.9	2	Japan	46.7
3	Mali	16.1	3	Italy	46.3
4	Chad	16.2	4	Germany	46.0
5	Angola	16.5	5	Portugal	44.4
6	Somalia	16.6	6	Martinique	44.1
7	Congo-Kinshasa	16.8	7	Bulgaria	43.7
8	Burkina Faso	17.1		Greece	43.7
	Gambia, The	17.1		Spain	43.7
10	Zambia	17.2	10	Hong Kong	43.5
11	Mozambique	17.3	11	Austria	43.4
12	Tanzania	17.4	12	Slovenia	43.3
13	Malawi	17.5	13	Channel Islands	43.0
	Timor-Leste	17.5	14	Croatia	42.9
15	Afghanistan	17.6		Lithuania	42.9
	Burundi	17.6	16	Latvia	42.8
17	Central African Rep.	17.9	17	Finland	42.6
	Nigeria	17.9	18	Switzerland	42.4
19	Benin	18.3	19	Netherlands	42.3
20	Cameroon	18.4	20	Andorra	42.0
	Ivory Coast	18.4		Bermuda	42.0
	Senegal	18.4		Hungary	42.0

Most old people

% of population aged 65 or over, 2015

1	Monaco	30.4
2	Japan	26.0
3	Italy	22.4
4	Germany	21.1
5	Portugal	20.7
6	Finland	20.3
7	Bulgaria	20.1
8	Greece	19.9
9	Sweden	19.6
10	Latvia	19.3
11	Denmark	19.0
12	Croatia	18.9
	France	18.9
	Spain	18.9
15	Austria	18.8
	Estonia	18.8
17	Lithuania	18.7
18	Malta	18.4
19	Belgium	18.1
	United Kingdom	18.1
21	Czech Republic	18.0
	Slovenia	18.0
	Switzerland	18.0
24	Netherlands	17.9

Most young people

% of population aged 0–19, 2015

1	Niger	60.5
2	Uganda	59.4
3	Chad	58.7
4	Mali	58.5
5	Somalia	57.7
6	Angola	57.5
7	Congo-Kinshasa	56.6
	Zambia	56.6
9	Gambia, The	56.5
	Timor-Leste	56.5
11	Burkina Faso	56.4
12	Afghanistan	56.2
13	Mozambique	56.0
14	Malawi	55.9
15	Tanzania	55.7
16	Central African Rep.	55.1
17	Burundi	55.0
18	Nigeria	54.4
19	Benin	53.8
20	Ivory Coast	53.7
21	Sierra Leone	53.6
22	Cameroon	53.5
	Senegal	53.5
24	Ethiopia	53.4

a Age at which there is an equal number of people above and below.

City living

Biggest cities[a]
Population, m, 2017

1	Tokyo, Japan	38.1		Shenzhen, China	11.0
2	Delhi, India	27.2	27	Bangalore, India	10.8
3	Shanghai, China	25.1	28	Jakarta, Indonesia	10.7
4	Beijing, China	21.9	29	London, UK	10.5
5	Mumbai, India	21.8	30	Chennai, India	10.4
6	São Paulo, Brazil	21.5	31	Lima, Peru	10.2
7	Mexico City, Mexico	21.3	32	Bogotá, Colombia	10.1
8	Osaka, Japan	20.4	33	Johannesburg, South Africa	9.8
9	Cairo, Egypt	19.5		Seoul, South Korea	9.8
10	Dhaka, Bangladesh	19.0	35	Bangkok, Thailand	9.6
11	New York, US	18.7	36	Hyderabad, India	9.5
12	Karachi, Pakistan	17.7	37	Nagoya, Japan	9.4
13	Buenos Aires, Argentina	15.5	38	Lahore, Pakistan	9.3
14	Kolkata, India	15.2	39	Chicago, US	8.8
15	Istanbul, Turkey	14.5	40	Tehran, Iran	8.6
16	Lagos, Nigeria	14.3	41	Wuhan, China	8.1
17	Chongqing, China	14.1	42	Chengdu, China	8.0
18	Guangzhou, China	13.5	43	Ahmedabad, India	7.8
19	Manila, Philippines	13.3		Nanjing, China	7.8
20	Rio de Janeiro, Brazil	13.1	45	Ho Chi Minh City, Vietnam	7.7
21	Kinshasa, Congo-Kinshasa	12.6	46	Dongguan, China	7.6
22	Los Angeles, US	12.4	47	Hong Kong	7.4
23	Moscow, Russia	12.3	48	Foshan, China	7.2
24	Tianjin, China	11.9		Kuala Lumpur, Malaysia	7.2
25	Paris, France	11.0	50	Baghdad, Iraq	7.0

City growth[b]
Average annual % change, 2015–20

Fastest

1	Samut Prakan, Thailand	8.2
2	Batam, Indonesia	7.3
3	Ouagadougou, Burkina Faso	7.0
4	Bujumbura, Burundi	6.9
5	Mwanza, Tanzania	6.6
	Nnewi, Nigeria	6.6
7	Abomey-Calavi, Benin	6.3
	Abuja, Nigeria	6.3
	Dar es Salaam, Tanzania	6.3
	Uyo, Nigeria	6.3
11	Xiamen, China	6.2
12	Bamako, Mali	6.0
	Denpasar, Indonesia	6.0
	Mogadishu, Somalia	6.0
15	Huambo, Angola	5.9
	Liuyang, China	5.9
17	Yinchuan, China	5.7
18	Hamah, Syria	5.6
	Port Harcourt, Nigeria	5.6

Slowest

1	Dnipropetrovsk, Ukraine	-1.0
2	Nizhny Novgorod, Russia	-0.9
3	Saratov, Russia	-0.8
4	Donetsk, Ukraine	-0.7
	Sendai, Japan	-0.7
6	Zaporizhia, Ukraine	-0.6
7	Perm, Russia	-0.4
	Yerevan, Armenia	-0.4
9	Busan, South Korea	-0.3
	Havana, Cuba	-0.3
11	Detroit, US	-0.2
	Fukuoka, Japan	-0.2
	Kharkiv, Ukraine	-0.2
	Sapporo, Japan	-0.2
	Tbilisi, Georgia	-0.2
16	Buffalo, US	-0.1
	Naples, Italy	-0.1
	Samara, Russia	-0.1
	Volgograd, Russia	-0.1

a Urban agglomerations. Data may change from year to year based on reassessments of agglomeration boundaries.
b Urban agglomerations with a population of at least 750,000 in 2015.

City liveability[a]

100 = ideal, 0 = intolerable, 2017

Best

1	Melbourne, Australia	97.5
2	Vienna, Austria	97.4
3	Vancouver, Canada	97.3
4	Toronto, Canada	97.2
5	Adelaide, Australia	96.6
	Calgary, Canada	96.6
7	Perth, Australia	95.9
	Tokyo, Japan	95.9
9	Auckland, New Zealand	95.7
	Osaka, Japan	95.7
11	Helsinki, Finland	95.6
12	Hamburg, Germany	95.0
13	Sydney, Australia	94.9
14	Montreal, Canada	94.8
15	Zurich, Switzerland	94.3

Worst

1	Damascus, Syria	30.7
2	Tripoli, Libya	36.6
3	Lagos, Nigeria	38.5
4	Dhaka, Bangladesh	38.7
5	Port Moresby, Papua New Guinea	39.6
6	Algiers, Algeria	40.9
	Karachi, Pakistan	40.9
8	Harare, Zimbabwe	42.6
9	Douala, Cameroon	44.0
10	Dakar, Senegal	48.3
11	Tehran, Iran	50.8
12	Colombo, Sri Lanka	51.0
	Kathmandu, Nepal	51.0
	Lusaka, Zambia	51.0

Tallest buildings[b]

Height, metres, 2017

a EIU liveability index, based on a range of factors including stability, health care, culture, education, infrastructure.   b Completed.

Migrants, refugees and asylum-seekers

Largest foreign-born[a] populations
m, 2017

1	United States	49.8	15	South Africa	4.0
2	Germany	12.2	16	Kazakhstan	3.6
	Saudi Arabia	12.2		Thailand	3.6
4	Russia	11.7	18	Pakistan	3.4
5	United Kingdom	8.8	19	Jordan	3.2
6	United Arab Emirates	8.3	20	Kuwait	3.1
7	Canada	7.9	21	Hong Kong	2.9
	France	7.9	22	Iran	2.7
9	Australia	7.0		Malaysia	2.7
10	Italy	5.9	24	Singapore	2.6
	Spain	5.9	25	Switzerland	2.5
12	India	5.2	26	Japan	2.3
13	Ukraine	5.0	27	Argentina	2.2
14	Turkey	4.9		Ivory Coast	2.2

Foreign-born[a] populations
As % of total population, 2017

1	United Arab Emirates	88.4	15	French Guiana	39.5
2	Kuwait	75.5	16	Hong Kong	39.1
3	Qatar	65.2	17	Saudi Arabia	37.0
4	Liechtenstein	65.1	18	Jordan	33.3
5	Macau	56.8	19	Lebanon	31.9
6	Monaco	54.9	20	Bermuda	30.9
7	Virgin Islands (US)	54.1	21	Switzerland	29.6
8	Andorra	53.3	22	Australia	28.8
9	Channel Islands	50.3	23	Brunei	25.3
10	Bahrain	48.4	24	New Caledonia	23.9
11	Guam	47.5	25	Israel	23.6
12	Singapore	46.0	26	New Zealand	22.7
13	Luxembourg	45.3	27	Guadeloupe	22.1
14	Oman	44.7	28	Canada	21.5

Annual growth rate of migrant populations
%, 2015–17

1	Uganda	17.3		Sweden	4.3
2	Romania	13.9	16	Central African Rep.	4.2
3	Tanzania	8.8	17	Somalia	3.8
4	Germany	8.7	18	Ireland	3.6
5	Sudan	8.3	19	Malta	3.5
	Turkey	8.3	20	Iceland	3.4
7	Niger	7.8		Norway	3.4
8	Bulgaria	7.0	22	Congo-Kinshasa	3.2
9	Oman	6.7		Gambia, The	3.2
10	Saudi Arabia	6.2	24	Cameroon	3.0
11	Austria	5.3	25	Hungary	2.9
12	Denmark	4.9	26	Brunei	2.8
13	Finland	4.4		Equatorial Guinea	2.8
14	Kuwait	4.3		South Africa	2.8

a Includes migrants.

Refugees and asylum-seekers

As % of migrant population, 2017

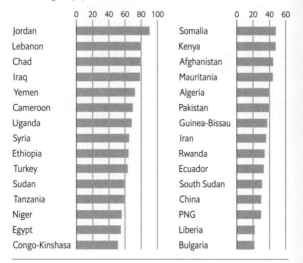

	0 20 40 60 80 100		0 20 40 60
Jordan		Somalia	
Lebanon		Kenya	
Chad		Afghanistan	
Iraq		Mauritania	
Yemen		Algeria	
Cameroon		Pakistan	
Uganda		Guinea-Bissau	
Syria		Iran	
Ethiopia		Rwanda	
Turkey		Ecuador	
Sudan		South Sudan	
Tanzania		China	
Niger		PNG	
Egypt		Liberia	
Congo-Kinshasa		Bulgaria	

Annual rate of change of refugee[a] population

%, 2015–17

1	Peru	57.1	21	Chile	11.6
2	Madagascar	54.9	22	Portugal	11.5
3	Austria	37.0	23	Botswana	11.4
4	Greece	30.9		Uruguay	11.4
5	Suriname	29.4	25	Lesotho	10.3
6	Germany	26.7	26	Tajikistan	10.1
7	Uganda	25.9	27	Italy	9.9
8	Spain	23.9	28	Colombia	9.8
9	Central African Rep.	21.7		Costa Rica	9.8
10	Slovenia	21.5	30	Australia	9.6
11	Albania	19.8	31	Mongolia	9.1
12	United States	18.9	32	Burundi	8.8
13	Mexico	15.9	33	Bangladesh	8.6
14	Tanzania	15.8	34	Somalia	8.3
15	Oman	15.7	35	Mozambique	7.9
16	Nicaragua	15.6	36	Morocco	7.8
17	Sudan	14.8	37	United Arab Emirates	7.7
18	Niger	14.3	38	Argentina	7.6
19	Jamaica	13.7	39	Japan	7.1
20	Bulgaria	12.8	40	Brazil	6.9

a Includes asylum-seekers.

Refugees[a] by country of origin
'000, 2016

1	Syria	5,524.4	11	Vietnam	329.4
2	Afghanistan	2,501.4	12	Iraq	316.0
3	South Sudan	1,436.7	13	Colombia	311.1
4	Somalia	1,012.3	14	Rwanda	286.1
5	Sudan	650.6	15	Ukraine	239.1
6	Congo-Kinshasa	537.5	16	Nigeria	229.3
7	Central African Rep.	490.9	17	China	207.7
8	Myanmar	490.3	18	Mali	156.4
9	Eritrea	459.4	19	Sri Lanka	117.5
10	Burundi	408.1	20	Pakistan	105.4

Countries with largest refugee[a] populations
'000, 2016

1	Turkey	2,869.4	11	Sudan	421.5
2	Pakistan	1,352.6	12	Chad	391.3
3	Lebanon	1,013.0	13	Cameroon	375.4
4	Iran	979.4	14	China	317.3
5	Uganda	940.8	15	France	304.5
6	Ethiopia	791.6	16	Tanzania	281.5
7	Jordan	685.2	17	Bangladesh	276.2
8	Germany	669.5	18	United States	273.0
9	Congo-Kinshasa	452.0	19	Yemen	269.8
10	Kenya	451.1	20	South Sudan	262.6

Applications for asylum by country of origin
'000, 2016

1	Syria	357.6	11	Somalia	41.4
2	Afghanistan	254.6	12	Ethiopia	40.8
3	Iraq	195.6	13	Albania	38.5
4	Iran	68.6	14	Venezuela	34.4
5	Pakistan	67.0	15	China	34.0
6	Congo-Kinshasa	65.1	16	Russia	32.4
7	Eritrea	62.8	17	Sudan	32.0
8	Nigeria	60.1	18	Serbia[b]	29.1
9	Ukraine	48.9	19	Bangladesh	28.4
10	El Salvador	43.3	20	Mexico	28.3

Countries where asylum applications were lodged
'000, 2016

1	Germany	745.5	11	Australia	33.5
2	United States	262.0	12	Egypt	30.7
3	France	125.7	13	Uganda	30.3
4	Italy	123.0	14	Hungary	29.4
5	Turkey	79.7	15	Switzerland	27.2
6	Greece	58.3	16	Russia	26.4
7	United Kingdom	54.9	17	Canada	23.6
8	Sweden	53.7	18	Belgium	23.5
9	Austria	39.9	19	Netherlands	21.3
10	South Africa	35.4	20	Malaysia	20.4

a According to UNHCR. Includes people in "refugee-like situations".
b Includes Kosovo.

The world economy

Biggest economies
GDP, $bn, 2016

1	United States	18,624	23	Sweden	514
2	China	11,222	24	Poland	471
3	Japan	4,949	25	Belgium	468
4	Germany	3,479	26	Thailand	412
5	United Kingdom	2,661	27	Nigeria	405
6	France[a]	2,466	28	Iran	404
7	India	2,274	29	Austria	391
8	Italy	1,860	30	Norway	371
9	Brazil	1,793	31	United Arab Emirates	349
10	Canada	1,536	32	Egypt	332
11	South Korea	1,411	33	Hong Kong	321
12	Russia	1,281	34	Israel	318
13	Australia	1,265	35	Singapore	310
14	Spain	1,238	36	Denmark	307
15	Mexico	1,077	37	Philippines	305
16	Indonesia	932	38	Ireland	304
17	Turkey	863	39	Malaysia	297
18	Netherlands	778	40	South Africa	296
19	Switzerland	669	41	Colombia	280
20	Saudi Arabia	645	42	Pakistan	279
21	Argentina	554	43	Chile	250
22	Taiwan	531	44	Finland	239

Biggest economies by purchasing power
GDP PPP, $bn, 2016

1	China	21,290	24	Poland	1,053
2	United States	18,624	25	Pakistan	986
3	India	8,705	26	Argentina	879
4	Japan	5,243	27	Netherlands	873
5	Germany	3,997	28	Malaysia	863
6	Russia	3,877	29	Philippines	806
7	Brazil	3,152	30	South Africa	742
8	Indonesia	3,032	31	Colombia	689
9	United Kingdom	2,812	32	United Arab Emirates	671
10	France[a]	2,735	33	Iraq	652
11	Mexico	2,367	34	Bangladesh	630
12	Italy	2,237	35	Algeria	610
13	Turkey	1,994	36	Vietnam	595
14	South Korea	1,934	37	Belgium	510
15	Saudi Arabia	1,755	38	Switzerland	503
16	Spain	1,691	39	Singapore	500
17	Canada	1,687		Sweden	500
18	Iran	1,549	41	Kazakhstan	451
19	Australia	1,197	42	Romania	442
20	Thailand	1,166	43	Chile	437
21	Taiwan	1,133	44	Venezuela	435
22	Egypt	1,132	45	Hong Kong	430
23	Nigeria	1,090	46	Austria	420

Note: For a list of 185 countries with their GDPs, see pages 250–53. "Advanced economies" refers to 39 countries as defined by the IMF.
a Includes overseas territories.   b IMF coverage.

Regional GDP

$bn, 2017		*% annual growth 2012–17*	
World	79,865	World	3.5
Advanced economies	48,188	Advanced economies	1.8
G7	36,746	G7	1.9
Euro area (19)	12,607	Euro area (19)	1.5
Other Asia	17,491	Other Asia	6.7
Latin America & Caribbean	5,493	Latin America & Caribbean	1.0
Other Europe & CIS	3,973	Other Europe & CIS	2.3
Middle East, N. Africa, Afghanistan & Pakistan	3,190	Middle East, N. Africa, Afghanistan & Pakistan	3.1
Sub-Saharan Africa	1,531	Sub-Saharan Africa	3.6

Regional purchasing power

GDP, % of total, 2017		*$ per person, 2017*	
World	100	World	17,225
Advanced economies	41.3	Advanced economies	49,165
G7	30.6	G7	50,769
Euro area (19)	11.6	Euro area (19)	43,547
Other Asia	32.5	Other Asia	11,496
Latin America & Caribbean	7.7	Latin America & Caribbean	15,700
Other Europe & CIS	8.1	Other Europe & CIS	21,968
Middle East, N. Africa, Afghanistan & Pakistan	7.5	Middle East, N. Africa, Afghanistan & Pakistan	13,999
Sub-Saharan Africa	3.0	Sub-Saharan Africa	3,922

Regional population

% of total (7.4bn), 2017		*No. of countries[b], 2017*	
World	100	World	190
Advanced economies	14.4	Advanced economies	23
G7	10.4	G7	7
Euro area (19)	4.6	Euro area (19)	19
Other Asia	48.5	Other Asia	30
Latin America & Caribbean	8.4	Latin America & Caribbean	32
Other Europe & CIS	6.3	Other Europe & CIS	24
Middle East, N. Africa, Afghanistan & Pakistan	9.3	Middle East, N. Africa, Afghanistan & Pakistan	22
Sub-Saharan Africa	13.1	Sub-Saharan Africa	45

Regional international trade

Exports of goods & services *% of total, 2017*		*Current-account balances* *$bn, 2017*	
World	100	World	371
Advanced economies	63.6	Advanced economies	396
G7	33.8	G7	-111
Euro area (19)	26.3	Euro area (19)	442
Other Asia	18.0	Other Asia	151
Latin America & Caribbean	5.1	Latin America & Caribbean	-85
Other Europe & CIS	6.3	Other Europe & CIS	-23
Middle East, N. Africa, Afghanistan & Pakistan	5.3	Middle East, N. Africa, Afghanistan & Pakistan	-28
Sub-Saharan Africa	1.6	Sub-Saharan Africa	-40

Living standards

Highest GDP per person
$, 2016

1	Monaco	161,700		31	New Caledonia	31,486
2	Liechtenstein	154,842		32	Italy	31,316
3	Luxembourg	97,758		33	Guadeloupe	30,000
4	Switzerland	79,613			Martinique	30,000
5	Macau	75,518		35	Guam	28,965
6	Norway	70,014		36	Andorra	28,585
7	Iceland	67,680		37	Brunei	28,498
8	Ireland	64,787		38	Puerto Rico	28,388
9	Bermuda	61,273		39	Malta	28,195
10	Qatar	58,642		40	Bahamas	28,155
11	United States	57,804		41	South Korea	27,776
12	Singapore	55,313		42	Kuwait	27,042
13	Denmark	53,842		43	Spain	26,734
14	Sweden	52,496		44	Réunion	24,444
15	Australia	52,487		45	Bahrain	22,983
16	Netherlands	45,738		46	Taiwan	22,483
17	Channel Islands[a]	45,000		47	Slovenia	21,299
18	Austria	44,938		48	Saudi Arabia	19,967
19	Hong Kong	43,956		49	Portugal	19,737
20	Finland	43,414		50	Czech Republic	18,425
21	Germany	42,481		51	French Polynesia	18,060
22	Canada	42,308		52	Estonia	17,960
23	Belgium	41,066		53	Greece	17,212
24	United Kingdom	40,436		54	Cyprus	16,713
25	Virgin Islands (US)[b]	40,000		55	French Guiana	16,667
26	New Zealand	39,443		56	Slovakia	16,631
27	Japan	38,757		57	Trinidad & Tobago	15,926
28	Israel	38,750		58	Barbados	15,880
29	France[c]	38,122		59	Uruguay	15,418
30	United Arab Emirates	37,499		60	Oman	15,187

Lowest GDP per person
$, 2016

1	South Sudan	250		17	North Korea	661
2	Burundi	299		18	Guinea	684
3	Malawi	302		19	Chad	696
4	Niger	364		20	Rwanda	712
5	Central African Rep.	382		21	Liberia	713
6	Mozambique	391		22	Ethiopia	714
7	Madagascar	402		23	Nepal	729
8	Somalia	435		24	Haiti	757
9	Gambia, The	483			Yemen	757
10	Congo-Kinshasa	500		26	Mali	780
11	Sierra Leone	511		27	Benin	787
12	Afghanistan	561		28	Tajikistan	799
13	Togo	587		29	Tanzania	857
14	Burkina Faso	608		30	Senegal	956
15	Uganda	610		31	Zimbabwe	995
16	Guinea-Bissau	647		32	Eritrea	1,001

a 2010   b 2004   c Includes overseas territories.

Highest purchasing power

GDP per person in PPP (US = 100), 2016

1	Monaco	331.8	35	Virgin Islands (US)	65.6
2	Liechtenstein	287.1	36	Italy	65.2
3	Qatar	218.0	37	Israel	63.5
4	Macau	186.1	38	Spain	63.2
5	Luxembourg	171.6	39	New Caledonia	62.1
6	Singapore	154.3	40	Puerto Rico	60.2
7	Brunei	141.7	41	Bermuda	59.0
8	United Arab Emirates	124.8	42	Czech Republic	57.8
9	Kuwait	124.0	43	Andorra	57.6
10	Ireland	119.8	44	Slovenia	54.8
11	Norway	119.7	45	Slovakia	54.6
12	Switzerland	103.5	46	Trinidad & Tobago	53.6
13	Hong Kong	102.0	47	Estonia	51.8
14	United States	100.0	48	Lithuania	51.5
15	Iceland	96.3	49	Portugal	49.9
16	Saudi Arabia	94.0	50	Bahamas	48.6
17	Netherlands	88.8	51	Hungary	48.2
18	Sweden	88.2	52	Malaysia	47.9
19	Australia	85.9	53	Poland	47.7
20	Germany	84.4	54	Russia	46.6
21	Denmark	83.7	55	Equatorial Guinea	45.0
22	Austria	83.4	56	Greece	44.7
23	Taiwan	83.0	57	Latvia	43.8
24	Bahrain	82.9	58	Kazakhstan	43.4
25	Canada	80.4		Turkey	43.4
26	Belgium	77.5	60	Cyprus	43.1
27	Malta	77.0	61	Chile	42.2
28	United Kingdom	73.9		Guam	42.2
29	Finland	73.2	63	Panama	41.9
30	France	73.1	64	Croatia	39.9
31	Oman	72.3	65	Romania	38.6
32	Japan	71.0	66	Uruguay	37.9
33	New Zealand	66.2	67	Bulgaria	35.4
34	South Korea	65.8	68	Argentina	34.7

Lowest purchasing power

GDP per person in PPP (US = 100), 2016

1	Central African Rep.	1.2	15	South Sudan	2.9
2	Burundi	1.3	16	Eritrea	3.0
3	Congo-Kinshasa	1.4		Ethiopia	3.0
4	Niger	1.7		Gambia, The	3.0
5	Malawi	2.0	19	Burkina Faso	3.1
6	Mozambique	2.1		Haiti	3.1
	Somalia	2.1	21	Afghanistan	3.3
8	Liberia	2.2		Rwanda	3.3
9	Madagascar	2.6	23	Guinea	3.4
	Sierra Leone	2.6	24	Chad	3.5
11	North Korea	2.7		Uganda	3.5
12	Guinea-Bissau	2.8		Zimbabwe	3.5
	Togo	2.8	27	Benin	3.7
	Yemen	2.8		Mali	3.7

The quality of life

Human development index[a]

Highest, 2015

1	Norway	94.9
2	Australia	93.9
	Switzerland	93.9
4	Germany	92.6
5	Denmark	92.5
	Singapore	92.5
7	Netherlands	92.4
8	Ireland	92.3
9	Iceland	92.1
10	Canada	92.0
	United States	92.0
12	Hong Kong	91.7
13	New Zealand	91.5
14	Sweden	91.3
15	Liechtenstein	91.2
16	United Kingdom	90.9
17	Japan	90.3
18	South Korea	90.1
19	Israel	89.9
20	Luxembourg	89.8
21	France	89.7
22	Belgium	89.6
23	Finland	89.5
24	Austria	89.3

Lowest, 2015

1	Central African Rep.	35.2
2	Niger	35.3
3	Chad	39.6
4	Burkina Faso	40.2
5	Burundi	40.4
6	Guinea	41.4
7	Mozambique	41.8
	South Sudan	41.8
9	Eritrea	42.0
	Sierra Leone	42.0
11	Guinea-Bissau	42.4
12	Liberia	42.7
13	Congo-Kinshasa	43.5
14	Mali	44.2
15	Ethiopia	44.8
16	Gambia, The	45.2
17	Ivory Coast	47.4
18	Malawi	47.6
19	Afghanistan	47.9
20	Yemen	48.2
21	Benin	48.5
22	Togo	48.7
23	Sudan	49.0
24	Haiti	49.3
	Uganda	49.3

Gini coefficient[b]

Highest, 2010–15

1	South Africa	63.4
2	Namibia	61.0
3	Haiti	60.8
4	Botswana	60.5
5	Central African Rep.	56.2
6	Zambia	55.6
7	Lesotho	54.2
8	Colombia	53.5
9	Paraguay	51.7
10	Brazil	51.5
	Swaziland	51.5
12	Guinea-Bissau	50.7
	Panama	50.7
14	Honduras	50.6
15	Chile	50.5
16	Rwanda	50.4

Lowest, 2010–15

1	Ukraine	24.1
2	Slovenia	25.6
3	Norway	25.9
4	Czech Republic	26.1
	Slovakia	26.1
6	Kazakhstan	26.3
7	Kyrgyzstan	26.8
	Moldova	26.8
9	Iceland	26.9
10	Finland	27.1
11	Belarus	27.2
12	Sweden	27.3
13	Romania	27.5
14	Belgium	27.6
15	Netherlands	28.0
16	Albania	29.0

a GDP or GDP per person is often taken as a measure of how developed a country is, but its usefulness is limited as it refers only to economic welfare. The UN Development Programme combines statistics on average and expected years of schooling and life expectancy with income levels (now GNI per person, valued in PPP US$). The HDI is shown here scaled from 0 to 100; countries scoring over 80 are considered to have very high human development, 70–79 high, 55–69 medium and those under 55 low.

b The lower its value, the more equally household income is distributed.

Household wealth
2016, $trn

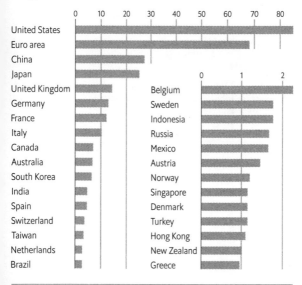

United States	
Euro area	
China	
Japan	
United Kingdom	Belgium
Germany	Sweden
France	Indonesia
Italy	Russia
Canada	Mexico
Australia	Austria
South Korea	Norway
India	Singapore
Spain	Denmark
Switzerland	Turkey
Taiwan	Hong Kong
Netherlands	New Zealand
Brazil	Greece

Number of millionaires
Persons with net worth above $1m, 2016, '000

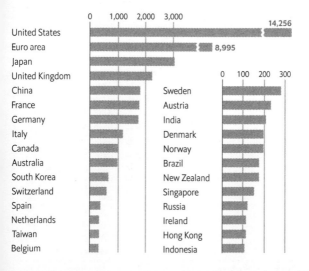

United States	14,256
Euro area	8,995
Japan	
United Kingdom	
China	Sweden
France	Austria
Germany	India
Italy	Denmark
Canada	Norway
Australia	Brazil
South Korea	New Zealand
Switzerland	Singapore
Spain	Russia
Netherlands	Ireland
Taiwan	Hong Kong
Belgium	Indonesia

Economic growth

Highest economic growth
Average annual % increase in real GDP, 2006–16

	0 2 4 6 8 10		0 2 4 6
Ethiopia		Zambia	
Turkmenistan		Congo-Kinshasa	
Qatar		Angola	
China		Iraq	
Myanmar		Bangladesh	
Uzbekistan		Uganda	
Timor-Leste		PNG	
Laos		Vietnam	
Rwanda		Sri Lanka	
Afghanistan		West Bank & Gaza	
Mongolia		Philippines	
India		Indonesia	
Panama		Niger	
Ghana		Azerbaijan	
Tajikistan		Malawi	
Tanzania		Macau	
Mozambique		Peru	
Cambodia		Burkina Faso	

Lowest economic growth
Average annual % change in real GDP, 2006–16

	8 6 4 2 – 0		0 + 2
Libya		Finland	
South Sudan[a]		Barbados	
Syria		Cyprus	
Yemen		Spain	
Virgin Islands (US)		Martinique[c]	
Greece		Denmark	
Puerto Rico[b]		Japan	
Andorra		Latvia	
Bermuda[b]		Euro area	
Central African Rep.		Hungary	
French Polynesia[c]		North Korea	
Ukraine		Trinidad & Tobago	
Italy		Estonia	
Bahamas		France	
Brunei		Slovenia	
Croatia		Netherlands	
Jamaica		Austria	
Portugal		Belgium	

a 2008–16   b 2006–13   c 2006–14

Highest economic growth
Average annual % increase in real GDP, 1996–2006

1	Equatorial Guinea	33.3	11	Mozambique	8.6
2	Liberia	13.9	12	Rwanda	8.5
3	Azerbaijan	13.4	13	Trinidad & Tobago	8.4
4	Myanmar	11.3	14	Iraq	8.2
5	Qatar[a]	11.0	15	Timor-Leste[b]	7.9
6	Bosnia & Herz.	9.6	16	Belarus	7.6
7	China	9.5		Latvia	7.6
8	Armenia	9.3	18	Tajikistan	7.5
	Chad	9.3	19	Kazakhstan	7.4
10	Cambodia	8.9			

Lowest economic growth
Average annual % change in real GDP, 1996–2006

1	Zimbabwe	-4.0	11	Channel Islands[c]	1.2
2	Guinea-Bissau	-0.9	12	Guyana	1.4
3	Gabon	0.2		Uruguay	1.4
4	Papua New Guinea	0.4	14	Germany	1.5
5	Congo-Kinshasa	0.5		Italy	1.5
6	Haiti	0.8		Paraguay	1.5
7	Ivory Coast	1.0	17	Burundi	1.7
	Jamaica	1.0	18	Eritrea	1.8
	Japan	1.0	19	Brunei	1.9
	North Korea	1.0	20	Fiji	2.0

Highest services growth
Average annual % increase in real terms, 2006–16

1	Ethiopia	12.8	10	Uzbekistan	8.9
2	Zimbabwe	11.0	11	Angola	8.8
3	Qatar	10.8	12	Equatorial Guinea	8.6
4	Afghanistan	10.7	13	Zambia	8.3
5	Myanmar	10.2	14	Mongolia	8.2
6	China	9.5	15	Mozambique	8.0
7	India	9.4	16	Macau	7.9
8	Rwanda	9.1	17	Congo-Kinshasa	7.8
	Turkmenistan	9.1		Nigeria	7.8

Lowest services growth
Average annual % change in real terms, 2006–16

1	Montenegro	-3.1		Ukraine	-0.3
2	Libya	-3.0	11	Italy	-0.1
3	Puerto Rico	-2.3	12	Jamaica	0.3
4	Greece	-2.1	13	Croatia	0.5
5	Yemen	-1.9		Virgin Islands (US)[d]	0.5
6	Syria	-1.7	15	Estonia	0.6
7	Andorra	-1.3		Finland	0.6
8	Bermuda	-0.5		Japan	0.6
9	Bahamas	-0.3		Portugal	0.6

a 2000–06   b 1999–2006   c 1998–2006   d 2007–16
Note: Rankings of highest and lowest industrial growth 2007–15 can be found on page 44.

Trading places

Biggest exporters
% of total world exports (goods, services and income), 2016

1	Euro area (19)	16.54		22	Luxembourg	1.41
2	United States	12.73		23	Australia	1.22
3	China	10.21		24	Thailand	1.21
4	Germany	7.67		25	Sweden	1.15
5	Japan	4.52		26	Hong Kong	1.13
6	United Kingdom	3.94		27	Poland	1.09
7	France	3.88		28	Austria	0.98
8	Netherlands	3.86		29	Brazil	0.97
9	South Korea	2.66		30	Saudi Arabia	0.95
10	Italy	2.63		31	Malaysia	0.89
11	Switzerland	2.43		32	Turkey	0.81
12	Canada	2.32		33	Denmark	0.80
13	Spain	1.96			Vietnam	0.80
14	India	1.88		35	Indonesia	0.72
15	Belgium	1.86		36	Norway	0.71
16	Ireland	1.80		37	Czech Republic	0.69
17	Mexico	1.72		38	Hungary	0.54
18	Singapore	1.68		39	Finland	0.45
19	Taiwan	1.61			Israel	0.45
20	United Arab Emirates	1.60		41	Iran	0.41
21	Russia	1.57			South Africa	0.41

Trade dependency
Trade[a] as % of GDP, 2016

Most			Least		
1	Vietnam	84.3	1	Bermuda	8.3
2	Slovakia	81.7	2	Nigeria	8.6
3	South Sudan	80.6	3	Cuba[b]	8.8
4	United Arab Emirates	74.8	4	Brazil	9.0
5	Singapore	74.4		Sudan	9.0
6	Hungary	66.6	6	Venezuela	9.3
7	Czech Republic	64.3	7	United States	9.8
8	Congo-Brazzaville[b]	61.2	8	Argentina	10.1
9	Slovenia	59.9		Burundi	10.1
10	Lithuania	58.9	10	Hong Kong	10.2
11	Belgium	58.5	11	Yemen[b]	10.4
12	Puerto Rico	58.1	12	Egypt	10.5
13	Netherlands	57.8	13	Timor-Leste	11.5
14	Estonia	54.8	14	Pakistan	11.6
15	Cambodia	54.3	15	Ethiopia	12.0
16	Taiwan	51.8	16	Japan	12.3
17	Malaysia	51.6	17	Central African Rep.	12.7
18	Belarus	51.1	18	Guinea-Bissau	12.9
	Lesotho	51.1	19	Bahamas	13.5
20	Bulgaria	49.0	20	Kenya	13.7
21	Ireland	48.9	21	Colombia	13.8

Notes: The figures are drawn wherever possible from balance of payment statistics, so have differing definitions from statistics taken from customs or similar sources. For Hong Kong and Singapore, only domestic exports and retained imports are used. Euro area data exclude intra-euro area trade.

a Average of imports plus exports of goods.   b 2015

Biggest traders of goods[a]
As % of world, 2017

Imports	Exports
China	United States
United States	China
Germany	Germany
Japan	Japan
Netherlands	United Kingdom
South Korea	France
France	Netherlands
Italy	South Korea
United Kingdom	Canada
Belgium	India
Canada	Italy
Mexico	Mexico
Russia	Belgium
UAE[b]	Spain
Spain	Switzerland
Taiwan	UAE[b]
India	Taiwan
Switzerland	Australia[b]
Australia	Poland
Poland	Russia
Thailand	Turkey
Brazil	Thailand
Malaysia	Vietnam

Biggest earners from services and income
% of world exports of services and income, 2016

1	Euro area (19)	18.21	19	South Korea	1.39
2	United States	18.14		Sweden	1.39
3	United Kingdom	6.10	21	Australia	1.12
4	Germany	5.81	22	Austria	1.05
5	Japan	5.05		Russia	1.05
6	China	5.03	24	Denmark	1.01
7	Netherlands	4.88	25	United Arab Emirates	0.98
8	France	4.80	26	Norway	0.92
9	Luxembourg	3.67	27	Thailand	0.86
10	Hong Kong	3.04	28	Taiwan	0.82
11	Switzerland	3.03	29	Poland	0.72
12	Singapore	2.66	30	Israel	0.58
13	Ireland	2.57	31	Finland	0.54
14	Spain	2.15		Malaysia	0.54
15	India	2.05	33	Brazil	0.52
16	Italy	1.99	34	Turkey	0.50
17	Belgium	1.94	35	Saudi Arabia	0.48
18	Canada	1.81	36	Philippines	0.47

a Individual countries only. b Estimate.

Balance of payments: current account

Largest surpluses
$m, 2016

1	Euro area (19)	428,779	26	Hungary	7,594
2	Germany	297,320	27	Malaysia	6,921
3	China	202,203	28	Papua New Guinea	4,860
4	Japan	193,996	29	Iraq	3,843
5	South Korea	99,243	30	Czech Republic	3,016
6	Taiwan	72,252	31	Luxembourg	2,894
7	Netherlands	65,573	32	Nigeria	2,713
8	Switzerland	63,205	33	Slovenia	2,337
9	Singapore	58,845	34	Botswana	1,985
10	Thailand	48,237	35	Cuba[a]	1,931
11	Italy	47,659	36	Brunei	1,766
12	Russia	24,401	37	Iceland	1,595
13	Spain	23,771	38	Ecuador	1,442
14	Denmark	22,458	39	Croatia	1,390
15	Sweden	21,675	40	Bulgaria	1,243
16	Iran	16,388	41	Portugal	1,200
17	Ireland	14,349	42	Guatemala	1,023
18	Norway	14,301	43	Bangladesh	928
19	United Arab Emirates	13,197	44	Malta	786
20	Hong Kong	12,711	45	Bermuda	766
21	Macau	12,215	46	Kuwait	642
22	Israel	11,879	47	Swaziland	640
23	Puerto Rico	8,639	48	Belgium	484
24	Austria	8,290	49	Estonia	447
25	Vietnam	8,235	50	Uruguay	417

Largest deficits
$m, 2016

1	United States	-451,692	22	Pakistan	-6,895
2	United Kingdom	-154,873	23	Peru	-5,303
3	Canada	-49,423	24	Libya	-4,705
4	Australia	-37,028	25	Congo-Brazzaville[a]	-4,627
5	Turkey	-33,137	26	Morocco	-4,531
6	Algeria	-26,179	27	New Zealand	-4,377
7	Saudi Arabia	-23,843	28	Sudan	-4,127
8	Brazil	-23,546	29	Romania	-3,961
9	Mexico	-22,828	30	Mozambique	-3,912
10	France	-21,124	31	Venezuela	-3,870
11	Egypt	-20,129	32	Afghanistan	-3,805
12	Indonesia	-16,952	33	Tunisia	-3,694
13	Argentina	-14,693	34	Jordan	-3,610
14	Oman	-12,319	35	Chile	-3,499
15	Colombia	-12,129	36	Kenya	-3,332
16	India	-12,114	37	Panama	-3,160
17	Lebanon	-9,863	38	Angola	-3,071
18	Kazakhstan	-8,874	39	Yemen[a]	-3,026
19	Qatar	-8,270	40	Ghana	-2,832
20	Ethiopia	-8,269	41	Guinea	-2,745
21	South Africa	-8,083	42	Trinidad & Tobago	-2,612

Note: Euro area data exclude intra-euro area trade.
a 2015

Largest surpluses as % of GDP
$m, 2016

1	Macau	26.9	26	Hong Kong	4.0
2	Papua New Guinea	21.5	27	Japan	3.9
3	Singapore	19.0		Norway	3.9
4	Swaziland	16.6	29	United Arab Emirates	3.8
5	Brunei	15.5	30	Guyana	3.7
6	Taiwan	13.6		Israel	3.7
7	Bermuda	12.7	32	Euro area (19)	3.6
	Botswana	12.7	33	Croatia	2.7
9	Thailand	11.7	34	Italy	2.6
10	Switzerland	9.5	35	Bulgaria	2.3
11	Germany	8.5		Malaysia	2.3
12	Netherlands	8.4	37	Cuba[a]	2.2
13	Puerto Rico	8.2		Iraq	2.2
14	Iceland	7.9	39	Austria	2.1
15	Denmark	7.3	40	Estonia	1.9
16	Malta	7.0		Russia	1.9
	South Korea	7.0		Spain	1.9
18	Hungary	5.9	43	China	1.8
19	French Polynesia[a]	5.5	44	Czech Republic	1.5
20	Slovenia	5.2		Ecuador	1.5
21	Luxembourg	4.9		Guatemala	1.5
22	Ireland	4.7		Paraguay	1.5
23	Sweden	4.2	48	Latvia	1.4
24	Iran	4.1	49	Guinea-Bissau	0.9
	Vietnam	4.1	50	Uruguay	0.8

Largest deficits as % of GDP
$m, 2016

1	South Sudan	-81.3	22	Trinidad & Tobago	-11.7
2	Congo-Brazzaville[a]	-54.1	23	Burundi	-11.3
3	Mozambique	-34.7		Ethiopia	-11.3
4	Guinea	-32.4	25	Togo[a]	-11.0
5	Liberia[a]	-27.1	26	Sierra Leone	-10.7
6	Libya	-25.4	27	West Bank & Gaza	-10.1
7	Timor-Leste	-21.2	28	Gambia, The	-9.9
8	Lebanon	-19.9	29	Bahamas	-9.8
	Maldives	-19.9	30	Benin	-9.4
10	Afghanistan	-19.6	31	Jordan	-9.3
11	Mauritania	-18.6	32	Chad	-9.2
12	Oman	-18.4	33	Central African Rep.	-9.1
13	Montenegro	-18.0	34	Cambodia	-8.8
14	Algeria	-16.5		Senegal[b]	-8.8
15	Namibia	-16.0		Tunisia	-8.8
16	Niger	-15.7	37	Lesotho	-8.1
17	Rwanda	-14.3	38	Yemen[a]	-8.0
18	Georgia	-13.5	39	Kosovo	-7.9
	Malawi	-13.5	40	Laos	-7.8
20	Kyrgyzstan	-12.1	41	Albania	-7.6
21	New Caledonia[a]	-12.0	42	Nicaragua	-7.5

a 2015   b 2014

Official reserves[a]

$m, end-2017

1	China	3,235,356	16	Mexico	175,448
2	Japan	1,264,006	17	France	155,892
3	Switzerland	810,847	18	United Kingdom	150,803
4	Euro area (19)	800,779	19	Italy	150,687
5	Saudi Arabia[b]	500,818	20	Czech Republic	147,975
6	Taiwan	469,083	21	Indonesia	130,201
7	United States	449,847	22	Poland	113,249
8	Russia	432,405	23	Israel	113,010
9	Hong Kong	431,370	24	Turkey	107,557
10	India	412,515	25	Algeria	104,822
11	South Korea	388,786	26	Malaysia	102,440
12	Brazil	373,944	27	United Arab Emirates	95,376
13	Singapore	284,978	28	Canada	86,678
14	Thailand	202,511	29	Philippines	81,379
15	Germany	199,387	30	Libya	78,905

Official gold reserves

Market prices, $m, end-2017

1	Euro area (19)	447,530	14	Portugal	15,876
2	United States	337,595	15	Saudi Arabia	13,403
3	Germany	140,030	16	United Kingdom	12,879
4	Italy	101,768	17	Kazakhstan	12,492
5	France	101,111	18	Lebanon	11,906
6	China	76,479	19	Spain	11,687
7	Russia	76,321	20	Austria	11,622
8	Switzerland	43,167	21	Belgium	9,439
9	Japan	31,762	22	Philippines	8,150
10	Netherlands	25,421	23	Algeria	7,207
11	Turkey	23,442	24	Venezuela	6,731
12	India	23,165	25	Thailand	6,390
13	Taiwan	17,583	26	Singapore	5,288

Workers' remittances

Inflows, $m, 2016

1	India	62,744	16	Lebanon	7,616
2	China	61,000	17	Guatemala	7,469
3	Philippines	31,145	18	Sri Lanka	7,257
4	Mexico	28,670	19	Morocco	7,088
5	France	24,373	20	Poland	6,712
6	Nigeria	20,112	21	Russia	6,678
7	Pakistan	19,761	22	Nepal	6,607
8	Germany	16,683	23	United States	6,547
9	Egypt	16,590	24	South Korea	6,393
10	Bangladesh	13,559	25	Thailand	6,273
11	Vietnam	11,880	26	Ukraine	6,146
12	Spain	10,281	27	Dominican Rep.	5,509
13	Belgium	9,867	28	Colombia	4,903
14	Italy	9,713	29	Hungary	4,609
15	Indonesia	8,977	30	El Salvador	4,594

a Foreign exchange, SDRs, IMF position and gold at market prices.   b August.

Exchange rates

The Economist's Big Mac index

Local currency under (-) / over (+) valuation
against the $[a], %, January 2018

Big Mac
price, $[b]

	Valuation	Big Mac price, $[b]
Switzerland		6.76
Norway		6.24
Sweden		6.12
United States[c]		5.28
Canada		5.26
Brazil		5.11
Denmark		4.93
Uruguay		4.90
Euro area[d]		4.84
Israel		4.80
Australia		4.71
New Zealand		4.51
United Kingdom		4.41
Singapore		4.39
Chile		4.29
South Korea		4.12
Costa Rica		4.03
Argentina		3.96
Colombia		3.83
UAE		3.81
Czech Republic		3.81
Sri Lanka		3.77
Thailand		3.72
Japan		3.43
Hungary		3.43
Pakistan		3.39
Peru		3.27
Saudi Arabia		3.20
China[e]		3.17
Poland		2.97
Vietnam		2.86
Turkey		2.83
India[f]		2.82
Indonesia		2.68
Philippines		2.64

Scale: 70 60 50 40 30 20 10 – 0 + 10 20 30

a Based on purchasing-power parity: local price of a Big Mac burger divided by United
States price. b At market exchange rates.   c Average of four cities.
d Weighted average of prices in euro area.   e Average of five cities.   f Maharaja Mac.

Inflation

Consumer-price inflation

Highest, 2017, %

1	Venezuela[a]	1,087.50
2	South Sudan[a]	187.9
3	Congo-Kinshasa[a]	41.5
4	Sudan[a]	32.4
5	Angola[a]	31.7
6	Libya	28.0
7	Argentina	25.7
8	Egypt	23.5
9	Suriname	22.0
10	Sierra Leone[a]	18.0
11	Burundi	16.6
12	Nigeria	16.5
13	Mozambique	15.3
14	Haiti	14.7
15	Ukraine	14.4
16	Azerbaijan	13.0
17	Uzbekistan[a]	12.5
18	Ghana	12.4
	Liberia[a]	12.4
20	Malawi	11.5
21	Turkey	11.1

Lowest, 2017, %

1	Chad	-0.9
	Saudi Arabia[a]	-0.9
3	Togo[a]	-0.7
4	Brunei	-0.1
5	Benin	0.1
	Iraq[a]	0.1
7	Israel	0.2
8	Ireland	0.3
9	Burkina Faso[a]	0.4
	Ecuador	0.4
	Qatar	0.4
12	Congo-Brazzaville	0.5
13	Japan	0.5
	Switzerland	0.5
15	Cameroon	0.6
	Singapore	0.6
	Taiwan	0.6
	Timor-Leste	0.6
19	Cyprus[a]	0.7
	Equatorial Guinea	0.7
	Thailand	0.7

Highest average annual consumer-price inflation, 2012–17, %

1	Venezuela[a]	188.9
2	South Sudan[a]	84.6
3	Sudan[a]	27.8
4	Argentina	21.9
5	Malawi	21.3
6	Angola[a]	17.5
7	Ukraine	16.7
8	Suriname	16.4
9	Iran	15.9
10	Ghana	14.8
11	Belarus	13.5
12	Libya	13.2
13	Egypt	12.2
14	Congo-Kinshasa[a]	11.5
	Nigeria	11.5
16	Sierra Leone[a]	11.3
17	Yemen[a]	10.1
18	Uzbekistan[a]	9.9
19	Zambia	9.8
20	Guinea	9.4
21	Liberia[a]	9.3
22	Haiti	9.2
23	Eritrea[a]	8.7
24	Turkey	8.6
25	Ethiopia[a]	8.5

Lowest average annual consumer-price inflation, 2012–17, %

1	Bulgaria	-0.5
2	Bosnia & Herz.	-0.4
	Cyprus[a]	-0.4
	Greece	-0.4
5	Switzerland	-0.3
	Zimbabwe[a]	-0.3
7	Brunei	-0.2
8	Benin	-0.1
9	Ireland	0.2
	Israel	0.2
11	Burkina Faso[a]	0.3
	Croatia	0.3
	Mali[a]	0.3
	Poland	0.3
15	Grenada	0.4
	Senegal	0.4
	Slovakia	0.4
18	Puerto Rico[a]	0.5
	Spain	0.5
20	El Salvador	0.6
	Italy	0.6
	Portugal	0.6
	Singapore	0.6
	Slovenia	0.6

a Estimate.

Commodity prices

	End 2017, % change on a year earlier			2012–17, % change	
1	Timber	48.0	1	Coconut oil	73.3
2	Wool (Aus)	30.3	2	Wool (Aus)	64.6
3	Copper	28.0	3	Zinc	57.4
4	Zinc	25.0	4	Lamb	30.3
5	Aluminium	22.8	5	Timber	20.0
6	Lead	18.5	6	Lead	7.5
7	Oil[a]	15.4	7	Cotton	5.0
8	Lamb	14.7	8	Aluminium	4.5
9	Nickel	14.0	9	Beef (US)	0.5
10	Gold	13.1	10	Beef (Aus)	-2.0
11	Cotton	12.1	11	Copper	-9.8
12	Rice	8.2	12	Coffee	-12.8
13	Wheat	7.3	13	Tin	-16.3
14	Beef (Aus)	4.8	14	Tea	-17.1
15	Beef (US)	3.8	15	Cocoa	-21.7
16	Tea	3.1	16	Gold	-22.8
17	Soya meal	2.3	17	Sugar	-23.5
18	Corn	2.0	18	Hides	-23.6
19	Soyabeans	-3.0	19	Palm oil	-26.5
20	Soya oil	-4.0	20	Wool (NZ)	-27.1
21	Tin	-8.6	21	Soya meal	-27.6
22	Coffee	-10.8	22	Nickel	-29.2
23	Hides	-13.9	23	Rice	-29.6
24	Cocoa	-16.8	24	Soya oil	-32.2
25	Palm oil	-18.0	25	Oil[a]	-32.4
26	Sugar	-19.7	26	Soyabeans	-33.4

The Economist's house prices

	Q3 2017[b], % change on a year earlier			Q4 2012–Q4 2017[b], % change	
1	Iceland	22.6	1	Turkey	74.9
2	Hong Kong	17.6	2	India	71.4
3	Czech Republic	12.4	3	Iceland	67.5
4	Ireland	12.1	4	Ireland	60.8
5	Portugal	10.4	5	Hong Kong	60.3
6	Netherlands	10.2	6	Sweden	53.1
7	Hungary	10.1	7	Colombia	52.4
8	Turkey	9.7	8	New Zealand	50.3
9	Latvia	9.5	9	Estonia	47.0
10	Canada	9.4	10	Hungary	46.4
11	New Zealand	8.6	11	Australia	45.7
12	Lithuania	8.4	12	China	42.9
13	Australia	8.3	13	Canada	42.1
14	Slovenia	7.9	14	Israel	38.1
15	China	7.6	15	United States	35.3
16	Sweden	7.5	16	Indonesia	35.0
17	India	7.3	17	United Kingdom	32.5
	Slovakia	7.3	18	Mexico	31.7
19	Spain	6.7	19	Latvia	31.0
20	Colombia	6.2	20	South Africa	30.3

a West Texas Intermediate.   b Or latest.

Debt

Highest foreign debt[a]

$bn, 2016

1	China	1,429.5		26	Venezuela	113.0
2	Brazil	543.3		27	Romania	95.9
3	Hong Kong	537.3		28	Panama	89.5
4	Russia	524.7		29	Israel	87.7
5	Singapore	504.2		30	Vietnam	87.0
6	India	456.1		31	Philippines	77.3
7	Mexico	422.7		32	Pakistan	72.7
8	Turkey	405.0		33	Peru	69.5
9	South Korea	358.7		34	Egypt	67.2
10	Indonesia	316.4		35	Iraq	64.2
11	Poland	227.4		36	Sudan	52.7
12	United Arab Emirates	218.7		37	Sri Lanka	46.6
13	Malaysia	200.4		38	Morocco	46.3
14	Argentina	190.5		39	Croatia	44.1
15	Saudi Arabia	189.3		40	Bahrain	42.6
16	Taiwan	172.2		41	Bangladesh	41.1
17	Chile	163.8		42	Bulgaria	39.7
	Kazakhstan	163.8		43	Kuwait	38.0
19	Qatar	158.2		44	Belarus	37.5
20	South Africa	146.0		45	Lebanon	36.9
21	Czech Republic	138.0		46	Angola	35.4
22	Hungary	136.1		47	Ecuador	34.1
23	Thailand	121.5		48	Nigeria	31.2
24	Colombia	120.3		49	Cuba	29.9
25	Ukraine	118.0		50	Serbia	29.6

Highest foreign debt burden[a]

Total foreign debt as % of GDP, 2016

1	Mongolia	213.8		21	Mauritania	82.9
2	Hong Kong	167.4		22	Belarus	79.2
3	Singapore	162.8		23	Serbia	77.3
4	Panama	162.2		24	Bulgaria	74.5
5	Mauritius	146.9		25	Lebanon	74.3
6	Bahrain	132.3		26	Tajikistan	71.7
7	Ukraine	126.5		27	Albania	71.1
8	Kazakhstan	122.5		28	Czech Republic	70.7
9	Kyrgyzstan	120.2		29	Jordan	70.2
10	Georgia	111.2		30	Macedonia	68.7
11	Papua New Guinea	109.7		31	Malaysia	67.6
12	Hungary	108.3		32	Tunisia	66.8
13	Qatar	103.8		33	Chile	66.3
14	Jamaica	103.0		34	United Arab Emirates	62.7
15	Mozambique	94.2		35	Bosnia & Herz.	62.5
16	Armenia	94.1		36	Paraguay	59.1
17	Moldova	89.9		37	Namibia	58.0
18	Laos	89.0		38	El Salvador	57.6
19	Croatia	85.9		39	Sri Lanka	57.3
20	Nicaragua	83.2		40	Sudan	55.2

a Foreign debt is debt owed to non-residents and repayable in foreign currency; the figures shown include liabilities of government, public and private sectors. Longer-established developed countries have been excluded.

Highest foreign debt[a]

As % of exports of goods and services, 2016

1	Sudan	1,099.8		15	Brazil	234.1
2	Mongolia	403.0		16	Niger	223.1
3	Venezuela	384.1		17	Chile	218.0
4	Kazakhstan	355.3		18	Mauritania	213.6
5	Laos	319.3		19	Turkey	208.7
6	Panama	302.8		20	Ukraine	208.3
7	Yemen	282.9		21	Jamaica	199.0
8	Central African Rep.	280.2		22	Qatar	198.9
9	Argentina	256.8		23	Sri Lanka	187.7
10	Mozambique	250.2		24	Georgia	184.4
11	Ethiopia	242.2		25	Zimbabwe	183.6
12	Papua New Guinea	236.0		26	Uruguay	181.3
13	Burundi	235.3		27	Kenya	179.6
14	Colombia	235.0		28	Kyrgyzstan	178.6

Highest debt service ratio[b]

Average, %, 2016

1	Syria	75.9		15	Turkey	32.8
2	Venezuela	59.3		16	Bosnia & Herz.	32.4
3	Brazil	50.6		17	Bahrain	30.1
4	Papua New Guinea	48.3		18	Panama	29.8
5	Kazakhstan	44.5		19	Mongolia	27.2
6	Sudan	39.2		20	Jamaica	27.1
7	Namibia	37.7		21	Hungary	26.9
8	Indonesia	37.6		22	Angola	26.5
9	Chile	36.8		23	Colombia	26.2
10	Ukraine	36.3		24	Armenia	25.9
11	Cuba	35.7		25	Zimbabwe	25.6
12	Argentina	34.6		26	Serbia	25.5
13	Georgia	34.2		27	Bulgaria	23.7
14	Croatia	33.6		28	Ecuador	23.6

Household debt[c]

As % of net disposable income, 2016

1	Denmark	285.2		13	Finland	133.1
2	Netherlands	270.1		14	Spain	118.0
3	Norway	229.6		15	Belgium	116.4
4	Australia	213.0		16	United States	111.5
5	Switzerland	212.8		17	France	109.9
6	Luxembourg	184.4		18	Greece	109.0
7	Sweden	180.1		19	Japan[d]	108.0
8	South Korea	178.9		20	Germany	93.4
9	Canada	178.4		21	Austria	91.6
10	Ireland	171.0		22	Italy	88.2
11	United Kingdom	152.7		23	Estonia	80.6
12	Portugal	137.2		24	Slovakia	73.5

b Debt service is the sum of interest and principal repayments (amortisation) due on
outstanding foreign debt. The debt service ratio is debt service as a percentage of
exports of goods, non-factor services, primary income and workers' remittances.
c OECD countries.   d 2015

Aid

Largest recipients of bilateral and multilateral aid
$bn, 2016

	0	2	4	6	8	10
Syria						
Afghanistan						
Ethiopia						
Turkey						
Pakistan						
Vietnam						
Jordan						
Cuba						
India						
Bangladesh						
Nigeria						
West Bank & Gaza						
Iraq						
Tanzania						
Kenya						
Congo-Kinshasa						
Egypt						
Morocco						
Yemen						
Uganda						
South Sudan						
Myanmar						

$ per person, 2016

#	Country	Value	#	Country	Value
1	West Bank & Gaza	527.7	21	Rwanda	96.4
2	Syria	481.2	22	Sierra Leone	93.7
3	Jordan	289.6	23	Moldova	92.4
4	Cuba	233.3	24	Guyana	90.3
5	Kosovo	203.7	25	Serbia	89.8
6	Lebanon	189.5	26	Kyrgyzstan	84.7
7	Timor-Leste	179.5	27	Somalia	81.7
8	Liberia	176.6	28	Macedonia	80.9
9	Montenegro	137.6	29	Burundi	70.5
10	South Sudan	130.0	30	Nicaragua	70.0
11	Bosnia & Herz.	126.6	31	Yemen	69.8
12	Georgia	124.4	32	Malawi	68.7
13	Fiji	121.0	33	Namibia	68.6
14	Afghanistan	117.3	34	Mauritania	67.6
15	Armenia	111.7	35	Mali	67.2
16	Swaziland	109.8	36	Papua New Guinea	65.3
17	Guinea-Bissau	109.6	37	Maldives	64.5
18	Central African Rep.	108.7	38	Bolivia	64.0
19	Mongolia	107.5	39	Iraq	61.4
20	Haiti	99.0	40	Laos	58.9

Largest bilateral and multilateral donors[a]

$bn, 2016

			As % of GDP					As % of GDP
1	United States	34.4	0.2		15	Switzerland	3.6	0.5
2	Germany	24.7	0.7		16	Australia	3.3	0.3
3	United Kingdom	18.1	0.7		17	Denmark	2.4	0.8
4	Japan	10.4	0.2		18	Belgium	2.3	0.5
5	France	9.6	0.4		19	South Korea	2.2	0.2
6	Saudi Arabia[b]	6.8	1.1		20	Austria	1.6	0.4
7	Turkey	6.5	0.1		21	Russia	1.3	0.1
8	Italy	5.1	0.3		22	Finland	1.1	1.0
9	Netherlands	5.0	0.6			Kuwait	1.1	0.4
10	Sweden	4.9	0.9		24	Ireland	0.8	0.3
11	Norway	4.4	1.1		25	Poland	0.7	0.1
12	Spain	4.3	0.3		26	Greece	0.4	0.3
13	United Arab Emirates	4.2	1.2			Israel	0.4	0.1
						Luxembourg	0.4	1.0
14	Canada	3.9	0.3			New Zealand	0.4	0.2

Biggest changes to aid

2016 compared with 2012, $m

Increases			Decreases		
1	Syria	7,198.0	1	Afghanistan	-2,602.4
2	Cuba	2,592.0	2	Ivory Coast	-2,249.9
3	Jordan	1,581.2	3	Vietnam	-1,220.2
4	Yemen	1,214.6	4	Congo-Kinshasa	-738.7
5	Myanmar	1,029.5	5	Brazil	-613.9
6	India	996.8	6	China	-610.6
7	Iraq	983.9	7	Sudan	-558.7
8	Pakistan	935.5	8	Mozambique	-540.3
9	Ethiopia	830.2	9	Tanzania	-504.4
10	Ukraine	751.1	10	Ghana	-483.3
11	Nigeria	584.5	11	Kenya	-464.8
12	Morocco	521.2	12	Serbia	-454.4
13	Turkey	500.8	13	Tunisia	-394.7
14	Lebanon	426.9	14	Zimbabwe	-346.9
15	South Sudan	403.8	15	Senegal	-339.4
16	Mexico	401.4	16	Azerbaijan	-209.3
17	West Bank & Gaza	395.7	17	Haiti	-199.1
18	Thailand	359.1	18	Kosovo	-196.7
19	Bangladesh	349.5	19	Georgia	-196.5
20	Colombia	342.4	20	Indonesia	-181.1
21	Egypt	316.9	21	Albania	-180.6
22	Nepal	296.2	22	Argentina	-175.2
23	Philippines	290.2	23	Lesotho	-163.4
24	Central African Rep.	271.6	24	Honduras	-154.5
25	Rwanda	269.7	25	Moldova	-147.1
26	Sierra Leone	253.4	26	Papua New Guinea	-142.4
27	Madagascar	253.3	27	Mauritius	-134.3
28	Liberia	248.3	28	Burkina Faso	-129.0
29	Burundi	218.0	29	Sri Lanka	-125.8

a China also provides aid, but does not disclose amounts.   b 2015

Industry and services

Largest industrial output
$bn, 2016

1	China	4,458	23	Iran	142
2	United States[a]	3,497	24	Poland	141
3	Japan	1,450		United Arab Emirates	141
4	Germany	955	26	Netherlands	140
5	India	588	27	Argentina	123
6	Canada[b]	495	28	Malaysia	114
7	South Korea	494	29	Sweden	112
8	United Kingdom	477	30	Ireland	111
9	France	431	31	Egypt	108
10	Italy	399	32	Norway	105
11	Russia	375	33	Austria	97
12	Indonesia	367	34	Philippines	94
13	Brazil	330	35	Belgium	93
14	Mexico	321	36	Colombia	84
15	Saudi Arabia	280	37	Qatar	79
16	Australia	274	38	South Africa	76
17	Spain	264	39	Nigeria	74
18	Turkey	243	40	Singapore	73
19	Taiwan	203	41	Chile	71
20	Venezuela[b]	180	42	Vietnam	67
21	Switzerland	167	43	Czech Republic	66
22	Thailand	146	44	Iraq	64

Highest growth in industrial output
Average annual % increase in real terms, 2006–16

1	Timor-Leste[c]	23.9	11	Qatar	9.1
2	Ethiopia	15.5	12	Montenegro	8.9
3	Myanmar	14.8	13	Tanzania	8.8
4	Laos	11.8	14	Bangladesh	8.7
5	Panama	11.5		Ghana	8.7
6	Liberia	11.0	16	Iraq	8.6
7	Uzbekistan	10.7	17	Niger	8.5
8	Rwanda	9.5	18	Cambodia	8.1
9	China	9.4	19	Burkina Faso	7.7
10	Congo-Kinshasa	9.2			

Lowest growth in industrial output
Average annual % change in real terms, 2006–16

1	Yemen	-7.0	12	Trinidad & Tobago	-1.7
2	Bermuda[d]	-6.3	13	Bahamas	-1.6
3	Greece	-5.4		Jamaica	-1.6
4	Cyprus	-4.8	15	Finland	-1.5
5	Ukraine	-4.0		Portugal	-1.5
6	Macau[e]	-3.4	17	Croatia	-1.2
7	Barbados	-3.1	18	Botswana	-0.9
8	Brunei	-2.6	19	Denmark	-0.8
9	Latvia	-2.0	20	Equatorial Guinea	-0.6
	Spain	-2.0	21	Norway	-0.5
11	Italy	-1.8		United Kingdom	-0.5

a 2015   b 2014   c 2006–15   d 2006–12   e 2008–16

Largest manufacturing output
$bn, 2016

1	China[a]	3,250		21	Netherlands	85
2	United States[a]	2,142			Poland	85
3	Japan	1,042		23	Saudi Arabia	83
4	Germany	718		24	Argentina	76
5	South Korea	376		25	Australia	74
6	India	337		26	Sweden	70
7	Italy	272		27	Malaysia	66
8	France	251		28	Austria	63
9	United Kingdom	239		29	Belgium	60
10	Indonesia	191			Philippines	60
11	Mexico	187		31	Venezuela[b]	58
12	Brazil	182		32	Egypt	56
13	Taiwan	177		33	Singapore	55
14	Canada[b]	176		34	Iran	50
15	Russia	159			Puerto Rico	50
	Spain	159		36	Czech Republic	48
17	Turkey	143		37	Denmark	41
18	Switzerland	119		38	Bangladesh	38
19	Thailand	112		39	Israel	37
20	Ireland	98		40	Romania	36

Largest services output
$bn, 2016

1	United States[a]	13,780		27	Nigeria	242
2	China	5,783		28	Thailand	227
3	Japan	3,404		29	Venezuela[b]	226
4	Germany	2,158		30	Iran	223
5	United Kingdom	1,872		31	Israel	222
6	France	1,737		32	Norway	215
7	Italy	1,234		33	Singapore	205
8	Canada[b]	1,163			United Arab Emirates	205
9	Brazil	1,138		35	Denmark	201
10	India	1,097		36	Egypt	181
11	Spain	828			Philippines	181
12	Australia	823			South Africa	181
13	South Korea	759		39	Ireland	169
14	Russia	726		40	Malaysia	157
15	Mexico	622		41	Colombia	156
16	Netherlands	546		42	Pakistan	147
17	Switzerland	477		43	Chile	145
18	Turkey	464		44	Finland	144
19	Indonesia	407		45	Portugal	135
20	Saudi Arabia	349		46	Greece	134
21	Sweden	337		47	New Zealand[b]	131
22	Belgium	322		48	Bangladesh	119
23	Argentina	303		49	Romania	107
24	Hong Kong	287		50	Peru	106
25	Poland	265		51	Czech Republic	105
26	Austria	247		52	Iraq	99

a 2015   b 2014

Agriculture and fisheries

Largest agricultural output
$bn, 2016

1	China	958		Italy	35
2	India	354	**17**	Thailand	34
3	United States[a]	184		Vietnam	34
4	Indonesia	125	**19**	Bangladesh	31
5	Brazil	85		Spain	31
	Nigeria	85	**21**	Sudan	30
7	Pakistan	65	**22**	Australia	29
8	Japan	57		Philippines	29
9	Russia	55	**24**	South Korea	28
10	Turkey	53	**25**	Canada[b]	26
11	Iran	40		Malaysia	26
12	Egypt	39	**27**	Ethiopia	25
13	Mexico	38	**28**	Venezuela[b]	24
14	France	36	**29**	Kenya	23
15	Argentina	35	**30**	Algeria	20

Most economically dependent on agriculture
% of GDP from agriculture, 2016

1	Sierra Leone	59.4	**15**	Rwanda	31.5
2	Chad	50.1		Tanzania	31.5
3	Guinea-Bissau	49.1	**17**	Burkina Faso	30.8
4	Central African Rep.	42.9	**18**	Malawi	28.1
5	Mali	42.1	**19**	Mauritania	27.4
6	Guyana	41.5	**20**	Cambodia	26.7
	Niger	41.5	**21**	Uganda	25.8
8	Togo	41.3	**22**	Benin	25.6
9	Burundi	39.8	**23**	Myanmar	25.5
10	Sudan	39.0	**24**	Tajikistan[a]	25.0
11	Ethiopia	37.2	**25**	Mozambique	24.8
12	Kenya	35.6	**26**	Madagascar	24.7
13	Liberia	34.2	**27**	Pakistan	24.6
14	Nepal	33.0	**28**	Ivory Coast	23.4

Least economically dependent on agriculture
% of GDP from agriculture, 2016

1	Macau	0.0	**14**	Bermuda[c]	0.8
	Singapore	0.0		Puerto Rico	0.8
3	Hong Kong	0.1		United Arab Emirates	0.8
4	Qatar	0.2	**17**	Denmark	0.9
5	Bahrain	0.3	**18**	Bahamas	1.0
	Luxembourg	0.3		Ireland	1.0
7	Andorra[a]	0.5	**20**	United States[a]	1.1
	Kuwait	0.5	**21**	Austria	1.2
	Trinidad & Tobago	0.5		Brunei	1.2
10	Germany	0.6		Japan	1.2
	United Kingdom	0.6	**24**	Israel	1.3
12	Belgium	0.7		Sweden	1.3
	Switzerland	0.7	**26**	Malta	1.4

a 2015   b 2014   c 2012

Fisheries and aquaculture production

Fish, crustaceans and molluscs, million tonnes, 2016

1	China	66.8	16	Malaysia	1.8
2	Indonesia	11.5	17	Egypt	1.7
3	India	10.8		Mexico	1.7
4	Vietnam	6.4	19	Morocco	1.4
5	United States	5.4	20	Brazil	1.3
6	Russia	4.9	21	Ecuador	1.2
7	Bangladesh	3.9		Spain	1.2
	Japan	3.9	23	Canada	1.1
	Peru	3.9		Iceland	1.1
10	Norway	3.4		Iran	1.1
11	Myanmar	3.1	26	Nigeria	1.0
12	Philippines	2.8		Taiwan	1.0
13	Chile	2.5	28	United Kingdom	0.9
	Thailand	2.5	29	Argentina	0.8
15	South Korea	1.9		Cambodia	0.8

Biggest producers

'000 tonnes, 2015

Cereals

1	China	572,045	6	Indonesia	95,010
2	United States	431,866	7	France	72,876
3	India	284,333	8	Ukraine	59,623
4	Brazil	106,030	9	Argentina	55,651
5	Russia	102,451	10	Bangladesh	54,904

Meat

1	China	85,248	6	India	7,070
2	United States	43,264	7	Mexico	6,353
3	Brazil	26,637	8	Spain	6,057
4	Russia	9,565	9	France	5,652
5	Germany	8,383	10	Argentina	5,311

Fruit

1	China	166,918	6	Mexico	18,628
2	India	87,400	7	Spain	17,839
3	Brazil	37,482	8	Italy	17,263
4	United States	24,857	9	Philippines	16,468
5	Indonesia	19,974	10	Turkey	14,658

Vegetables

1	China	625,140	6	Iran	18,886
2	India	119,485	7	Russia	17,786
3	United States	36,507	8	Vietnam	15,353
4	Turkey	29,311	9	Mexico	14,817
5	Egypt	18,907	10	Italy	14,403

Roots and tubers

1	China	172,604	5	Thailand	32,864
2	Nigeria	111,638	6	Brazil	27,772
3	India	53,610	7	Ghana	25,951
4	Russia	33,646	8	Indonesia	25,729

Commodities

Wheat

Top 10 producers, 2016–17
'000 tonnes

1	EU28	144,200
2	China	128,900
3	India	86,000
4	Russia	72,500
5	United States	62,800
6	Australia	34,400
7	Canada	31,700
8	Ukraine	26,800
9	Pakistan	25,600
10	Turkey	20,600

Top 10 consumers, 2016–17
'000 tonnes

1	EU28	126,500
2	China	121,200
3	India	97,300
4	Russia	37,600
5	United States	31,800
6	Pakistan	24,600
7	Egypt	20,500
8	Turkey	19,100
9	Iran	17,300
10	Brazil	11,300

Rice[a]

Top 10 producers, 2016–17
'000 tonnes

1	China	144,953
2	India	109,698
3	Indonesia	36,858
4	Bangladesh	34,578
5	Vietnam	27,400
6	Thailand	19,200
7	Burma	12,650
8	Philippines	11,686
9	Brazil	8,383
10	Japan	7,780

Top 10 consumers, 2016–17
'000 tonnes

1	China	141,448
2	India	95,776
3	Indonesia	37,800
4	Bangladesh	35,000
5	Vietnam	22,000
6	Philippines	12,900
7	Thailand	12,000
8	Burma	10,000
9	Japan	8,500
10	Brazil	8,000

Sugar[b]

Top 10 producers, 2016
'000 tonnes

1	Brazil	38,990
2	India	24,790
3	EU28	15,470
4	China	9,990
5	Thailand	9,260
6	United States	7,750
7	Mexico	6,090
8	Russia	5,770
9	Pakistan	5,610
10	Australia	4,620

Top 10 consumers, 2016
'000 tonnes

1	India	24,760
2	EU28	18,770
3	China	15,780
4	Brazil	11,100
5	United States	10,330
6	Indonesia	6,430
7	Russia	5,700
8	Pakistan	4,990
9	Mexico	4,490
10	Egypt	3,400

Coarse grains[c]

Top 5 producers, 2016–17
'000 tonnes

1	United States	403,000
2	China	228,000
3	EU28	153,100
4	Brazil	101,000
5	Argentina	56,300

Top 5 consumers, 2016–17
'000 tonnes

1	United States	328,100
2	China	236,200
3	EU28	157,900
4	Brazil	67,100
5	Mexico	47,700

a Milled. b Raw. c Includes: maize (corn), barley, sorghum, oats, rye, millet, triticale and other. d Tonnes at 65 degrees brix.

Tea

Top 10 producers, 2016		*Top 10 consumers, 2016*	
'000 tonnes		*'000 tonnes*	
1 China	2,402	1 China	2,134
2 India	1,252	2 India	1,052
3 Kenya	473	3 Turkey	320
4 Sri Lanka	349	4 Pakistan	174
5 Turkey	243	5 Russia	154
6 Vietnam	240	6 United States	128
7 Indonesia	144	7 United Kingdom	110
8 Myanmar	102	8 Japan	105
9 Argentina	90	9 Egypt	85
10 Japan	80	10 Bangladesh	82

Coffee

Top 10 producers, 2017		*Top 10 consumers, 2016–17*	
'000 tonnes		*'000 tonnes*	
1 Brazil	3,060	1 EU28	2,543
2 Vietnam	1,770	2 United States	1,547
3 Colombia	840	3 Brazil	1,230
4 Indonesia	720	4 Japan	475
5 Honduras	501	5 Russia	278
6 Ethiopia	459	6 Indonesia	276
7 India	350	7 Canada	227
8 Uganda	306	8 Ethiopia	224
9 Peru	258	9 Philippines	180
10 Mexico	240	10 Mexico	142

Cocoa

Top 10 producers, 2016–17		*Top 10 consumers, 2016–17*	
'000 tonnes		*'000 tonnes*	
1 Ivory Coast	2,020	1 Ivory Coast	577
2 Ghana	970	2 Netherlands	565
3 Indonesia	290	3 Indonesia	455
4 Ecuador	270	4 Germany	410
5 Cameroon	246	5 United States	390
6 Nigeria	245	6 Ghana	250
7 Brazil	174	7 Brazil	227
8 Peru	115	8 Malaysia	216
9 Dominican Rep.	57	9 France	143
10 Colombia	55	10 Spain	115

Orange juice[d]

Top 5 producers, 2016–17		*Top 5 consumers, 2016–17*	
'000 tonnes		*'000 tonnes*	
1 Brazil	1,152	1 EU28	717
2 United States	215	2 United States	510
3 Mexico	171	3 China	96
4 EU28	102	4 Canada	82
5 China	44	5 Japan	70

Copper

Top 10 producers[a], 2016 *'000 tonnes*		*Top 10 consumers[b], 2016* *'000 tonnes*	
1 Chile	5,553	1 China	11,642
2 Peru	2,354	2 EU28	3,357
3 China	1,851	3 United States	1,811
4 United States	1,431	4 Germany	1,243
5 Congo-Kinshasa	1,024	5 Japan	973
6 Australia	948	6 South Korea	759
7 EU28	889	7 Italy	596
8 Mexico	766	8 Brazil	511
9 Russia	740	9 Taiwan	507
10 Zambia	738	10 India	499

Lead

Top 10 producers[a], 2016 *'000 tonnes*		*Top 10 consumers[b], 2016* *'000 tonnes*	
1 China	2,230	1 China	4,655
2 Australia	453	2 EU28	1,784
3 United States	342	3 United States	1,610
4 Peru	314	4 South Korea	622
5 Mexico	241	5 India	567
6 Russia	192	6 Germany	374
7 EU28	175	7 United Kingdom	285
8 India	139	8 Japan	264
9 Bolivia	90	9 Spain	262
10 Sweden	75	10 Mexico	252

Zinc

Top 10 producers[a], 2016 *'000 tonnes*		*Top 10 consumers[c], 2016* *'000 tonnes*	
1 China	5,270	1 China	6,693
2 Peru	1,334	2 EU28	2,100
3 Australia	860	3 United States	789
4 United States	798	4 India	672
5 EU28	690	5 South Korea	619
6 Mexico	661	6 Germany	483
7 India	653	7 Japan	470
8 Bolivia	487	8 Belgium	353
9 Kazakhstan	366	9 Spain	283
10 Canada	322	10 Italy	268

Tin

Top 5 producers[a], 2016 *'000 tonnes*		*Top 5 consumers[b], 2016* *'000 tonnes*	
1 China	153.1	1 China	191.4
2 Myanmar	95.0	2 EU28	53.2
3 Indonesia	60.0	3 United States	29.5
4 Peru	18.8	4 Japan	26.1
5 Brazil	18.0	5 Germany	18.2

Nickel

Top 10 producers[a], 2016		*Top 10 consumers[b], 2016*	
'ooo tonnes		*'ooo tonnes*	
1 Philippines	311.1	**1** China	875.7
2 Canada	235.7	**2** EU28	344.1
3 Russia	221.4	**3** Japan	161.9
4 New Caledonia	208.8	**4** United States	136.2
5 Australia	203.1	**5** South Korea	103.3
6 Indonesia	172.7	**6** Taiwan	65.9
7 China	90.0	**7** Finland	64.0
8 Brazil	74.4	**8** Germany	57.6
9 Cuba	51.6	**9** India	57.4
10 South Africa	49.0	**10** Italy	56.0

Aluminium

Top 10 producers[d], 2016		*Top 10 consumers[e], 2016*	
'ooo tonnes		*'ooo tonnes*	
1 China	31,870	**1** China	31,615
2 Russia	3,561	**2** EU28	7,137
3 Canada	3,209	**3** United States	5,121
4 United Arab Emirates	2,471	**4** Germany	2,197
5 EU28	2,313	**5** Japan	1,742
6 India	1,909	**6** South Korea	1,453
7 Australia	1,635	**7** India	1,378
8 Norway	1,247	**8** Turkey	949
9 Bahrain	971	**9** Italy	909
10 Saudi Arabia	869	**10** United Arab Emirates	835

Precious metals

Gold[a]		*Silver[a]*	
Top 10 producers, 2016		*Top 10 producers, 2016*	
tonnes		*tonnes*	
1 China	453.5	**1** Mexico	5,409
2 Australia	287.3	**2** Peru	4,273
3 Russia	253.5	**3** China	3,496
4 United States	225.7	**4** EU28	2,184
5 Indonesia	170.5	**5** Chile	1,497
6 Peru	168.5	**6** Poland	1,482
7 Canada	165.0	**7** Russia	1,449
8 South Africa	150.0	**8** Australia	1,418
9 Mexico	134.1	**9** Bolivia	1,353
10 Ghana	95.0	**10** Kazakhstan	1,180

Platinum		*Palladium*	
Top 3 producers, 2015		*Top 3 producers, 2015*	
tonnes		*tonnes*	
1 South Africa	142.1	**1** South Africa	76.1
2 Russia	20.8	**2** Russia	69
3 Zimbabwe	12.5	**3** United States/Canada	24.6

a Mine production.   b Refined consumption.   c Slab consumption.
d Primary refined production.   e Primary refined consumption.

Rubber (natural and synthetic)

Top 10 producers, 2016		*Top 10 consumers, 2016*	
'000 tonnes		*'000 tonnes*	
1 Thailand	4,747	1 China	9,166
2 China	3,756	2 EU28	3,642
3 Indonesia	3,208	3 India	1,623
4 EU28	2,473	4 United States	2,844
5 United States	2,368	5 Japan	1,543
6 Japan	1,566	6 Thailand	1,152
7 South Korea	1,546	7 Indonesia	583
8 Russia	1,517	8 Malaysia	908
9 Vietnam	1,032	9 Brazil	966
10 Taiwan	707	10 South Korea	381

Cotton

Top 10 producers, 2016–17		*Top 10 consumers, 2016–17*	
'000 tonnes		*'000 tonnes*	
1 India	5,865	1 China	8,000
2 China	4,900	2 India	5,148
3 United States	3,738	3 Pakistan	2,147
4 Pakistan	1,663	4 Turkey	1,455
5 Brazil	1,530	5 Bangladesh	1,409
6 Australia	891	6 Vietnam	1,168
7 Uzbekistan	789	7 United States	708
8 Turkey	703	8 Indonesia	700
9 Turkmenistan	296	9 Brazil	690
10 Burkina Faso	285	10 Mexico	420

Major oil seeds[a]

Top 5 producers, 2016–17		*Top 5 consumers, 2016–17*	
'000 tonnes		*'000 tonnes*	
1 United States	126,934	1 China	141,281
2 Brazil	117,014	2 United States	65,607
3 Argentina	62,818	3 Brazil	55,854
4 China	56,336	4 EU28	53,499
5 India	37,026	5 Argentina	51,840

Major vegetable oils[b]

Top 5 producers, 2016–17		*Top 5 consumers, 2016–17*	
'000 tonnes		*'000 tonnes*	
1 Indonesia	36,000	1 China	31,149
2 China	23,385	2 EU28	23,415
3 Malaysia	18,952	3 India	19,667
4 EU28	16,273	4 United States	13,234
5 United States	11,033	5 Indonesia	9,104

a Soyabeans, rapeseed (canola), cottonseed, sunflowerseed and groundnuts
(peanuts). b Palm, soyabean, rapeseed and sunflowerseed oil.
c Includes crude oil, shale oil, oil sands and natural gas liquids. d Opec member.
e Opec membership suspended 30 November 2016.

Oil[c]

Top 10 producers, 2017
'000 barrels per day

1	United States	13,057
2	Saudi Arabia[d]	11,951
3	Russia	11,257
4	Iran[d]	4,982
5	Canada	4,831
6	Iraq[d]	4,520
7	United Arab Emirates[d]	3,935
8	China	3,846
9	Kuwait[d]	3,025
10	Brazil	2,734

Top 10 consumers, 2017
'000 barrels per day

1	United States	19,880
2	China	12,799
3	India	4,690
4	Japan	3,988
5	Saudi Arabia[d]	3,918
6	Russia	3,224
7	Brazil	3,017
8	South Korea	2,796
9	Germany	2,447
10	Canada	2,428

Natural gas

Top 10 producers, 2017
Billion cubic metres

1	United States	734.5
2	Russia	635.6
3	Iran[d]	223.9
4	Canada	176.3
5	Qatar[d]	175.7
6	China	149.2
7	Norway	123.2
8	Australia	113.5
9	Saudi Arabia[d]	111.4
10	Algeria[d]	91.2

Top 10 consumers, 2017
Billion cubic metres

1	United States	739.5
2	Russia	424.8
3	China	240.4
4	Iran[d]	214.4
5	Japan	117.1
6	Canada	115.7
7	Saudi Arabia[d]	111.4
8	Germany	90.2
9	Mexico	87.6
10	United Kingdom	78.8

Coal

Top 10 producers, 2017
Million tonnes oil equivalent

1	China	1,747.2
2	United States	371.3
3	Australia	297.4
4	India	294.2
5	Indonesia[e]	271.6
6	Russia	206.3
7	South Africa	143.0
8	Colombia	61.4
9	Poland	49.6
10	Kazakhstan	47.9

Top 10 consumers, 2017
Million tonnes oil equivalent

1	China	1,892.6
2	India	424.0
3	United States	332.1
4	Japan	120.5
5	Russia	92.3
6	South Korea	86.3
7	South Africa	82.2
8	Germany	71.3
9	Indonesia[e]	57.2
10	Poland	48.7

Oil reserves[c]

Top proved reserves, end 2017
% of world total

1	Venezuela[d]	17.9	6	Russia	6.3
2	Saudi Arabia[d]	15.7	7	Kuwait[d]	6.0
3	Canada	10.0	8	United Arab Emirates[d]	5.8
4	Iran[d]	9.3	9	Libya[d]	2.9
5	Iraq[d]	8.8		United States	2.9

Energy

Largest producers
Million tonnes of oil equivalent, 2015

1	China	2,601		16	Venezuela	191
2	United States	2,107		17	Kuwait	174
3	Russia	1,411		18	Algeria	169
4	Saudi Arabia	720		19	Kazakhstan	163
5	Canada	518			Nigeria	163
6	Australia	365		21	France	132
7	Iran	364		22	United Kingdom	129
8	India	359		23	Colombia	125
9	Indonesia	330		24	South Africa	119
10	Brazil	262		25	Germany	114
11	Qatar	256		26	Angola	100
12	United Arab Emirates	244			Malaysia	100
13	Norway	240		28	Turkmenistan	92
14	Iraq	219		29	Egypt	83
15	Mexico	196		30	Oman	80

Largest consumers
Million tonnes of oil equivalent, 2015

1	China	3,017		16	Italy	168
2	United States	2,343		17	Turkey	144
3	Russia	747		18	Australia	142
4	India	637		19	Spain	140
5	Japan	473		20	Thailand	128
6	Canada	362		21	South Africa	123
7	Germany	333		22	Taiwan	114
8	Brazil	320		23	United Arab Emirates	111
9	South Korea	287		24	Poland	98
10	Iran	273		25	Argentina	97
11	Saudi Arabia	269		26	Netherlands	95
12	France	259		27	Egypt	89
13	United Kingdom	205		28	Singapore	87
14	Mexico	192			Ukraine	87
15	Indonesia	173		30	Malaysia	79

Energy efficiency[a]
GDP per unit of energy use, 2014

	Most efficient			Least efficient	
1	South Sudan	32.8	1	Congo-Kinshasa	1.9
2	Hong Kong	26.8	2	Trinidad & Tobago	2.2
3	Ireland[b]	21.6	3	Iceland[b]	2.5
4	Sri Lanka	20.7		Mozambique	2.5
5	Switzerland[b]	19.3	5	Ethiopia	2.9
6	Panama	18.4		Togo	2.9
7	Colombia	17.9		Turkmenistan	2.9
	Malta	17.9	8	Ukraine	3.4
9	Dominican Rep.	17.2	9	Bahrain	4.1
10	Mauritius	16.4	10	Haiti	4.2
11	Denmark[b]	16.1	11	South Africa	4.6

a 2011 PPP $ per kg of oil equivalent.   b 2015   c 2014

Net energy importers

% of commercial energy use, 2014

Highest

1	Hong Kong	98.7
2	Malta	98.4
3	Lebanon	97.9
4	Singapore	97.7
5	Jordan	96.8
6	Luxembourgb	96.3
7	Cyprus	94.0
8	Japanb	93.0
9	Morocco	90.7
10	Moldova	90.0
11	Belarus	86.8
12	Dominican Rep.	86.7

Lowest

1	South Sudan	-1,058.1
2	Norwayb	-581.3
3	Angola	-541.0
4	Congo-Brazzaville	-496.6
5	Qatar	-399.0
6	Kuwait	-391.1
7	Brunei	-357.4
8	Azerbaijan	-310.4
9	Colombia	-274.1
10	Iraq	-229.4
11	Gabon	-213.4
12	Oman	-206.2

Largest consumption per person

Kg of oil equivalent, 2015

1	Qatarc	18,563
2	Iceland	17,479
3	Trinidad & Tobagoc	14,447
4	Bahrainc	10,594
5	Kuwaitc	8,957
6	Bruneic	8,632
7	United Arab Emiratesc	7,769
8	Canada	7,604
9	Saudi Arabiac	6,937
10	United States	6,801
11	Luxembourg	6,548

12	Omanc	6,142
13	Finland	5,925
14	Norway	5,816
15	Australia	5,476
16	South Korea	5,413
17	Singaporec	5,122
18	Sweden	5,103
19	Russiac	4,943
20	Turkmenistanc	4,893
21	Belgium	4,688
22	New Zealand	4,445

Sources of electricity

As % of total, 2015

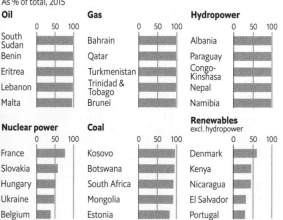

Oil

South Sudan
Benin
Eritrea
Lebanon
Malta

Gas

Bahrain
Qatar
Turkmenistan
Trinidad & Tobago
Brunei

Hydropower

Albania
Paraguay
Congo-Kinshasa
Nepal
Namibia

Nuclear power

France
Slovakia
Hungary
Ukraine
Belgium

Coal

Kosovo
Botswana
South Africa
Mongolia
Estonia

Renewables
excl. hydropower

Denmark
Kenya
Nicaragua
El Salvador
Portugal

Labour markets

Labour-force participation
% of working-age population[a] working or looking for work, 2017 or latest

Highest			Lowest		
1	Qatar	86.8	1	Yemen	32.7
2	Rwanda	85.0	2	Jordan	33.3
3	Madagascar	84.9	3	Bosnia & Herz.	34.7
4	Cambodia	84.5	4	Syria	34.8
5	Nepal	81.9	5	Puerto Rico	36.8
6	Tanzania	81.5	6	Algeria	37.3
7	Zimbabwe	79.3	7	Timor-Leste	37.5
8	Niger	78.6	8	Iran	38.4
9	United Arab Emirates	78.3	9	South Africa	39.6
10	Ethiopia	78.2	10	Tunisia	39.8
11	Laos	77.8	11	Swaziland	40.0
12	Burundi	77.7	12	Sudan	40.5
13	North Korea	76.6	13	Moldova	40.6
	Vietnam	76.6	14	Montenegro	40.7
15	Eritrea	76.2	15	Gabon	41.3
16	Togo	76.1	16	Greece	41.6
17	Ghana	75.1	17	Egypt	42.2
	Iceland	75.1	18	Macedonia	42.4
19	Peru	73.8	19	Iraq	42.7
20	Cameroon	73.0	20	Italy	43.1
21	Malawi	72.3	21	Libya	43.2
22	Angola	71.3	22	French Polynesia	43.4
	Bahrain	71.3		Somalia	43.4
24	Congo-Kinshasa	69.8	24	Lebanon	44.2
25	Macau	69.4	25	Mauritania	44.4
26	Uganda	69.2		Morocco	44.4
27	Benin	69.1	27	Croatia	45.8
28	Zambia	69.0		Turkey	45.8

Most male workforce
Highest % men in workforce, 2017

1	Yemen	93.3
2	Syria	90.0
3	Oman	89.5
4	United Arab Emirates	87.9
5	Qatar	86.0
6	Saudi Arabia	85.9
7	Jordan	84.4
8	Afghanistan	83.4
9	Algeria	83.2
10	Iran	82.9
11	Iraq	81.0
12	Egypt	80.2
13	Bahrain	79.7
	Somalia	79.7
15	Libya	78.3
	Pakistan	78.3

Most female workforce
Highest % women in workforce, 2017

1	Mozambique	53.5
2	Burundi	52.6
3	Nepal	52.0
4	Rwanda	51.5
5	Lithuania	51.2
6	Latvia	50.8
7	Sierra Leone	50.6
8	Angola	49.9
	Cambodia	49.9
10	Laos	49.8
	Virgin Islands (US)	49.8
	Zimbabwe	49.8
13	Barbados	49.7
	Belarus	49.7
	Moldova	49.7
16	Guinea	49.6

a Aged 15 and over.

Highest rate of unemployment
% of labour force[a], 2017

1	West Bank & Gaza	27.9	26	Yemen	13.8
2	South Africa	27.7	27	Iran	13.1
3	Kosovo[b]	27.5	28	Brazil	12.9
4	Lesotho	27.3	29	Sudan	12.8
5	Swaziland	26.4	30	Bahamas	12.6
6	Bosnia & Herz.	25.6	31	Jamaica	12.5
7	Mozambique	25.0	32	Egypt	12.1
8	Namibia	23.3	33	Guyana	11.8
9	Macedonia	23.0	34	Puerto Rico	11.7
10	Greece	21.4	35	Georgia	11.6
11	French Polynesia	20.8	36	Kenya	11.5
12	Gabon	19.6		South Sudan	11.5
13	Armenia	18.2	38	Italy	11.3
14	Botswana	18.1		Turkey	11.3
15	Libya	17.7	40	Congo-Brazzaville	11.0
16	Spain	17.4	41	Croatia	10.8
17	Montenegro	16.0		Cyprus	10.8
	Oman	16.0	43	Tajikistan	10.3
19	Syria	15.2	44	Mauritania	10.2
	Tunisia	15.2	45	Algeria	10.0
21	Jordan	14.9	46	Barbados	9.7
22	New Caledonia	14.8		France	9.7
23	Serbia	14.1	48	Gambia, The	9.5
24	Haiti	14.0		Ukraine	9.5
25	Albania	13.9	50	Channel Islands	9.4

Highest rate of youth unemployment
% of labour force[a] aged 15–24, 2017 estimates

1	South Africa	57.4	21	Tunisia	35.8
2	French Polynesia	55.6	22	Botswana	35.7
3	Bosnia & Herz.	55.4	23	Syria	34.9
4	Swaziland	54.8	24	Saudi Arabia	34.7
5	Kosovo[b]	52.4	25	Egypt	34.4
6	Oman	48.2	26	Montenegro	33.1
7	Macedonia	46.9	27	Serbia	32.8
8	Libya	46.0	28	Brazil	30.5
9	Namibia	45.5	29	Iran	30.3
10	West Bank & Gaza	44.5	30	Albania	30.0
11	Greece	42.8	31	Jamaica	29.7
12	Mozambique	42.7	32	Georgia	29.3
13	Jordan	39.8	33	Barbados	29.0
14	Spain	39.4	34	Sudan	28.4
15	Armenia	39.0	35	Brunei	28.2
16	Lesotho	38.5	36	Guyana	26.3
17	New Caledonia	38.1	37	Kenya	26.2
18	Italy	36.9	38	Croatia	25.9
19	Gabon	36.5	39	Bahamas	25.7
20	Haiti	36.0	40	Yemen	25.5

a ILO definition.   b 2016

Minimum wage
Gross monthly pay[a], $, 2016

1	Luxembourg	2,190	15	Poland	1,055
2	Belgium	1,913	16	Croatia	895
	Ireland	1,913	17	Lithuania	847
4	Netherlands	1,911	18	Slovakia	832
5	Germany	1,851	19	Hungary	831
6	France	1,825	20	Estonia	795
7	United Kingdom	1,724	21	Czech Republic	770
8	Slovenia	1,350	22	Romania	764
9	United States	1,257	23	Latvia	755
10	Turkey	1,226	24	Macedonia	754
11	Malta	1,218	25	Serbia	692
12	Spain	1,157	26	Bulgaria	620
13	Greece	1,119	27	Costa Rica	542
14	Portugal	1,057	28	Albania	510

Average hours worked
Per employed person per week, 2016

1	Nepal[b]	53.6	13	Panama	44.2
2	Myanmar[b]	50.8	14	Costa Rica	43.9
3	Qatar	50.0	15	Colombia	43.8
4	Bangladesh	49.0	16	Egypt	43.6
5	Mongolia	48.0	17	Guatemala	43.3
6	Pakistan	47.4		South Africa	43.3
7	Turkey	46.4	19	Thailand	43.2
8	Macau	46.0	20	South Korea	43.0
9	Ivory Coast	45.7	21	Argentina	42.9
	Mexico	45.7		Mali	42.9
11	Malaysia	45.5	23	Kosovo	42.6
	Namibia	45.5		Uruguay	42.6

Poverty pay
% of workers paid $1.90[c] or less per day, 2016

1	Afghanistan	83.2		Nigeria	47.4
2	Central African Rep.	74.9	17	Sierra Leone	45.8
3	Congo-Kinshasa	73.9	18	Niger	43.4
4	Burundi	71.3	19	Benin	42.9
5	Madagascar	71.0	20	Togo	41.3
6	Malawi	63.2	21	Gambia, The	38.7
7	Zimbabwe	60.7	22	Burkina Faso	38.0
8	Guinea-Bissau	58.5	23	Liberia	37.7
9	Mozambique	54.3	24	Chad	37.0
	North Korea	54.3		Eritrea	37.0
11	Zambia	51.1	26	Guinea	36.7
12	Mali	49.8	27	Lesotho	36.1
13	Rwanda	49.3		Tanzania	36.1
14	Laos	48.9	29	Haiti	35.6
15	Bangladesh	47.4	30	Yemen	34.9

a Constant 2011 $PPP.   b 2015   c At purchasing power parity.

Business costs and foreign direct investment

Office rents

Rent, taxes and operating expenses, Q1 2017, $ per sq. ft.

	0	50	100	150	200	250	300
Hong Kong (Central)							
London (West End), UK							
New York (Midtown Manhattan), US							
Hong Kong (West Kowloon)							
Beijing (CBD), China							
Beijing (Finance Street), China							
Tokyo (Marunouchi Otemachi), Japan							
New York (Midtown-South Manhattan), US							
New Delhi (Connaught Place, CBD), India							
Shanghai (Pudong), China							
London (City), UK							
Moscow, Russia							
Shanghai (Puxi), China							
San Francisco (Downtown), US							
Dubai, United Arab Emirates							
Boston (Downtown), US							
Seoul (CBD), South Korea							
Paris, France							
Sydney, Australia							
Mumbai (Bandra Kurla Complex), India							

Foreign direct investment[a]

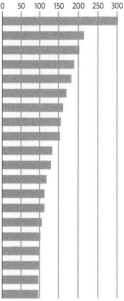

Inflows, $m, 2016			*Outflows, $m, 2016*	
1	United States	391,104	1 United States	299,003
2	United Kingdom	253,826	2 China	183,100
3	China	133,700	3 Netherlands	173,658
4	Hong Kong	108,126	4 Japan	145,242
5	Netherlands	91,956	5 Canada	66,403
6	Singapore	61,597	6 Hong Kong	62,460
7	Brazil	58,680	7 France	57,328
8	Australia	48,190	8 Ireland	44,548
9	India	44,486	9 Spain	41,789
10	Russia	37,668	10 Germany	34,558
11	Canada	33,721	11 Luxembourg	31,643
12	Belgium	33,103	12 Switzerland	30,648
13	Italy	28,955	13 South Korea	27,274
14	France	28,352	14 Russia	27,272
15	Luxembourg	26,857	15 Singapore	23,888
16	Mexico	26,739	16 Sweden	22,851
17	Ireland	22,304	17 Italy	22,794
18	Sweden	19,584	18 Finland	22,760

Note: CBD is Central Business District.
a Investment in companies in a foreign country.

Business creativity and research

Entrepreneurial activity
Percentage of population aged 18–64 who are either a nascent entrepreneur[a] or owner-manager of a new business, average 2012–17

Highest		Lowest	
1 Zambia	40.7	1 Suriname	3.6
2 Senegal	38.6	2 Bulgaria	4.0
3 Nigeria	37.5	Kosovo	4.0
4 Uganda	32.2	4 Japan	4.1
5 Malawi	31.8	5 Italy	4.3
6 Ecuador	31.7	6 France	4.9
7 Ghana	31.2	7 Germany	5.0
8 Cameroon	30.1	8 Russia	5.3
9 Botswana	28.6	9 Belgium	5.4
10 Burkina Faso	28.3	Denmark	5.4
11 Bolivia	27.4	11 Spain	5.6
12 Namibia	25.7	12 Finland	6.0
13 Angola	25.4	13 Norway	6.1
14 Lebanon	25.1	14 Greece	6.2
15 Chile	24.6	15 Morocco	6.3
16 Peru	24.1	16 Slovenia	6.5
17 Colombia	21.8	17 Macedonia	6.6
Madagascar	21.8	18 Algeria	6.8
19 Guatemala	19.0	19 Sweden	7.2
20 Thailand	18.8	20 Czech Republic	7.3
21 Brazil	18.5	United Arab Emirates	7.3
22 Barbados	18.1	22 Bosnia & Herz.	7.4
23 Philippines	18.0	23 Switzerland	7.5
24 Vietnam	16.9	Tunisia	7.5
25 Trinidad & Tobago	16.4	25 Georgia	7.9
26 El Salvador	16.3	26 Taiwan	8.0

Brain drains[b]

Highest, 2017		Lowest, 2017	
1 Venezuela	1.6	1 Switzerland	6.0
2 Bosnia & Herz.	1.8	2 United Arab Emirates	5.8
Haiti	1.8	3 United States	5.7
Serbia	1.8	4 Norway	5.5
5 Moldova	1.9	Singapore	5.5
6 Romania	2.0	6 Netherlands	5.3
7 Croatia	2.1	United Kingdom	5.3
Yemen	2.1	8 Luxembourg	5.2
9 Benin	2.2	Qatar	5.2
Ukraine	2.2	10 Finland	5.1
11 Hungary	2.4	Germany	5.1
Mongolia	2.4	Hong Kong	5.1
		Malaysia	5.1
		14 Canada	5.0
		Chile	5.0
		Iceland	5.0

a An individual who has started a new firm which has not paid wages for over three months.
b Scores: 1 = talented people leave for other countries; 7 = they stay and pursue opportunities in the country.

Total spending on R&D

$bn, 2016			% of GDP, 2016	
1 United States	511.1		**1** Israel	4.25
2 China	235.9		**2** South Korea	4.23
3 Japan	155.4		**3** Switzerland[a]	3.37
4 Germany	102.2		**4** Sweden	3.25
5 South Korea	59.8		**5** Taiwan	3.16
6 France	55.4		**6** Japan	3.14
7 United Kingdom	44.8		**7** Austria	3.09
8 Brazil[b]	28.2		**8** Germany	2.94
9 Canada	24.6		**9** Denmark	2.87
10 Italy	23.9		**10** Finland	2.75
11 Australia[a]	23.4		**11** United States	2.74
12 Switzerland[a]	22.9		**12** Belgium	2.49
13 Taiwan	16.8		**13** Singapore[a]	2.28
14 Sweden	16.7		**14** France	2.25
15 Netherlands	15.8		**15** China	2.11
16 Spain	14.7		**16** Iceland	2.08
17 Russia	14.1		**17** Norway	2.04
18 Israel	13.5		**18** Netherlands	2.03
19 India[a]	13.3		**19** Slovenia	2.00
20 Austria	12.1		**20** Australia[a]	1.90

Innovation index[c]

2017, 100=maximum score

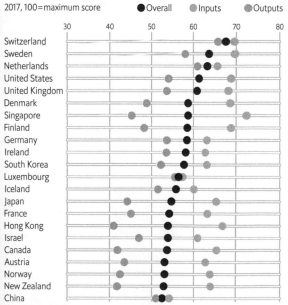

a 2015   b 2014
c The innovation index averages countries' capacity for innovation (inputs) and success
in innovation (outputs), based on 79 indicators.

Businesses and banks

Largest non-financial companies

By market capitalisation,
$bn, end December 2017

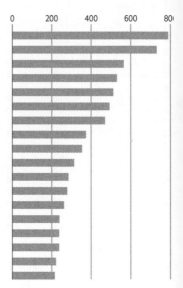

Apple, US
Alphabet, US
Amazon, US
Microsoft, US
Facebook, US
Tencent, China
Alibaba, China
Johnson & Johnson, US
Exxon Mobil, US
Walmart, US
Samsung Electronics, Japan
Royal Dutch, Netherlands
Nestlé, Switzerland
Home Depot, US
AT&T, US
Chevron, US
Procter & Gamble, US
Pfizer, US

By net profit
$bn, 2017

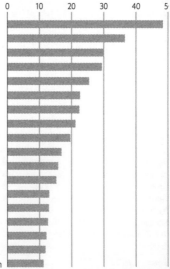

Apple, US
Samsung Electronics, S. Korea
Verizon Communications, US
AT&T, US
Microsoft, US
Comcast, US
Toyota Motor, Japan
Pfizer, US
Exxon Mobil, US
China Mobile, China
Facebook, US
Procter & Gamble, US
Volkswagen, Germany
Royal Dutch, Netherlands
Alphabet, US
Gazprom, Russia
Daimler, Germany
Taiwan Semiconductor, Taiwan

Largest banks

By market capitalisation, \$bn, end December 2017

1	JPMorgan Chase	United States	366.3
2	Industrial & Commercial Bank of China	China	339.6
3	Bank of America	United States	303.7
4	Wells Fargo	United States	296.8
5	China Construction Bank	China	230.4
6	HSBC	United Kingdom	210.8
7	Citigroup	United States	191.2
8	Agricultural Bank of China	China	151.3
9	Bank of China	China	144.7
10	Royal Bank of Canada	Canada	113.6
11	China Merchants Bank	China	112.5
12	Commonwealth Bank of Australia	Australia	109.7
13	Banco Santander	Spain	106.3
14	TD Bank Group	Canada	104.8
15	BNP Paribas	France	93.4

By assets, \$bn, end December 2017

1	Industrial & Commercial Bank of China	China	4,009
2	China Construction Bank	China	3,400
3	Agricultural Bank of China	China	3,236
4	Bank of China	China	2,992
5	Mitsubishi UFJ	Japan	2,890
6	JPMorgan Chase	United States	2,534
7	HSBC	United Kingdom	2,522
8	BNP Paribas	France	2,357
9	Bank of America	United States	2,281
10	Japan Post	Japan	1,983
11	Wells Fargo	United States	1,952
12	Mizuho	Japan	1,930
13	Sumitomo Mitsui Financial	Japan	1,874
14	Crédit Agricole	France	1,864
15	Citigroup	United States	1,842

Largest sovereign-wealth funds

By assets, \$bn, April 2018

1	Government Pension Fund, Norway	1,035
2	China Investment Corporation	900
3	Abu Dhabi Investment Authority, UAE	828
4	Kuwait Investment Authority	524
5	SAMA Foreign Holdings, Saudi Arabia	494
6	Hong Kong Monetary Authority Investment Portfolio	457
7	SAFE Investment Company, China[a]	441
8	Government of Singapore Investment Corporation	390
9	Temasek Holdings, Singapore[a]	321
10	Qatar Investment Authority	320

Note: Countries listed refer to the company's domicile.

a Estimate.

Stockmarkets

Largest market capitalisation
$bn, end 2017

1	NYSE	22,081		21	Singapore Exchange	787
2	Nasdaq – US	10,039		22	Moscow Exchange	623
3	Japan Exchange Group	6,223		23	Stock Exchange of Thailand	549
4	Shanghai SE	5,090		24	Indonesia SE	521
5	London SE Group	4,455		25	Bursa Malaysia	456
6	Euronext	4,393		26	Saudi SE (Tadawul)	451
7	Hong Kong Exchanges	4,351		27	Bolsa Mexicana de Valores	417
8	Shenzhen SE	3,622		28	Bolsa de Comercio de Santiago	295
9	TMX Group	2,367		29	Philippine SE	290
10	National Stock Exchange of India	2,351		30	Oslo Bors	287
11	BSE India	2,332		31	Tel-Aviv SE	231
12	Deutsche Börse	2,262		32	Borsa Istanbul	228
13	Korea Exchange[a]	1,772		33	Warsaw SE	201
14	SIX Swiss Exchange	1,686		34	Wiener Börse	151
15	Nasdaq OMX Nordic Exchanges[b]	1,533		35	Irish SE	147
16	Australian Securities Exchange[c]	1,508		36	Qatar SE	131
17	Johannesburg SE	1,231		37	Abu Dhabi Securities Exchange	125
18	Taiwan SE	1,073		38	Bolsa de Valores de Colombia	121
19	BM&FBOVESPA	955				
20	BME Spanish Exchanges	889				

Stockmarket gains and losses
$ terms, % change December 30th 2016 to December 29th 2017

	Best performance				Worst performance	
1	Argentina (MERV)	49.4		1	Pakistan (KSE)	-19.9
2	Austria (ATX)	48.7		2	Saudi Arabia (SE Tadawul)	-0.1
3	Poland (WIG)	48.0		3	Russia (RTS)	6.2
4	Chile (IGPA)	47.0		4	China (SSEB)	6.7
5	Greece (Athex comp)	41.9		5	Canada (S&P TSX)	13.5
6	Czech Republic (PX)	41.0		6	China (SSEA)	13.7
7	Hungary (BUX)	39.5		7	Mexico (IPC)	13.9
8	South Korea (KOSPI)	37.4		8	Colombia (IGBC)	14.2
9	Turkey (BIST)	36.9		9	Sweden (OMXS30)	15.3
10	India BSE (SENSEX) 30	36.0		10	Australia (All Ord.)	16.6
11	Hong Kong (Hang Seng)	34.9		11	United Kingdom (FTSE 100)	17.8
12	Denmark (OMXCB)	32.0		12	Israel (TA 125)	18.5
13	South Africa (FTSE JSE)	29.8		13	Switzerland (SMI)	19.0
14	Italy (FTSE MIB)	29.4		14	Indonesia (IDX)	19.2
15	Netherlands (AEX)	28.3		15	United States (S&P 500)	19.4
16	United States (NAScomp)	28.2		16	Euro Area (EURO STOXX 50)	21.2
17	Germany (DAX)[d]	28.1		17	Malaysia (KLCI)	21.3
18	Singapore (STI)	27.7		18	Spain (IBEX 35)	22.3
19	Belgium (BEL 20)	25.6		19	Japan (NIKKEI 225)	23.3
20	United states (DJIA)	25.1		20	Euro area (FTSE Euro 100)	23.8

a Includes Kosdaq.   b Armenia, Copenhagen, Helsinki, Iceland, Riga, Stockholm, Tallinn and Vilnius stock exchanges.   c Includes investment funds.   d Total return index.

Value traded[a]

$bn, 2017

1	Nasdaq – US	33,407
2	NYSE	16,140
3	BATS Global Markets – US	12,302
4	Shenzhen SE	9,164
5	BATS Chi-x Europe	7,888
6	Shanghai SE	7,594
7	Japan Exchange Group Inc.	6,621
8	London SE Group	4,867
9	Euronext	2,875
10	Hong Kong Exchanges	2,078
11	Korea Exchange[b]	1,953
12	Deutsche Börse	1,568
13	TMX Group	1,244
14	SIX Swiss Exchange	1,051
15	National Stock Exchange of India	1,017
16	Australian Securities Exchange[c]	944
17	Nasdaq Nordic Exchanges[d]	898
18	Taiwan SE	793
19	BME Spanish Exchanges	734
20	BM&FBOVESPA	664
21	Johannesburg SE	414
22	Borsa Istanbul	395
23	Stock Exchange of Thailand	339
24	Moscow Exchange	297
25	Taipei Exchange	254
26	Saudi SE (Tadawul)	224
27	Singapore Exchange	214
28	BSE India	183
29	Bursa Malaysia	143
30	Indonesia SE	135
31	Oslo Bors	132
32	Bolsa Mexicana de Valores	114
33	Tel-Aviv SE	76
34	Warsaw SE	72

Number of listed companies[e]

End 2017

1	BSE India	5,616
2	Japan Exchange Group	3,604
3	TMX Group	3,328
4	BME Spanish Exchanges	3,136
5	Nasdaq – US	2,949
6	London SE Group	2,498
7	NYSE	2,286
8	Australian Securities Exchange[c]	2,147
9	Korea Exchange[b]	2,134
10	Hong Kong Exchanges	2,118
11	Shenzhen SE	2,089
12	National Stock Exchange of India	1,897
13	Shanghai SE	1,396
14	Euronext	1,255
15	Nasdaq Nordic Exchanges[d]	984
16	Taiwan SE	924
17	Bursa Malaysia	904
18	Warsaw SE	890
19	Singapore Exchange	750
20	Taipei Exchange	743
21	Stock Exchange of Thailand	688
22	Indonesia SE	566
23	Wiener Börse	536
24	Deutsche Börse	499
25	Tel-Aviv SE	457
26	Hanoi SE	384
27	Borsa Istanbul	375
28	Johannesburg SE	366
29	Hochiminh Stock Exchange	344
30	BM&FBOVESPA	343
31	Tehran SE	326
32	Dhaka SE	302
33	Colombo SE	296
34	Bolsa de Comercio de Santiago	293
35	Chittagong SE	270
36	Philippine SE	267
37	SIX Swiss Exchange	263
38	Bolsa de Valores de Lima	258
39	The Egyptian Exchange	255

Note: Figures are not entirely comparable due to different reporting rules and calculations. a Includes electronic and negotiated deals. b Includes Kosdaq. c Includes investment funds. d Armenia, Copenhagen, Helsinki, Iceland, Riga, Stockholm, Tallinn and Vilnius stock exchanges. e Domestic and foreign.

Public finance

Government debt
As % of GDP, 2017

1	Japan	224.1	16	Germany	71.7
2	Greece	185.1	17	Netherlands	68.7
3	Italy	154.6	18	Poland	67.8
4	Portugal	148.1	19	Iceland	64.5
5	Belgium	121.9	20	Israel	60.8
	France	121.9	21	Slovakia	58.4
7	United Kingdom	118.0	22	Denmark	50.3
8	Spain	114.8		Sweden	50.3
9	United States	105.4	24	Latvia	48.4
10	Austria	101.0	25	South Korea	44.5
11	Canada	93.8	26	Czech Republic	43.9
12	Hungary	91.8	27	Australia	43.0
13	Slovenia	88.6	28	Norway	42.4
14	Ireland	82.2	29	Switzerland	41.5
15	Finland	73.9	30	New Zealand	36.0

Government spending
As % of GDP, 2017

1	France	56.3	16	Netherlands	42.5
2	Finland	53.7	17	Iceland	41.9
3	Belgium	52.4	18	Poland	41.2
4	Denmark	51.9	19	Spain	41.0
5	Norway	50.0	20	United Kingdom	40.8
6	Sweden	49.1	21	New Zealand	40.4
7	Austria	48.9		Slovakia	40.4
8	Italy	48.8	23	Canada	40.3
9	Greece	48.2	24	Estonia	40.2
10	Euro area (16)	47.1	25	Israel	40.1
11	Hungary	46.5	26	Czech Republic	38.8
12	Portugal	45.9	27	Japan	38.7
13	Germany	43.9	28	Latvia	38.0
14	Slovenia	43.1	29	United States	37.7
15	Luxembourg	42.9	30	Australia	36.0

Tax revenue
As % of GDP, 2016

1	Denmark	45.9	14	Slovenia	37.0
2	France	45.3	15	Iceland	36.4
3	Belgium	44.2	16	Estonia	34.7
4	Finland	44.1	17	Portugal	34.4
	Sweden	44.1	18	Czech Republic	34.0
6	Italy	42.9	19	Poland	33.6
7	Austria	42.7	20	Spain	33.5
8	Hungary	39.4	21	United Kingdom	33.2
9	Netherlands	38.8	22	Slovakia	32.7
10	Greece	38.6	23	New Zealand	32.1
11	Norway	38.0	24	Canada	31.7
12	Germany	37.6	25	Israel	31.2
13	Luxembourg	37.1	26	Japan[a]	30.7

Note: Includes only OECD countries. a 2015

Democracy

Democracy index
Most democratic = 10, 2017

Most			Least		
1	Norway	9.87	1	North Korea	1.08
2	Iceland	9.58	2	Syria	1.43
3	Sweden	9.39	3	Chad	1.50
4	New Zealand	9.26	4	Central African Rep.	1.52
5	Denmark	9.22	5	Congo-Kinshasa	1.61
6	Canada	9.15	6	Turkmenistan	1.72
	Ireland	9.15	7	Equatorial Guinea	1.81
8	Australia	9.09	8	Saudi Arabia	1.93
9	Finland	9.03		Tajikistan	1.93
	Switzerland	9.03	10	Uzbekistan	1.95
11	Netherlands	8.89	11	Guinea-Bissau	1.98
12	Luxembourg	8.81	12	Yemen	2.07
13	Germany	8.61	13	Sudan	2.15
14	United Kingdom	8.53	14	Libya	2.32
15	Austria	8.42	15	Burundi	2.33
16	Mauritius	8.22	16	Eritrea	2.37
17	Malta	8.15		Laos	2.37
18	Uruguay	8.12	18	Iran	2.45
19	Spain	8.08	19	Afghanistan	2.55
20	South Korea	8.00	20	Azerbaijan	2.65

Parliamentary seats
Lower or single house, seats per 100,000 population, April 2018

Most			Fewest		
1	Liechtenstein	62.5	1	India	0.04
2	Monaco	60.0	2	United States	0.13
3	Andorra	28.0	3	Pakistan	0.18
4	Maldives	21.3	4	Nigeria	0.19
5	Iceland	21.0	5	Bangladesh	0.21
6	Malta	17.0		China	0.21
7	Montenegro	13.5		Indonesia	0.21
8	Barbados	10.0	8	Brazil	0.25
	Luxembourg	10.0	9	Philippines	0.28
10	Bahamas	9.8	10	Russia	0.31

Women in parliament
Lower or single house, women as % of total seats, April 2018

1	Rwanda	61.3	12	Norway	41.4
2	Cuba	53.2	13	Mozambique	39.6
3	Bolivia	53.1	14	Spain	39.1
4	Namibia	46.2	15	France	39.0
5	Nicaragua	45.7	16	Argentina	38.9
6	Costa Rica	45.6	17	Ethiopia	38.8
7	Sweden	43.6	18	New Zealand	38.3
8	Mexico	42.6	19	Iceland	38.1
9	South Africa	42.4	20	Belgium	38.0
10	Finland	42.0		Ecuador	38.0
11	Senegal	41.8	22	Macedonia	37.5

Education

Primary enrolment
Number enrolled as % of relevant age group

Highest			Lowest		
1	Madagascar	144	1	Eritrea	54
2	Malawi	139	2	Equatorial Guinea	62
3	Rwanda	137	3	South Sudan	67
4	Nepal	134	4	Niger	74
5	Benin	132		Sudan	74
6	Burundi	131	6	Syria	76
7	Togo	124	7	Mali	77
8	Sweden	123	8	Tanzania	81
9	Suriname	121	9	Senegal	83
10	Cameroon	119	10	Puerto Rico	87
	Bangladesh	119	11	Chad	88
	Cameroon	119		Turkmenistan	88
13	Saudi Arabia	116	13	Lebanon	89
				Romania	89
			15	Bermuda	90
			16	Burkina Faso	91

Highest secondary enrolment
Number enrolled as % of relevant age group

1	Belgium	164	12	Iceland	119
2	Australia	154	13	Portugal	118
3	Finland	152	14	Saudi Arabia	117
4	Sweden	140	15	Liechtenstein	116
5	Netherlands	133	16	New Zealand	114
6	Denmark	129		Norway	114
7	Spain	128	18	Canada	113
8	Costa Rica	126		Kazakhstan	113
	Ireland	126	20	Latvia	112
10	United Kingdom	125		Uruguay	112
11	Thailand	121			

Highest tertiary enrolment[a]
Number enrolled as % of relevant age group

1	Australia	122		Puerto Rico	85
2	Greece	117	12	Ireland	84
3	Turkey	95	13	Austria	83
4	South Korea	93		Ukraine	83
5	Spain	91	15	New Zealand	82
6	Chile	90		Russia	82
7	Belarus	87	17	Denmark	81
	Finland	87		Norway	81
9	Argentina	86	19	Netherlands	80
10	United States	85		Slovenia	80

Notes: Latest available year 2013–17. The gross enrolment ratios shown are the actual number enrolled as a percentage of the number of children in the official primary age group. They may exceed 100 when children outside the primary age group are receiving primary education.
a Tertiary education includes all levels of post-secondary education including courses leading to awards not equivalent to a university degree, courses leading to a first university degree and postgraduate courses.

Least literate[a]

% adult population

1	Niger	19.1	26	Papua New Guinea	63.4
2	Chad	22.3	27	Togo	63.7
3	Guinea	30.5	28	Timor-Leste	64.1
4	South Sudan	32.0	29	Nepal	64.7
5	Mali	33.1	30	Rwanda	68.3
6	Central African Rep.	36.8	31	Morocco	69.4
7	Burkina Faso	37.7	32	Yemen	70.0
8	Afghanistan	38.2	33	Angola	71.2
9	Benin	38.4	34	Madagascar	71.6
10	Senegal	42.8	35	India	72.2
11	Iraq	43.7	36	Bangladesh	72.8
12	Ivory Coast	43.9	37	Eritrea	73.8
13	Liberia	47.6		Uganda	73.8
14	Sierra Leone	48.4	39	Cameroon	74.9
15	Ethiopia	49.0	40	Myanmar	75.6
16	Mauritania	52.1	41	Egypt	75.8
17	Gambia, The	55.6	42	Ghana	76.6
18	Pakistan	57.0		Lesotho	76.6
19	Sudan	58.6	44	Congo-Kinshasa	77.0
20	Mozambique	58.8	45	Tanzania	77.9
21	Nigeria	59.6	46	Cambodia	78.3
22	Guinea-Bissau	59.8	47	Kenya	78.7
23	Haiti	60.7	48	Tunisia	79.0
24	Burundi	61.6	49	Guatemala	79.1
25	Malawi	62.1	50	Congo-Brazzaville	79.3

Education spending[b]

% of GDP[b]

Highest			Lowest		
1	Iceland	7.8	1	West Bank & Gaza	1.3
2	Norway	7.7	2	Monaco	1.4
	Sweden	7.7	3	Bermuda	1.5
4	Denmark	7.6	4	South Sudan	1.8
5	Timor-Leste	7.5	5	Cambodia	1.9
	Zimbabwe	7.5	6	Guinea-Bissau	2.1
7	Bolivia	7.3		Madagascar	2.1
8	Finland	7.2	8	Myanmar	2.2
	Malta	7.2	9	Congo-Kinshasa	2.3
10	Costa Rica	7.1		Uganda	2.3
	Senegal	7.1	11	Guinea	2.4
	Swaziland	7.1	12	Bangladesh	2.5
13	Moldova	6.7		Lebanon	2.5
14	Belgium	6.6	14	Mauritania	2.6
	Tunisia	6.6	15	Bahrain	2.7
16	Mozambique	6.5		Gabon	2.7
17	New Zealand	6.3	17	Armenia	2.8
18	Ghana	6.2		Cameroon	2.8
	Oman	6.2		Gambia, The	2.8
20	Cyprus	6.1		Guatemala	2.8

a Latest year 2012–16.   b Latest year 2013–17.

Marriage and divorce

Highest marriage rates
Number of marriages per 1,000 population, 2016 or latest available year

1	Egypt	11.0	23	United States	6.9
2	West Bank & Gaza	10.8	24	Hong Kong	6.8
3	Kazakhstan	9.9		Jamaica	6.8
4	China	9.6	26	Bahrain	6.7
5	Uzbekistan	9.2		Georgia	6.7
6	Tajikistan	9.1		Romania	6.7
7	Iran	8.7	29	Latvia	6.6
8	Belarus	8.6	30	Cyprus	6.4
9	Jordan	8.5		Israel	6.4
	Russia	8.5		Macedonia	6.4
11	Albania	8.2	33	Guyana	6.3
12	Kyrgyzstan	7.9	34	Montenegro	6.2
	Mauritius	7.9	35	Armenia	5.9
14	Turkey	7.7	36	Bahamas	5.8
15	Lithuania	7.6		Macau	5.8
16	Bermuda	7.3	38	Channel Islands[a]	5.6
	Guam	7.3	39	Costa Rica	5.5
18	Moldova	7.2		Cuba	5.5
19	Azerbaijan	7.1		Liechtenstein	5.5
	Singapore	7.1		South Korea	5.5
21	Malta	7.0		Sweden	5.5
	Ukraine	7.0			

Lowest marriage rates
Number of marriages per 1,000 population, 2016 or latest available year

1	Qatar	1.5		Kuwait	3.9
2	Martinique	2.5	23	Andorra	4.1
3	Uruguay	2.7	24	New Zealand	4.3
4	Argentina	2.8	25	Finland	4.5
	Peru	2.8		Norway	4.5
6	Guadeloupe	3.0	27	Czech Republic	4.6
	Venezuela	3.0		Greece	4.6
8	Portugal	3.1		Mexico	4.6
9	Italy	3.2		Puerto Rico	4.6
	Slovenia	3.2	31	Croatia	4.7
11	Réunion	3.3	32	Australia	4.8
12	Belgium	3.5		Bosnia & Herz.	4.8
	Suriname	3.5		Estonia	4.8
14	Chile	3.6		Ireland	4.8
	France	3.6	36	Germany	4.9
	Luxembourg	3.6		Guatemala	4.9
	New Caledonia	3.6	38	Japan	5.0
	Panama	3.6		Switzerland	5.0
	Spain	3.6	40	Poland	5.1
20	Netherlands	3.8		Serbia	5.1
21	Bulgaria	3.9			

Note: The data are based on latest available figures (no earlier than 2012) and hence will be affected by the population age structure at the time. Marriage rates refer to registered marriages only and, therefore, reflect the customs surrounding registry and efficiency of administration.   a Jersey only.

Highest divorce rates

Number of divorces per 1,000 population, 2016 or latest available year[a]

1	Russia	4.7		13	Georgia	2.6
2	Guam	3.6			Liechtenstein	2.6
3	Belarus	3.5		15	Czech Republic	2.5
4	Lithuania	3.2			Estonia	2.5
	Puerto Rico	3.2			Finland	2.5
6	Latvia	3.1			Sweden	2.5
7	Denmark	3.0			United States	2.5
	Kazakhstan	3.0		20	Luxembourg	2.4
	Moldova	3.0		21	Jordan	2.3
	Ukraine	3.0		22	Belgium	2.2
11	Cuba	2.8			Dominican Rep.	2.2
12	Costa Rica	2.7			Portugal	2.2

Lowest divorce rates

Number of divorces per 1,000 population, 2016 or latest available year[a]

1	Bosnia & Herz.	0.4			Slovenia	1.2
	Guatemala	0.4		17	Albania	1.3
	Peru	0.4			Azerbaijan	1.3
	Qatar	0.4			Greece	1.3
5	Ireland	0.6			Mongolia	1.3
	Jamaica	0.6			Serbia	1.3
7	Malta	0.9			Suriname	1.3
	Montenegro	0.9		23	Croatia	1.4
	Uzbekistan	0.9			Italy	1.4
10	Macedonia	1.0		25	Bulgaria	1.5
	Mexico	1.0			Kyrgyzstan	1.5
	Tajikistan	1.0			Mauritius	1.5
13	Martinique	1.1			Romania	1.5
	Panama	1.1		29	Barbados	1.6
15	Armenia	1.2				

Mean age of women at first marriage

Years, 2016 or latest available year[b]

Youngest			Oldest		
1	South Sudan	14.6	1	Barbados	35.3
2	Niger	17.2	2	Slovenia	34.1
3	Central African Rep.	17.3	3	French Polynesia	33.8
4	Bangladesh	18.8	4	Martinique	33.3
	Chad	18.8	5	Hungary	32.8
6	Mozambique	18.9		New Caledonia	32.8
7	Madagascar	19.0	7	Ireland	32.4
	Mali	19.0	8	Bulgaria	32.3
9	Burkina Faso	19.5		Netherlands	32.3
10	Malawi	19.9	10	Czech Republic	32.0
11	Zimbabwe	20.2		France	32.0
12	Somalia	20.4		French Guiana	32.0
13	Equatorial Guinea	20.5	13	Norway	31.9
	Laos	20.5			
	Uganda	20.5			

a No earlier than 2012.   b No earlier than 2002.

Households, living costs and giving

Number of households

Biggest, m, 2016 or latest

1	China	452.8	21	Turkey	22.4
2	India	268.6	22	Ethiopia	21.9
3	United States	124.5	23	South Korea	19.1
4	Indonesia	65.3	24	Spain	18.4
5	Brazil	62.1	25	Ukraine	17.7
6	Russia	56.5	26	South Africa	15.3
7	Japan	53.3	27	Poland	14.2
8	Germany	40.5	28	Canada	14.1
9	Nigeria	38.3	29	Argentina	13.5
10	Bangladesh	37.1	30	Colombia	13.3
11	Mexico	32.8	31	Congo-Kinshasa	11.5
12	France	29.1	32	Tanzania	11.2
13	United Kingdom	28.6	33	Myanmar	11.1
14	Pakistan	28.1	34	Kenya	10.8
15	Vietnam	27.1	35	North Korea	9.6
16	Italy	25.8	36	Australia	8.9
17	Iran	24.1	37	Uganda	8.2
18	Egypt	23.4	38	Venezuela	7.9
19	Philippines	22.9	39	Peru	7.8
20	Thailand	22.5		Taiwan	7.8

Average household size, people

Biggest, 2016 or latest

1	Guinea	8.6
2	Angola	8.5
3	Senegal	8.2
4	Chad	7.9
	Equatorial Guinea	7.9
	Gambia, The	7.9
7	Gabon	7.8
	Guinea-Bissau	7.8
9	Congo-Kinshasa	6.9
	Oman	6.9
	Pakistan	6.9
12	Mauritania	6.7
	Yemen	6.7
14	Iraq	6.3
	Papua New Guinea	6.3
	Tajikistan	6.3
	Turkmenistan	6.3
18	Maldives	6.2
19	Libya	6.1
	Mali	6.1
21	Benin	6.0
	Niger	6.0

Smallest, 2016 or latest

1	Germany	2.0
	Sweden	2.0
3	Finland	2.1
	Lithuania	2.1
5	France	2.2
	Netherlands	2.2
7	Austria	2.3
	Czech Republic	2.3
	Estonia	2.3
	Italy	2.3
	United Kingdom	2.3
12	Belgium	2.4
	Denmark	2.4
	Hungary	2.4
	Japan	2.4
	Latvia	2.4
	Slovenia	2.4
18	Greece	2.5
	Portugal	2.5
	Spain	2.5
	Ukraine	2.5

a The cost of living index shown is compiled by the Economist Intelligence Unit for use by companies in determining expatriate compensation: it is a comparison of the cost of maintaining a typical international lifestyle in the country rather than a comparison of the purchasing power of a citizen of the country. The index is based on typical urban prices an international executive and family will face abroad. The prices

Cost of living[a]

December 2017, US=100

Highest	
Singapore	
France	
Hong Kong	
Norway	
South Korea	
Switzerland	
Denmark	
Israel	
Australia	
Japan	
United States	
Iceland	
Austria	
Finland	
Ireland	
New Zealand	
Jordan	
Italy	
United Kingdom	

Lowest	
Syria	
Venezuela	
Kazakhstan	
Nigeria	
Algeria	
Pakistan	
India	
Romania	
Egypt	
Iran	
Bulgaria	
Paraguay	
Saudi Arabia	
Zambia	
Nepal	
Morocco	
Panama	
Sri Lanka	
Uzbekistan	

World Giving Index[b]

Top givers, % of population, 2017

1	Myanmar	65		Norway	45
2	Indonesia	60		Zambia	45
	Kenya	60	**21**	Denmark	44
4	New Zealand	57		Uganda	44
5	Australia	56	**23**	Ghana	43
	United States	56		Hong Kong	43
7	Canada	54		South Africa	43
8	Ireland	53	**26**	Austria	42
9	Netherlands	51		Mauritius	42
	United Arab Emirates	51		Mongolia	42
11	United Kingdom	50		Nigeria	42
12	Sierra Leone	49	**30**	Dominican Rep.	41
13	Malta	48		Israel	41
14	Iceland	46		Kuwait	41
	Liberia	46		Singapore	41
	Thailand	46		Sweden	41
17	Germany	45		Switzerland	41
	Iran	45			

a are for products of international comparable quality found in a supermarket or department store. Prices found in local markets and bazaars are not used unless the available merchandise is of the specified quality and the shopping area itself is safe for executive and family members. New York City prices are used as the base, so United States = 100.

b Three criteria are used to assess giving: in the previous month those surveyed either gave money to charity, gave time to those in need or helped a stranger.

Transport: roads and cars

Longest road networks
Km, 2016 or latest

1	United States	6,772,347	25	Romania	229,210
2	India	5,625,656	26	Vietnam	228,645
3	China	4,773,500	27	Colombia	219,159
4	Brazil	1,691,473	28	Malaysia	216,604
5	Russia	1,563,876	29	Hungary	206,632
6	Canada	1,409,008	30	Nigeria	198,233
7	Japan	1,226,559	31	Philippines	197,090
8	France	1,079,398	32	Thailand	195,978
9	South Africa	891,932	33	Peru	173,209
10	Australia	872,848	34	Egypt	167,774
11	Spain	667,058	35	Ukraine	163,028
12	Germany	643,134	36	Belgium	155,357
13	Indonesia	537,838	37	Congo-Kinshasa	154,633
14	Italy	494,844	38	Netherlands	139,448
15	Sweden	432,009	39	Czech Republic	130,390
16	Poland	423,997	40	Austria	124,591
17	United Kingdom	422,310	41	Algeria	119,386
18	Turkey	394,390	42	Greece	116,986
19	Mexico	382,478	43	Ghana	109,515
20	Iran	312,761	44	South Korea	105,758
21	Saudi Arabia	274,861	45	Belarus	99,606
22	Bangladesh	266,216	46	Zimbabwe	97,724
23	Pakistan	265,991	47	Kazakhstan	96,643
24	Argentina	230,923	48	Venezuela	96,156

Densest road networks
Km of road per km² land area, 2016 or latest

1	Monaco	38.5		Switzerland	1.7
2	Macau	13.6		United Kingdom	1.7
3	Malta	9.7	26	Italy	1.6
4	Bermuda	8.9	27	Cyprus	1.4
5	Bahrain	5.3		Ireland	1.4
6	Belgium	5.1		Poland	1.4
7	Singapore	4.8		Sri Lanka	1.4
8	Barbados	3.7	31	Estonia	1.3
9	Netherlands	3.4		Lithuania	1.3
10	Japan	3.2		Spain	1.3
11	Puerto Rico	3.0	34	Taiwan	1.2
12	Liechtenstein	2.5	35	Latvia	1.1
13	Hungary	2.2		Mauritius	1.1
14	France	2.0		South Korea	1.1
	Jamaica	2.0	38	Romania	1.0
	Luxembourg	2.0		Sweden	1.0
17	Guam	1.9	40	Greece	0.9
	Hong Kong	1.9		Israel	0.9
	Slovenia	1.9		Portugal	0.9
20	Germany	1.8		Slovakia	0.9
21	Czech Republic	1.7		West Bank & Gaza	0.9
	Denmark	1.7	45	Qatar	0.8
	India	1.7			

Most crowded road networks
Number of vehicles per km of road network, 2015 or latest

1	United Arab Emirates	523.0	26	Liechtenstein	77.3
2	Monaco	427.3	27	Germany	75.3
3	Hong Kong	322.1	28	Tunisia	74.6
4	Kuwait	273.3	29	Armenia	73.3
5	Macau	238.0	30	Dominican Rep.	71.6
6	Singapore	235.5	31	Portugal	69.2
7	South Korea	198.5	32	Barbados	68.8
8	Taiwan	180.6		Switzerland	68.8
9	Israel	157.2	34	Netherlands	67.4
10	Jordan	156.6	35	Japan	63.1
11	Bahrain	140.3	36	Croatia	63.0
12	Puerto Rico	123.6	37	Malaysia	61.4
13	Guatemala	113.8	38	Morocco	60.6
14	Guam	112.9	39	Argentina	59.5
15	Mauritius	110.2	40	Chile	57.4
16	Malta	104.8	41	Poland	57.2
17	Qatar	103.8	42	Ukraine	55.8
18	Brunei	99.3	43	Georgia	54.9
19	Syria	98.8	44	Slovakia	54.8
20	Mexico	97.7	45	Moldova	53.9
21	United Kingdom	90.5	46	Bermuda	53.7
22	Bulgaria	89.5	47	Greece	53.0
23	Italy	85.4	48	Ecuador	51.3
24	Luxembourg	80.8	49	Bahamas	48.1
25	Thailand	79.0	50	Fiji	47.7

Most congested cities
Time spent in congestion on roads, hours per year, 2017

Highest car ownership
Number of cars per 1,000 population, 2015

1	Puerto Rico	811	26	Greece	456
2	Iceland	754	27	Bulgaria	445
3	Brunei	737	28	Portugal	442
4	Malta	688	29	Lithuania	429
5	New Zealand	655	30	Ireland	422
6	Luxembourg	635	31	Denmark	420
7	Italy	629	32	Cyprus	406
8	Canada	608	33	Guam	400
9	Australia	562	34	Malaysia	386
10	Germany	550	35	Kuwait	383
11	Austria	546	36	United States	380
12	Poland	542	37	Slovakia	377
13	Switzerland	536	38	Bahrain	357
14	Estonia	520		Croatia	357
15	Slovenia	518	40	Libya	344
16	United Kingdom	510	41	Latvia	340
17	France	495	42	Hungary	326
18	Belgium	490		South Korea	326
	Netherlands	490	44	Belarus	320
20	Norway	489	45	Israel	318
21	Czech Republic	487	46	Russia	307
22	Spain	483	47	Barbados	300
23	Japan	478	48	Taiwan	279
24	Sweden	476	49	Qatar	269
25	Finland	475	50	Romania	260

Lowest car ownership
Number of cars per 1,000 population, 2015

1	Ethiopia	1		Kenya	17
	Sudan	1	24	Ivory Coast	18
3	Bangladesh	2		Togo	18
	Burundi	2	26	Benin	19
5	Malawi	3	27	Cuba	20
6	Haiti	4		Ghana	20
	Honduras	4		Nicaragua	20
	Liberia	4	30	Vietnam	21
	Tanzania	4	31	Senegal	22
	Uganda	4		Yemen	22
11	Mauritania	5	33	Angola	26
12	Madagascar	8		Bolivia	26
13	Mali	9	35	Sri Lanka	32
14	Mozambique	10	36	Afghanistan	33
15	Burkina Faso	11		Philippines	33
	Cameroon	11	38	Guatemala	42
17	Congo-Kinshasa	14	39	Egypt	46
	Pakistan	14		Iraq	46
19	Zambia	15	41	Peru	47
20	Nigeria	16	42	Zimbabwe	51
21	El Salvador	17	43	Indonesia	52
	India	17		Jamaica	52

Car production

Number of cars produced, m, 2016

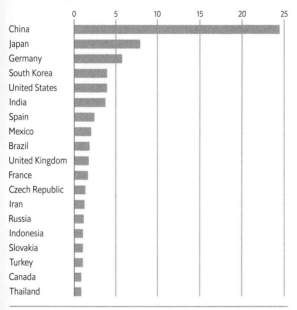

China	
Japan	
Germany	
South Korea	
United States	
India	
Spain	
Mexico	
Brazil	
United Kingdom	
France	
Czech Republic	
Iran	
Russia	
Indonesia	
Slovakia	
Turkey	
Canada	
Thailand	

Cars sold

New car registrations, '000, 2016

1	China	24,962	**23**	Saudi Arabia	438
2	United States	6,096	**24**	Netherlands	415
3	Japan	4,391	**25**	Thailand	402
4	Germany	3,442	**26**	Sweden	379
5	India	3,228	**27**	South Africa	370
6	United Kingdom	2,539	**28**	Austria	353
7	France	2,110	**29**	Switzerland	314
8	Italy	1,969	**30**	Czech Republic	272
9	Brazil	1,844	**31**	Israel	271
10	Iran	1,592	**32**	Chile	270
11	South Korea	1,495	**33**	Denmark	222
12	Russia	1,393		Portugal	222
13	Spain	1,235	**35**	Taiwan	208
14	Mexico	1,017	**36**	Colombia	205
15	Australia	915	**37**	Pakistan	203
16	Indonesia	825	**38**	Norway	159
17	Turkey	723	**39**	Philippines	156
18	Argentina	663	**40**	Morocco	155
19	Canada	639	**41**	Vietnam	153
20	Belgium	547	**42**	United Arab Emirates	150
21	Malaysia	520	**43**	Peru	142
22	Poland	485	**44**	Egypt	133

Transport: planes and trains

Most air travel
Passengers carried, m, 2016

1	United States	822.9	16	France	65.4
2	China	488.0	17	Thailand	60.5
3	United Kingdom	145.1	18	Malaysia	53.8
4	Ireland	125.6	19	Mexico	53.3
5	Germany	124.7	20	Philippines	40.1
6	India	119.6	21	Vietnam	37.9
7	Japan	117.7	22	Netherlands	37.7
8	Turkey	100.4	23	Singapore	35.0
9	Indonesia	96.5	24	Saudi Arabia	34.5
10	Brazil	94.1	25	Colombia	32.3
11	United Arab Emirates	92.2	26	Qatar	31.2
12	Canada	85.4	27	Italy	28.9
13	Russia	77.5	28	Switzerland	25.9
14	Australia	72.6	29	Hungary	21.4
15	Spain	66.7	30	South Africa	19.5

Busiest airports
Total passengers, m, 2017

1	Atlanta, Hartsfield	103.9
2	Beijing, Capital	95.8
3	Dubai Intl.	88.2
4	Los Angeles, Intl.	84.6
5	Chicago, O'Hare	79.8
6	London, Heathrow	78.0
7	Tokyo, Haneda	76.5
8	Hong Kong, Intl.	72.7
9	Shanghai, Pudong Intl.	70.0
10	Paris, Charles de Gaulle	69.5
11	Amsterdam, Schiphol	68.5
12	Dallas, Ft Worth	67.1
13	Guangzhou Baiyun, Intl	65.9
14	Frankfurt, Main	64.5
15	Istanbul, Ataturk	63.9

Total cargo, m tonnes, 2017

1	Hong Kong, Intl.	5.0
2	Memphis, Intl.	4.3
3	Shanghai, Pudong Intl.	3.8
4	Dubai, Intl.	2.8
	Seoul, Incheon	2.8
6	Anchorage, Intl.	2.7
7	Louisville, Intl.	2.6
8	Taiwan, Taoyuan Intl.	2.3
	Tokyo, Narita	2.3
10	Frankfurt, Main	2.2
	Los Angeles, Intl.	2.2
	Paris, Charles de Gaulle	2.2
	Singapore, Changi	2.2
14	Miami, Intl.	2.1
15	Beijing, Capital	2.0

Average daily aircraft movements, take-offs and landings, 2017

1	Atlanta, Hartsfield	2,421		Toronto, Pearson Intl.	1,275
2	Chicago, O'Hare	2,356	16	Houston, George Bush	
3	Los Angeles, Intl.	1,924		Intercontinental	1,234
4	Dallas, Ft Worth	1,795		San Francisco	1,234
5	Beijing, Capital	1,632	18	Mexico City, Intl.[a]	1,228
6	Denver, Intl.	1,577	19	New York, JFK	1,223
7	Charlotte/Douglas, Intl.	1,517	20	Tokyo, Haneda[a]	1,221
8	Las Vegas, McCarran Intl.	1,488	21	Newark	1,214
9	Amsterdam, Schiphol	1,404	22	Guangzhou Baiyun, Intl	1,192
10	Shanghai, Pudong Intl.	1,351	23	Phoenix, Skyharbor Intl.	1,181
11	Paris, Charles de Gaulle	1,320	24	Dubai, Intl.	1,146
12	London, Heathrow	1,304	25	Minneapolis–Saint Paul	1,140
13	Frankfurt, Main	1,303	26	Miami	1,132
14	Istanbul, Ataturk[a]	1,275	27	Munich	1,108

a 2016

Longest railway networks
'000 km, 2016 or latest

1	United States	228.2	21	Turkey	10.1
2	Russia	85.4	22	Sweden	9.7
3	China	67.1	23	Czech Republic	9.5
4	India	66.0	24	Pakistan	9.3
5	Canada	52.1	25	Iran	8.6
6	Germany	33.4	26	Hungary	7.7
7	Australia	32.8	27	Finland	5.9
8	France	30.0	28	Belarus	5.5
9	Brazil	29.8		Chile	5.5
10	Argentina	28.5	30	Thailand	5.3
11	Mexico	26.7	31	Egypt	5.2
12	Ukraine	21.6	32	Austria	4.9
13	South Africa	20.5	33	Indonesia	4.7
14	Japan	19.2	34	Sudan	4.3
15	Poland	18.4		Uzbekistan	4.3
16	Italy	16.8	36	Norway	4.2
17	United Kingdom	16.2	37	South Korea	4.1
18	Spain	15.7	38	Bulgaria	4.0
19	Kazakhstan	15.5		Switzerland	4.0
20	Romania	10.8			

Most rail passengers
Km per person per year, 2016 or latest

1	Switzerland	2,295	13	India	865
2	Japan	1,637	14	Ukraine	838
3	Russia	1,440	15	Czech Republic	703
4	Austria	1,311		Finland	703
5	France	1,309	17	Belarus	677
6	Netherlands	1,045	18	Italy	657
7	Denmark	1,032	19	Sweden	636
8	Kazakhstan	1,015	20	Luxembourg	622
9	Germany	982	21	Slovakia	591
10	United Kingdom	957	22	Norway	582
11	Belgium	906	23	Spain	568
12	Taiwan	874	24	Hungary	550

Most rail freight
Million tonne-km per year, 2016 or latest

1	United States	2,547,253	13	Belarus	41,107
2	Russia	2,342,590	14	France	33,116
3	China	1,920,285	15	Poland	28,720
4	India	681,696	16	Iran	27,243
5	Canada	540,141	17	Uzbekistan	22,937
6	Brazil	267,700	18	Japan	20,255
7	Kazakhstan	188,159	19	Austria	16,052
8	Ukraine	187,557	20	Lithuania	13,790
9	South Africa	134,600	21	Turkmenistan	13,327
10	Mexico	73,879	22	Mongolia	12,371
11	Germany	72,913	23	Argentina	12,111
12	Australia	59,649	24	Latvia	11,838

Transport: shipping

Merchant fleets

Number of vessels, by country of domicile, January 2017

1	China	5,206	11	Turkey	1,563
2	Greece	4,199	12	Hong Kong	1,532
3	Japan	3,901	13	United Kingdom	1,368
4	Germany	3,090	14	Netherlands	1,256
5	Singapore	2,599	15	India	986
6	United States	2,106	16	Vietnam	943
7	Norway	1,842	17	Taiwan	926
8	Indonesia	1,840	18	Denmark	920
9	Russia	1,707	19	United Arab Emirates	883
10	South Korea	1,656	20	France	790

Ships' flags

Largest registered fleets, 2016

% of world total

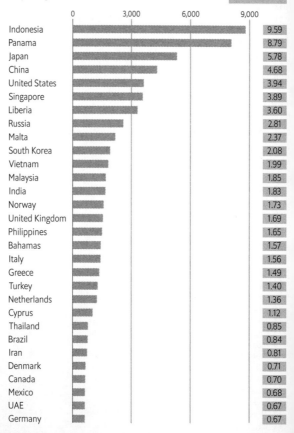

	% of world total
Indonesia	9.59
Panama	8.79
Japan	5.78
China	4.68
United States	3.94
Singapore	3.89
Liberia	3.60
Russia	2.81
Malta	2.37
South Korea	2.08
Vietnam	1.99
Malaysia	1.85
India	1.83
Norway	1.73
United Kingdom	1.69
Philippines	1.65
Bahamas	1.57
Italy	1.56
Greece	1.49
Turkey	1.40
Netherlands	1.36
Cyprus	1.12
Thailand	0.85
Brazil	0.84
Iran	0.81
Denmark	0.71
Canada	0.70
Mexico	0.68
UAE	0.67
Germany	0.67

Crime and punishment

Murders
Homicides per 100,000 pop., 2015 or latest

1	El Salvador	105.4
2	Honduras	57.5
3	Venezuela	56.3
4	Virgin Islands (US)	49.3
5	Jamaica	42.1
6	Lesotho	41.2
7	Bahamas	37.7
8	South Africa	33.8
9	Trinidad & Tobago	30.9
10	Guatemala	29.4
11	Brazil	28.4
12	Colombia	26.5
13	Guyana	19.4
14	Dominican Rep.	17.4
15	Swaziland	17.3
16	Namibia	17.1
17	Puerto Rico	16.8
18	Mexico	16.5
19	Macedonia	16.0
20	Botswana	15.0

Robberies
Per 100,000 pop., 2015 or latest

1	Costa Rica	1,096
2	Argentina	1,020
3	Chile	593
4	Ecuador	571
5	Uruguay	566
6	Brazil	496
7	Paraguay	317
8	Swaziland	310
9	Peru	264
10	Colombia	210
11	Maldives	208
	Panama	208
13	Belgium	196
14	Guyana	191
15	Trinidad & Tobago	182
16	France	163
17	Portugal	149
18	Dominican Rep.	144
19	Bolivia	141
20	Spain	140

Prisoners
Total prison pop., 2018 or latest

1	United States	2,121,600
2	China	1,649,804
3	Brazil	675,850
4	Russia	600,721
5	India	419,623
6	Thailand	334,279
7	Indonesia	240,391
8	Turkey	232,179
9	Iran	230,000
10	Mexico	204,749
11	Philippines	178,661
12	South Africa	158,111
13	Colombia	115,488
14	Vietnam	115,035
15	Ethiopia	113,727
16	Egypt	106,000
17	Peru	85,727
18	Pakistan	84,315
19	United Kingdom	83,673
20	Morocco	82,512
21	Argentina	81,975
22	Myanmar	79,668
23	Bangladesh	79,280
24	Poland	74,896
25	Nigeria	71,522
26	France	68,974
27	Germany	64,351

Per 100,000 pop., 2018 or latest

1	United States	655
2	El Salvador	614
3	Turkmenistan	583
4	Virgin Islands (US)	542
5	Maldives	514
6	Cuba	510
7	Thailand	483
8	Bahamas	438
	Guam	438
10	Rwanda	434
11	Russia	415
12	Panama	390
13	Costa Rica	374
14	Brazil	325
15	Uruguay	321
16	Bermuda	319
17	Belarus	314
18	Puerto Rico	313
19	Barbados	300
20	Namibia	295
21	Turkey	287
22	Iran	284
23	Swaziland	282
24	South Africa	280
25	Guyana	278
26	Trinidad & Tobago	270
27	Peru	267

War and terrorism

Defence spending
As % of GDP, 2017

1	Oman	12.1		13	Azerbaijan	4.0
2	Saudi Arabia	11.3		14	Armenia	3.9
3	Afghanistan	10.3		15	Iran	3.7
4	Iraq	10.1		16	Cambodia	3.5
5	Congo-Brazzaville	6.2			Lebanon	3.5
	Israel	6.2		18	Colombia	3.3
7	Algeria	5.7			Namibia	3.3
8	Jordan	4.9			Singapore	3.3
9	Kuwait	4.8			South Sudan	3.3
10	Bahrain	4.4		22	Morocco	3.2
11	Mali	4.3			Pakistan	3.2
12	Russia[a]	4.2				

Defence spending

$bn, 2017				*Per person, $, 2017*		
1	United States	602.8		1	Saudi Arabia	2,684
2	China	150.5		2	Oman	2,537
3	Saudi Arabia	76.7		3	Israel	2,235
4	Russia[a]	61.2		4	Kuwait	1,986
5	India	52.5		5	United States	1,845
6	United Kingdom	50.7		6	Singapore	1,736
7	France	48.6		7	Norway	1,143
8	Japan	46.0		8	Australia	1,075
9	Germany	41.7		9	Bahrain	1,049
10	South Korea	35.7		10	United Kingdom	783
11	Brazil	29.4		11	Brunei	731
12	Australia	25.0		12	France	725
13	Italy	22.9		13	South Korea	697
14	Israel[b]	21.6		14	Denmark	679
15	Iraq	19.4		15	Sweden	599

Armed forces
'000, 2018[c]

		Regulars	Reserves				Regulars	Reserves
1	China	2,035	510		16	Colombia	293	35
2	India	1,395	1,155		17	Mexico	277	82
3	United States	1,348	858		18	Japan	247	56
4	North Korea	1,280	600		19	Sri Lanka	243	6
5	Russia[a]	900	2,000		20	Saudi Arabia	227	0
6	Pakistan	654	0		21	Taiwan	215	1,657
7	South Korea	625	3,100		22	Ukraine	204	900
8	Iran	523	350		23	France	203	32
9	Vietnam	482	5,000		24	Eritrea	202	120
10	Egypt	439	479		25	Morocco	196	150
11	Myanmar	406	0		26	South Sudan	185	0
12	Indonesia	396	400		27	Germany	179	28
13	Thailand	361	200		28	Israel	177	465
14	Turkey	355	379		29	Italy	175	18
15	Brazil	335	1,340		30	Afghanistan	174	0

a National defence budget only.   b Includes US Foreign Military Assistance.   c Estimates.

Arms exporters
$m, 2017

1	United States	12,394
2	Russia	6,148
3	France	2,162
4	Germany	1,653
5	Israel	1,263
6	United Kingdom	1,214
7	Netherlands	1,167
8	China	1,131
9	Spain	814
10	Italy	660
11	South Korea	587
12	Turkey	244
13	Ukraine	240
14	Switzerland	186
15	Norway	134
16	Czech Republic	110
17	Indonesia	102
18	Australia	97
19	Canada	87
20	Sweden	83

Arms importers
$m, 2017

1	Saudi Arabia	4,111
2	India	3,358
3	Egypt	2,355
4	Australia	1,806
5	Indonesia	1,196
6	China	1,117
7	South Korea	918
8	Algeria	905
9	United Kingdom	899
10	UAE	848
11	Italy	794
12	Oman	783
13	Iraq	712
14	Pakistan	710
15	Vietnam	690
16	Qatar	670
17	United States	547
18	Israel	528
19	Japan	500
20	Taiwan	493

Terrorist attacks
Number of incidences, 2016

Space and peace

Manned space missions
Firsts and selected events

1957	Man-made satellite
	Dog in space, Laika
1961	Human in space, Yuri Gagarin
1963	Woman in space, Valentina Tereshkova
1964	Space crew, one pilot and two passengers
1965	Spacewalk, Alexei Leonov
	Eight days in space achieved (needed to travel to moon and back)
1968	Live television broadcast from space
1968	Moon orbit
1969	Moon landing
1971	Space station, Salyut
	Drive on the Moon
1973	Space laboratory, Skylab
1978	Non-American, non-Soviet, Vladimir Remek (Czechoslovakia)
1982	Space shuttle, Columbia (first craft to carry four crew members)
1986	Space shuttle explosion, Challenger
	Mir space station activated
1990	Hubble telescope deployed
2001	Dennis Tito, paying space tourist
2003	China manned space flight, Yang Liwei
2004	SpaceShipOne, successful private manned suborbital space flight
2010	SpaceX, privately funded spacecraft to complete an orbital flight
2014	Rosetta probe landed on comet 67P after 12-year mission
2015	United States becomes first country to have space probes explore all nine planets
2017	Falcon 9, first reuse of orbital class rocket
2018	SpaceX launch car and mannequin towards Mars

Orbital launches

2017		Commercial	Non-commercial[a]	Total	*2005–17*
1	United States	21	8	29	247
2	Russia	7	11	18	348
3	China	0	18	18	181
4	Europe	8	3	11	103
5	Japan	0	7	7	43
6	India	0	5	5	42

Global Peace Index[b]

Most peaceful, 2018			*Least peaceful, 2018*		
1	Iceland	1.096	**1**	Syria	3.600
2	New Zealand	1.192	**2**	Afghanistan	3.585
3	Austria	1.274	**3**	South Sudan	3.508
4	Portugal	1.318	**4**	Iraq	3.425
5	Denmark	1.353	**5**	Somalia	3.367
6	Canada	1.372	**6**	Yemen	3.305
7	Czech Republic	1.381	**7**	Libya	3.262
8	Singapore	1.382	**8**	Congo-Kinshasa	3.251
9	Japan	1.391	**9**	Central African Rep.	3.236

a Government and non-profit launches.
b Ranks 163 countries using 23 indicators which gauge the level of safety and security in society, the extent of domestic or international conflict and the degree of militarisation.

Environment

Biggest emitters of carbon dioxide
Million tonnes, 2014

1	China	10,291.9	31	Iraq	168.4
2	United States	5,254.3	32	Netherlands	167.3
3	India	2,238.4	33	Vietnam	166.9
4	Russia	1,705.3	34	Pakistan	166.3
5	Japan	1,214.0	35	Algeria	145.4
6	Germany	719.9	36	Qatar	107.9
7	Iran	649.5	37	Philippines	105.7
8	Saudi Arabia	601.0	38	Uzbekistan	105.2
9	South Korea	587.2	39	Czech Republic	96.5
10	Canada	537.2	40	Nigeria	96.3
11	Brazil	529.8	41	Kuwait	95.4
12	South Africa	489.8	42	Belgium	93.4
13	Mexico	480.3	43	Colombia	84.1
14	Indonesia	464.2	44	Chile	82.6
15	United Kingdom	419.8	45	Bangladesh	73.2
16	Australia	361.3	46	Romania	70.0
17	Turkey	346.0	47	Turkmenistan	68.4
18	Italy	320.4	48	Greece	67.3
19	Thailand	316.2	49	Israel	64.6
20	France	303.3	50	Belarus	63.5
21	Poland	285.7	51	Peru	61.7
22	Taiwan	271.8	52	Oman	61.2
23	Kazakhstan	248.3	53	Morocco	59.9
24	Malaysia	242.8	54	Austria	58.7
25	Spain	234.0	55	Libya	57.0
26	Ukraine	227.3	56	Singapore	56.4
27	United Arab Emirates	211.4	57	Norway	47.6
28	Argentina	204.0	58	Finland	47.3
29	Egypt	201.9	59	Trinidad & Tobago	46.3
30	Venezuela	185.2	60	Hong Kong	46.2

Largest amount of carbon dioxide emitted per person
Tonnes, 2014

1	Qatar	45.4	18	South Korea	11.6
2	Trinidad & Tobago	34.2	19	Taiwan	11.5
3	Kuwait	25.2	20	Singapore	10.3
4	Bahrain	23.4	21	Netherlands	9.9
5	United Arab Emirates	23.3	22	Japan	9.5
6	Brunei	22.1	23	Norway	9.3
7	Saudi Arabia	19.5	24	Czech Republic	9.2
8	Luxembourg	17.4		Libya	9.2
9	United States	16.5	26	South Africa	9.0
10	New Caledonia	16.0	27	Germany	8.9
11	Australia	15.4	28	Bermuda	8.8
	Oman	15.4	29	Finland	8.7
13	Canada	15.1	30	Belgium	8.3
14	Estonia	14.8		Iran	8.3
15	Kazakhstan	14.4	32	Malaysia	8.0
16	Turkmenistan	12.5	33	Israel	7.9
17	Russia	11.9	34	New Zealand	7.7

Most polluted capital cities
Annual mean particulate matter concentration[a], micrograms per cubic metre
2016 or latest

1	Delhi, India	143.1		13	Yaoundé, Cameroon	49.0
2	Cairo, Egypt	116.6		14	Ankara, Turkey	46.9
3	Kampala, Uganda	104.3		15	Skopje, Macedonia	44.5
4	Doha, Qatar	93.4		16	La Paz, Bolivia	44.4
5	Kabul, Afghanistan	86.0		17	Lima, Peru	38.8
6	Dhaka, Bangladesh	81.6		18	Tunis, Tunisia	38.0
7	Baghdad, Iraq	73.6		19	Antananarivo, Madagascar	36.8
8	Beijing, China	73.0		20	Colombo, Sri Lanka	35.6
	Riyadh, Saudi Arabia	73.0		21	Guatemala City, Guatemala	35.2
10	Abu Dhabi, UAE	61.5				
11	Ulaanbaatar, Mongolia	57.0		22	Muscat, Oman	34.7
12	Brasília, Brazil	54.1				

Environmental Performance Index[b]
2017, 100=highest, 0=lowest

Best				Worst		
1	Switzerland	87.4		1	Burundi	27.4
2	France	84.0		2	Bangladesh	29.6
3	Denmark	81.6		3	Congo-Kinshasa	30.4
4	Malta	80.9		4	India	30.6
5	Sweden	80.5		5	Nepal	31.4
6	United Kingdom	79.9		6	Haiti	33.7
7	Luxembourg	79.1			Madagascar	33.7
8	Austria	79.0		8	Lesotho	33.8
9	Ireland	78.8		9	Niger	35.7
10	Finland	78.6		10	Central African Rep.	36.4
	Iceland	78.6		11	Angola	37.4
12	Germany	78.4		12	Pakistan	37.5
	Spain	78.4		13	Afghanistan	37.7

Lowest access to electricity
% of population, 2015

1	Burundi	7.3		16	Rwanda	22.8
2	Chad	7.7		17	Mozambique	24.0
3	South Sudan	7.9		18	Lesotho	27.9
4	Malawi	10.8		19	Somalia	28.3
5	Central African Rep.	13.4		20	Guinea	31.0
6	Liberia	13.8		21	Zambia	31.1
7	Guinea-Bissau	14.0		22	Ethiopia	33.4
8	Congo-Kinshasa	16.4		23	Zimbabwe	33.7
9	Sierra Leone	16.5		24	North Korea	37.4
10	Niger	16.6		25	Mali	37.6
11	Burkina Faso	18.5		26	Sudan	38.0
	Tanzania	18.5		27	Haiti	38.2
	Uganda	18.5		28	Mauritania	39.5
14	Madagascar	19.0		29	Benin	40.0
15	Papua New Guinea	22.2		30	Kenya	41.6

a Particulates less than 2.5 microns in diameter.
b Ranked on 24 indicators covering environmental health and ecosystem vitality.

Largest forested land
Sq km, 2015

1	Russia	8,149,305
2	Brazil	4,935,380
3	Canada	3,470,690
4	United States	3,100,950
5	China	2,083,213
6	Congo-Kinshasa	1,525,780
7	Australia	1,247,510
8	Indonesia	910,100
9	Peru	739,730
10	India	706,820
11	Mexico	660,400
12	Colombia	585,017
13	Angola	578,560
14	Bolivia	547,640
15	Zambia	486,350
16	Venezuela	466,830
17	Tanzania	460,600
18	Mozambique	379,400
19	Papua New Guinea	335,590
20	Myanmar	290,410
21	Sweden	280,730
22	Argentina	271,120
23	Japan	249,580
24	Gabon	230,000
25	Congo-Brazzaville	223,340
26	Finland	222,180
27	Malaysia	221,950
28	Central African Rep.	221,700
29	Sudan	192,099
30	Cameroon	188,160

Most forested
% of land area, 2015

1	Suriname	98.3
2	Gabon	89.3
3	Guyana	84.0
4	Laos	81.3
5	Papua New Guinea	74.1
6	Finland	73.1
7	Brunei	72.1
8	Guinea-Bissau	70.1
9	Sweden	68.9
10	Japan	68.5
11	Malaysia	67.6
12	Congo-Kinshasa	67.3
13	Congo-Brazzaville	65.4
	Zambia	65.4
15	South Korea	63.4
16	Panama	62.1
17	Slovenia	62.0
18	Montenegro	61.5
19	Brazil	59.0
20	Peru	57.8
21	Equatorial Guinea	55.9
	Puerto Rico	55.9
23	Fiji	55.7
24	Costa Rica	54.0
	Latvia	54.0
26	Cambodia	53.6
27	Venezuela	52.9
28	Colombia	52.7
	Estonia	52.7
30	Tanzania	52.0

Deforestation
Biggest % change in forested land, 1995–2015

Decrease			Increase		
1	Togo	-67.9	1	Iceland	119.2
2	Nigeria	-53.9	2	Bahrain	106.9
3	Uganda	-51.8	3	French Polynesia	93.8
4	Mauritania	-38.7	4	Uruguay	70.2
5	Honduras	-36.8	5	Dominican Rep.	53.1
6	Pakistan	-36.6	6	Kuwait	50.6
7	Sudan	-35.7	7	Rwanda	45.0
8	North Korea	-33.5	8	Cuba	42.4
9	Zimbabwe	-31.5	9	Egypt	41.7
10	Niger	-30.2	10	Tunisia	40.7
11	Chad	-25.2	11	Vietnam	40.1
	El Salvador	-25.2	12	Ireland	37.1
	Nicaragua	-25.2	13	Puerto Rico	34.6
14	Mali	-25.1	14	Azerbaijan	32.2
15	Kyrgyzstan	-24.8	15	Montenegro	32.1
16	Timor-Leste	-24.6	16	Moldova	27.2
17	Paraguay	-24.4	17	China	24.7

Biodiversity and habitat index

Scores on biodiversity[a], 2017, 0=lowest, 100=highest

Best			Worst		
1	Zambia	98.8	1	Afghanistan	13.4
2	Botswana	98.3	2	Haiti	14.4
3	Germany	96.9	3	Lesotho	17.4
4	United Kingdom	96.7	4	Libya	20.7
5	Luxembourg	96.5	5	Singapore	21.5
6	Poland	96.4	6	Maldives	23.6
7	France	96.3	7	Jordan	23.9
8	Venezuela	96.2	8	Turkey	25.2
			9	Bosnia & Herz.	26.9

Species listed as endangered

Mammals, 2017

1	Indonesia	191	12	Peru	50
2	Madagascar	121	13	Myanmar	49
3	India	94	14	Cameroon	47
4	Mexico	93	15	Ecuador	45
5	Brazil	81		Laos	45
6	China	74	17	Papua New Guinea	40
7	Malaysia	72		Tanzania	40
8	Australia	63	19	Cambodia	39
9	Thailand	59		Philippines	39
10	Vietnam	56	21	Argentina	37
11	Colombia	54		Bangladesh	37

Fish, 2017

1	United States	251	12	Thailand	107
2	India	228	13	Colombia	98
3	Mexico	181		Malawi	98
4	Tanzania	176	15	Congo-Kinshasa	94
5	Indonesia	163	16	Philippines	93
6	China	134	17	Brazil	90
7	Turkey	131	18	Malaysia	87
8	Australia	123	19	Vietnam	82
9	Cameroon	121	20	Greece	80
10	South Africa	120		Spain	80
11	Madagascar	110	22	Japan	77

Plants, 2017

1	Ecuador	1,857	11	India	390
2	Madagascar	789	12	New Caledonia	349
3	Malaysia	717	13	Peru	327
4	Tanzania	631	14	Sri Lanka	292
5	China	574	15	Colombia	259
6	Cameroon	535	16	Philippines	243
7	Brazil	533	17	Kenya	234
8	United States	475		Spain	234
9	Indonesia	437	19	Jamaica	214
10	Mexico	430	20	Panama	209

a Based on six indicators, such as protection of species and percentage of biomes in protected areas.

Worst natural catastrophes
2016

Country/region	Type of disaster	Deaths[a]
1 Caribbean/United States	Hurricane Matthew	734
2 Ecuador	Earthquake	663
3 North Korea	Typhoon/flooding	538
4 Italy	Earthquake	299
5 China	Floods along Yangtze river	289
China	Flooding, Hebei & elsewhere	289
7 India	Monsoon floods	228
8 Sri Lanka	Cyclone rains	191
9 India	Monsoon floods	151
10 Pakistan	River floods	141
11 Japan	Earthquake	137
12 Nepal	River floods	122
13 Taiwan	Earthquake	117
14 Philippines/Taiwan/China	Typhoon Nepartak	111
15 Indonesia	Earthquake	103
16 Ethiopia	Floods/landslide	100
Taiwan/Thailand	Cold wave	100
18 China	Thunderstorms/hail	99
19 Pakistan	River floods	92
20 Japan/China	Typhoon Lionrock	79
21 Mexico/Belize	Hurricane Earl	67
22 China	River floods	66
23 Indonesia	River floods/landslides	62
24 India	Monsoon floods	61

People internally displaced[b] by natural disasters
'000, 2016

1 China	7,434.3		22 Israel	75.2
2 Philippines	5,929.9		23 Somalia	70.0
3 India	2,400.3		24 Dominican Rep.	52.3
4 Indonesia	1,246.5		25 Madagascar	51.0
5 United States	1,107.3		26 Niger	46.0
6 Cuba	1,079.2		27 Yemen	44.9
7 Japan	863.6		28 Kenya	40.3
8 Bangladesh	613.7		29 Tanzania	35.9
9 Myanmar	509.2		30 Nepal	31.3
10 Sri Lanka	500.2		31 Italy	31.0
11 Ethiopia	347.2		32 Colombia	30.8
12 Ecuador	289.4		33 Senegal	24.2
13 Haiti	180.2		34 Angola	19.1
14 Congo-Kinshasa	130.2		35 Malaysia	18.5
15 Sudan	122.7		36 Nicaragua	18.4
16 North Korea	107.0		37 Burkina Faso	17.9
17 Canada	92.7		38 Peru	17.0
18 Thailand	90.2		39 Chile	16.4
19 Vietnam	80.5		40 Brazil	13.6
20 Nigeria	77.7		41 Pakistan	12.7
21 Fiji	76.1		42 Uruguay	12.3

a Includes "missing".   b Includes mandatory evacuations.

Life expectancy

Highest life expectancy
Years, 2015–20

1	Monaco[a]	89.4	25	Guadeloupe	81.7	
2	Hong Kong	84.2		Ireland	81.7	
3	Macau	84.1	27	Finland	81.6	
4	Japan	84.0	28	Greece	81.5	
5	Switzerland	83.6		Portugal	81.5	
6	Spain	83.4	30	Belgium	81.4	
7	Italy	83.3		Bermuda	81.4	
	Singapore	83.3	32	Channel Islands	81.3	
9	Australia	83.2		Germany	81.3	
10	Iceland	83.0	34	Slovenia	81.2	
11	Andorra[a]	82.9	35	Malta	81.1	
12	France	82.8	36	Denmark	80.9	
13	Israel	82.7	37	Cyprus	80.7	
	Sweden	82.7	38	Réunion	80.6	
15	Canada	82.6	39	French Guiana	80.3	
16	Norway	82.4	40	Puerto Rico	80.2	
	South Korea	82.4		Taiwan	80.2	
18	Martinique	82.3	42	Costa Rica	80.1	
19	Netherlands	82.1	43	Cuba	80.0	
	New Zealand	82.1		Virgin Islands (US)	80.0	
21	Luxembourg	82.0	45	Chile	79.9	
22	Austria	81.9	46	Guam	79.8	
	Liechtenstein[a]	81.9		Lebanon	79.8	
24	United Kingdom	81.8	48	United States	79.6	

Highest male life expectancy
Years, 2015–20

1	Monaco[a]	85.6	11	Andorra[a]	80.7
2	Iceland	81.6		Canada	80.7
	Switzerland	81.6		Japan	80.7
4	Australia	81.3	14	Spain	80.6
	Singapore	81.3	15	New Zealand	80.5
6	Hong Kong	81.2		Norway	80.5
7	Italy	81.1	17	Netherlands	80.3
	Macau	81.1	18	United Kingdom	80.0
9	Israel	81.0	19	France	79.9
	Sweden	81.0			

Highest female life expectancy
Years, 2015–20

1	Monaco[b]	93.5		Switzerland	85.4
2	Hong Kong	87.2	10	Singapore	85.3
	Japan	87.2	11	Andorra[b]	85.2
4	Macau	87.0		Martinique	85.2
5	Spain	86.1	13	Australia	85.0
6	France	85.7	14	Guadeloupe	84.8
7	Italy	85.4	15	Liechtenstein[b]	84.7
	South Korea	85.4	16	Bermuda	84.6

a 2017 estimate. b 2016 estimate.

Lowest life expectancy

Years, 2015–20

1	Sierra Leone	52.3		26	Zambia	62.3
2	Central African Rep.	53.3		27	Ghana	63.2
	Chad	53.3		28	Liberia	63.3
4	Nigeria	54.1		29	Mauritania	63.4
5	Ivory Coast	54.4		30	Haiti	63.7
6	Lesotho	54.7			South Africa	63.7
7	Somalia	56.9		32	Malawi	63.8
8	South Sudan	57.5		33	Afghanistan	64.2
9	Burundi	58.0		34	Sudan	64.8
	Equatorial Guinea	58.0		35	Namibia	65.0
	Guinea-Bissau	58.0		36	Yemen	65.2
12	Swaziland	58.5		37	Congo-Brazzaville	65.3
13	Mali	58.7		38	Eritrea	65.7
14	Cameroon	58.8		39	Papua New Guinea	65.8
15	Mozambique	59.2		40	Ethiopia	66.0
16	Congo-Kinshasa	60.2		41	Madagascar	66.5
17	Uganda	60.3		42	Gabon	66.7
18	Niger	60.5			Pakistan	66.7
	Togo	60.5			Tanzania	66.7
20	Burkina Faso	60.9		45	Guyana	66.8
	Guinea	60.9			Myanmar	66.8
22	Benin	61.3		47	Laos	67.2
23	Gambia, The	61.5		48	Kenya	67.3
24	Angola	61.8		49	Rwanda	67.6
25	Zimbabwe	61.9			Senegal	67.6

Lowest male life expectancy

Years, 2015–20

1	Central African Rep.	51.4		11	South Sudan	56.5
2	Sierra Leone	51.7		12	Equatorial Guinea	56.8
3	Chad	52.1		13	Mozambique	57.0
4	Lesotho	52.4		14	Cameroon	57.8
5	Ivory Coast	53.0		15	Mali	58.0
6	Nigeria	53.3			Uganda	58.0
7	Somalia	55.3		17	Congo-Kinshasa	58.7
	Swaziland	55.3		18	Angola	59.0
9	Burundi	56.1		19	Niger	59.5
10	Guinea-Bissau	56.3		20	Zambia	59.6

Lowest female life expectancy

Years, 2015–20

1	Sierra Leone	52.9			Mali	59.5
2	Chad	54.6		11	Guinea-Bissau	59.8
3	Nigeria	54.9		12	Cameroon	59.9
4	Central African Rep.	55.3		13	Burundi	60.0
5	Ivory Coast	55.9		14	Mozambique	61.3
6	Lesotho	56.8		15	Swaziland	61.4
7	South Sudan	58.6			Togo	61.4
8	Somalia	58.7		17	Guinea	61.5
9	Equatorial Guinea	59.5				

Death rates and infant mortality

Highest death rates
Number of deaths per 1,000 population, 2015–20

#	Country	Rate	#	Country	Rate
1	Bulgaria	15.3	49	South Africa	9.5
2	Latvia	15.1	50	Niger	9.4
3	Ukraine	14.9		Uruguay	9.4
4	Lithuania	14.3	52	Swaziland	9.3
5	Russia	13.6	53	Channel Islands	9.1
6	Belarus	13.5		Spain	9.1
7	Georgia	13.1		Sweden	9.1
8	Hungary	13.0	56	Benin	9.0
	Romania	13.0		France	9.0
10	Central African Rep.	12.9		North Korea	9.0
11	Croatia	12.8		United Kingdom	9.0
	Serbia	12.8	60	Kazakhstan	8.9
13	Chad	12.6		Malta	8.9
14	Sierra Leone	12.5	62	Guinea	8.8
15	Lesotho	12.4	63	Netherlands	8.7
16	Estonia	12.2	64	Bermuda	8.6
17	Nigeria	12.0		Martinique	8.6
18	Ivory Coast	11.8		Togo	8.6
19	Moldova	11.7		Virgin Islands (US)	8.6
20	Germany	11.3	68	Haiti	8.5
21	Bosnia & Herz.	11.2		Uganda	8.5
22	Somalia	11.0	70	Angola	8.4
23	Barbados[a]	10.9		United States	8.4
	Greece	10.9	72	Burkina Faso	8.3
25	Japan	10.8		Guyana	8.3
	Portugal	10.8		Mauritius	8.3
27	Czech Republic	10.7	75	Myanmar	8.2
28	Italy	10.6	76	Cuba	8.1
	South Sudan	10.6		Thailand	8.1
30	Poland	10.5	78	Puerto Rico	8.0
31	Burundi	10.4		Switzerland	8.0
32	Guinea-Bissau	10.2	80	Gambia, The	7.9
33	Slovakia	10.1		Ghana	7.9
34	Equatorial Guinea	10.0		Norway	7.9
	Montenegro	10.0	83	Mauritania	7.8
36	Macedonia	9.9		Zimbabwe	7.8
	Slovenia	9.9	85	Albania	7.7
38	Belgium	9.8	86	Argentina	7.6
	Finland	9.8		Liberia	7.6
	Mali	9.8		Zambia	7.6
	Monaco[a]	9.8	89	Canada	7.5
	Trinidad & Tobago	9.8		China	7.5
43	Armenia	9.7	91	Gabon	7.4
	Austria	9.7		India	7.4
	Cameroon	9.7		Liechtenstein[a]	7.4
	Mozambique	9.7		Suriname	7.4
47	Congo-Kinshasa	9.6		Taiwan	7.4
	Denmark	9.6			

Note: Both death and, in particular, infant mortality rates can be underestimated in certain countries where not all deaths are officially recorded.   a 2017 estimate.

Highest infant mortality
Number of deaths per 1,000 live births, 2015–20

1	Central African Rep.	81	23	Afghanistan	52
	Chad	81		Guinea	52
3	Sierra Leone	80	25	Togo	50
4	Guinea-Bissau	70	26	Lesotho	49
5	Burundi	69	27	Liberia	47
	Somalia	69	28	Zambia	46
7	Mali	66	29	Gambia, The	45
	South Sudan	66		Papua New Guinea	45
9	Congo-Kinshasa	65	31	Sudan	44
10	Mozambique	64		Swaziland	44
	Pakistan	64	33	Turkmenistan	43
12	Mauritania	63	34	Haiti	42
	Nigeria	63		Myanmar	42
14	Benin	61		Yemen	42
	Equatorial Guinea	61	37	Zimbabwe	41
16	Angola	59	38	Ghana	40
	Malawi	59		Laos	40
18	Cameroon	58	40	Congo-Brazzaville	39
19	Ivory Coast	57		Tanzania	39
	Niger	57	42	Ethiopia	37
21	Uganda	55		Rwanda	37
22	Burkina Faso	54			

Lowest death rates
No. of deaths per 1,000 pop., 2015–20

1	Qatar	1.6
2	United Arab Emirates	1.7
3	Bahrain	2.4
4	Oman	2.5
5	Kuwait	2.9
6	French Guiana	3.0
7	Maldives	3.3
8	West Bank & Gaza	3.5
9	Saudi Arabia	3.6
10	Brunei	3.7
11	Jordan	3.8
12	Macau	3.9
13	Iran	4.5
14	Lebanon	4.7
15	Algeria	4.8
	Guatemala	4.8
	Honduras	4.8
	Nicaragua	4.8
19	Iraq	4.9
	Mexico	4.9
21	Costa Rica	5.0
	Malaysia	5.0

Lowest infant mortality
No. of deaths per 1,000 live births, 2015–20

1	Hong Kong	1
2	Austria	2
	Czech Republic	2
	Finland	2
	Germany	2
	Iceland	2
	Ireland	2
	Italy	2
	Japan	2
	Monaco[a]	2
	Norway	2
	Portugal	2
	Singapore	2
	Slovenia	2
	South Korea	2
	Spain	2
	Sweden	2

Death and disease

Diabetes
Prevalence in pop. aged 18–99, %
2017 age-standardised estimate[a]

1	New Caledonia	22.6
2	French Polynesia	22.0
3	Mauritius	21.3
4	Guam	20.9
5	Papua New Guinea	17.7
	Saudi Arabia	17.7
7	United Arab Emirates	17.2
8	Egypt	16.8
9	Malaysia	16.4
10	Bahrain	16.3
	Qatar	16.3
12	Kuwait	15.5
13	Sudan	15.2
14	Fiji	13.9
15	Réunion	13.4
16	Barbados	13.3

Cardiovascular disease
No. of deaths per 100,000 pop.,
2016

1	Bulgaria	966.0
2	Ukraine	947.4
3	Latvia	835.8
4	Belarus	792.7
5	Russia	787.7
6	Romania	766.8
7	Lithuania	763.3
8	Georgia	732.2
9	Estonia	657.5
10	Croatia	656.4
11	Serbia	654.7
12	Hungary	643.3
13	Macedonia	625.4
14	Moldova	596.7
15	Montenegro	560.5
16	Greece	539.3

Cancer
Deaths per 100,000 pop., 2016

1	Hungary	338.0
2	Croatia	324.4
3	Italy	305.1
4	Japan	304.1
5	Denmark	294.2
6	Germany	292.6
7	Netherlands	287.0
8	Virgin Islands (US)	285.4
9	Greece	283.7
10	Slovenia	281.0
11	Latvia	274.4
12	Serbia	274.2
13	United Kingdom	273.7
14	France	271.3
15	Belgium	271.1
16	Portugal	270.3
17	Uruguay	267.0
18	Poland	264.1
19	Czech Republic	262.1
20	Lithuania	261.4
21	Estonia	256.6
22	Andorra	254.7
23	Sweden	250.7
24	Bosnia & Herz.	249.5
25	Bulgaria	246.4
26	Romania	242.4

Tuberculosis
Deaths per 100,000 pop., 2016

1	Central African Rep.	258.9
2	Lesotho	154.3
3	Somalia	97.8
4	Burundi	96.2
5	Congo-Kinshasa	88.2
6	Zambia	72.7
7	Eritrea	64.9
8	Swaziland	62.5
9	Guinea-Bissau	62.3
10	Zimbabwe	61.0
11	Uganda	59.5
12	Mozambique	58.7
13	South Sudan	56.3
14	Ethiopia	47.8
15	Congo-Brazzaville	44.6
16	Angola	43.2
17	South Africa	42.3
18	Afghanistan	41.7
19	Guinea	40.8
20	Rwanda	39.3
21	Botswana	36.7
22	Malawi	35.9
23	Namibia	35.8
24	Indonesia	34.9
25	Morocco	34.7
26	Sierra Leone	34.5

a Assumes that every country and region has the same age profile.
Note: Statistics are not available for all countries. The number of cases diagnosed and reported depends on the quality of medical practice and administration and can be under-reported in a number of countries.

Measles immunisation
Lowest % of children aged 12–23 months, 2016

1	South Sudan	20
2	Equatorial Guinea	30
3	Ukraine	42
4	Somalia	46
5	Montenegro	47
6	Angola	49
	Central African Rep.	49
8	Nigeria	51
9	Haiti	53
10	Guinea	54
11	Chad	58
	Madagascar	58
13	Pakistan	61
14	Afghanistan	62
	Syria	62
16	Gabon	64
17	Iraq	66

DPT[a] immunisation
Lowest % of children aged 12–23 months, 2016

1	Equatorial Guinea	19
	Ukraine	19
3	South Sudan	26
4	Somalia	42
	Syria	42
6	Chad	46
7	Central African Rep.	47
8	Nigeria	49
9	Guinea	57
10	Haiti	58
11	Iraq	63
12	Angola	64
13	Afghanistan	65
14	South Africa	66
15	Niger	67
16	Mali	68
17	Yemen	71

HIV/AIDS prevalence
Prevalence in adults aged 15–49, %, 2016

1	Swaziland	27.2
2	Lesotho	25.0
3	Botswana	21.9
4	South Africa	18.9
5	Namibia	13.8
6	Zimbabwe	13.5
7	Zambia	12.4
8	Mozambique	12.3
9	Malawi	9.2
10	Uganda	6.5
11	Equatorial Guinea	6.2
12	Kenya	5.4
13	Tanzania	4.7
14	Central African Rep.	4.0
15	Cameroon	3.8
16	Gabon	3.6
17	Bahamas	3.3
18	Congo-Brazzaville	3.1
	Guinea-Bissau	3.1
	Rwanda	3.1
21	Nigeria	2.9
22	Ivory Coast	2.7
	South Sudan	2.7
24	Haiti	2.1
	Togo	2.1
26	Angola	1.9

AIDS
Deaths per 100,000 population, 2016

1	Lesotho	470
2	Swaziland	314
3	South Africa	311
4	Mozambique	213
5	Botswana	212
6	Namibia	187
7	Zimbabwe	184
8	Malawi	170
9	Equatorial Guinea	164
10	Zambia	151
11	Central African Rep.	149
12	Cameroon	117
13	Congo-Brazzaville	97
	Guinea-Bissau	97
15	Kenya	90
16	Ivory Coast	83
17	Uganda	82
18	Tanzania	78
19	South Sudan	77
20	Nigeria	73
21	Chad	68
22	Gabon	67
23	Togo	64
24	Ghana	50
25	Haiti	48
26	Gambia, The	43
27	Liberia	42

a Diphtheria, pertussis and tetanus.

Health

Highest health spending
As % of GDP, 2015

1	Sierra Leone	18.3
2	United States	16.8
3	Liberia	15.2
4	Switzerland	12.1
5	Andorra	12.0
6	Maldives	11.5
7	Germany	11.2
8	France	11.1
9	Sweden	11.0
10	Cuba	10.9
	Japan	10.9
12	Netherlands	10.7
13	Belgium	10.5
14	Canada	10.4
15	Afghanistan	10.3
	Austria	10.3
	Denmark	10.3
	Zimbabwe	10.3
19	Moldova	10.2
20	Armenia	10.1
21	Norway	10.0
22	United Kingdom	9.9
23	Malta	9.6

Lowest health spending
As % of GDP, 2015

1	Monaco	2.0
2	South Sudan	2.5
3	Bangladesh	2.6
	Brunei	2.6
5	Equatorial Guinea	2.7
	Gabon	2.7
	Pakistan	2.7
8	Laos	2.8
9	Angola	2.9
10	Sri Lanka	3.0
11	Qatar	3.1
	Timor-Leste	3.1
13	Venezuela	3.2
14	Eritrea	3.3
	Indonesia	3.3
16	Iraq	3.4
17	United Arab Emirates	3.5
18	Fiji	3.6
	Nigeria	3.6
20	Oman	3.8
	Papua New Guinea	3.8
	Thailand	3.8

Highest pop. per doctor
2016 or latest[a]

1	Tanzania	45,455
2	Somalia	34,483
3	Chad	22,727
4	Burkina Faso	21,277
5	Mozambique	18,182
6	Rwanda	15,625
7	Senegal	14,706
8	Guinea	13,333
9	Zimbabwe	12,987
10	Timor-Leste	12,821
11	Zambia	10,989
12	Uganda	10,753
13	Gambia, The	9,346
14	Cambodia	6,993
	Madagascar	6,993
16	Benin	6,536
17	Indonesia	4,975
18	Kenya	4,902
19	Afghanistan	3,390
20	Yemen	3,215
21	Botswana	2,604
22	Gabon	2,463
23	Thailand	2,128

Lowest pop. per doctor
2016 or latest[a]

1	Cuba	133
2	Monaco	150
3	Greece	160
4	Austria	191
5	Georgia	209
6	Portugal	226
7	Lithuania	228
	Norway	228
9	Switzerland	235
10	Germany	239
	Sweden	239
12	Belarus	246
13	Italy	249
14	Bulgaria	250
15	Russia	252
16	Argentina	256
	Malta	256
18	Spain	258
19	Iceland	264
20	Andorra	271
21	Czech Republic	272
22	Denmark	274
23	China	276

a 2012–16

Obesity[a]

Adult population 18 years or over, 2015   ● Men   ● Women

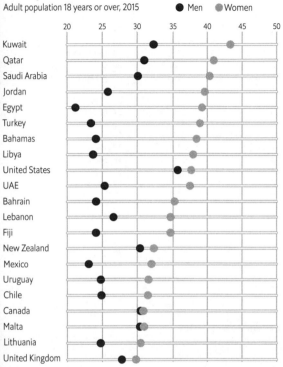

Kuwait	
Qatar	
Saudi Arabia	
Jordan	
Egypt	
Turkey	
Bahamas	
Libya	
United States	
UAE	
Bahrain	
Lebanon	
Fiji	
New Zealand	
Mexico	
Uruguay	
Chile	
Canada	
Malta	
Lithuania	
United Kingdom	

Food deficit

Average kilocalories needed[b] per person per day, 2016 or latest

Highest deficit			Lowest deficit	
1	Haiti	546	**1** Turkey	1
2	Zambia	405	**2** Argentina	2
3	Central African Rep.	380	**3** Tunisia	3
4	North Korea	343	**4** South Korea	4
5	Namibia	325	**5** Cuba	7
6	Chad	261	**6** Saudi Arabia	9
7	Zimbabwe	259	Venezuela	9
8	Liberia	256	**8** Brazil	10
9	Tajikistan	250	**9** Azerbaijan	12
10	Tanzania	238	Brunei	12
11	Ethiopia	236	Egypt	12
12	Rwanda	232	**12** Jordan	13
			South Africa	13
			14 Malaysia	14

a Defined as body mass index of 30 or more – see page 248.
b To lift the undernourished from their status.

Telephones and the internet

Mobile telephones
Subscribers per 100 population, 2016

1	Macau	321.8	26	Suriname	144.5
2	Hong Kong	240.8	27	Mauritius	143.7
3	United Arab Emirates	214.7	28	Qatar	142.1
4	Bahrain	210.1	29	Kazakhstan	142.0
5	Maldives	189.9	30	Georgia	140.9
6	Thailand	173.8	31	Malaysia	140.8
7	Costa Rica	171.5	32	Gambia, The	139.2
8	Montenegro	165.6	33	Poland	138.7
9	Austria	163.8	34	Ghana	135.8
10	Russia	159.2	35	Ukraine	135.2
11	Trinidad & Tobago	158.7	36	Latvia	134.5
12	Oman	155.2	37	Finland	133.9
13	Italy	153.0	38	Switzerland	133.8
14	El Salvador	151.9	39	Cyprus	133.4
15	Turkmenistan	151.4	40	Kuwait	133.1
16	Singapore	150.5	41	Luxembourg	132.7
17	Gabon	149.6	42	Japan	130.6
18	Uruguay	148.6	43	Serbia	130.2
19	Saudi Arabia	148.5	44	Chile	130.1
20	Indonesia	147.7	45	Israel	129.0
21	South Africa	147.1	46	Slovakia	128.4
22	Botswana	146.2	47	Kyrgyzstan	127.8
23	Argentina	145.3	48	Panama	127.5
24	Estonia	144.6		Sweden	127.5
	Lithuania	144.6		Vietnam	127.5

Landline telephones
Per 100 population, 2016

1	Monaco	121.0	23	Ireland	40.1
2	France	60.3	24	Netherlands	39.9
3	Hong Kong	59.1	25	Belgium	38.5
4	Taiwan	58.5	26	Iran	38.2
5	South Korea	55.2	27	New Zealand	37.8
6	Malta	54.6	28	Cyprus	37.7
7	Germany	53.8		United States	37.7
8	United Kingdom	50.9	30	Serbia	37.5
9	Japan	50.2	31	Singapore	35.5
10	Andorra	50.1	32	Slovenia	35.2
11	Iceland	49.5	33	Croatia	34.1
12	Barbados	49.0		Italy	34.1
13	Luxembourg	48.0	35	Australia	33.9
14	Belarus	47.6	36	Uruguay	32.3
15	Switzerland	47.2	37	Hungary	32.0
16	Greece	46.5	38	Sweden	31.6
17	Portugal	46.2	39	Bahamas	31.0
18	Liechtenstein	43.5	40	Mauritius	30.9
19	Spain	42.4	41	Lebanon	30.2
20	Canada	41.8	42	Moldova	28.9
21	Austria	40.9	43	Estonia	28.2
22	Israel	40.8	44	Denmark	27.3

Internet users
Per 100 population, 2016

1	Iceland	98.2	26	Belgium	86.5
2	Liechtenstein	98.1	27	France	85.6
	Luxembourg	98.1	28	Ireland	85.0
4	Bahrain	98.0	29	Austria	84.3
	Bermuda	98.0	30	Macau	81.6
6	Andorra	97.9	31	Singapore	81.0
7	Norway	97.3	32	Spain	80.6
8	Denmark	97.0	33	Slovakia	80.5
9	Monaco	95.2	34	Puerto Rico	80.3
10	United Kingdom	94.8	35	Bahamas	80.0
11	Qatar	94.3	36	Latvia	79.8
12	Japan	93.2	37	Israel	79.7
13	South Korea	92.8		Taiwan	79.7
14	United Arab Emirates	90.6	39	Barbados	79.5
15	Netherlands	90.4	40	Hungary	79.3
16	Brunei	90.0	41	Malaysia	78.8
17	Canada	89.8	42	Kuwait	78.4
18	Sweden	89.7	43	Azerbaijan	78.2
19	Germany	89.6	44	Malta	77.3
20	Switzerland	89.1	45	Guam	77.0
21	New Zealand	88.5	46	Czech Republic	76.5
22	Australia	88.2	47	United States	76.2
23	Finland	87.7	48	Lebanon	76.1
24	Hong Kong	87.5	49	Cyprus	75.9
25	Estonia	87.2	50	Slovenia	75.5

Broadband
Fixed-broadband subscriptions per 100 population, 2016

1	Monaco	48.3	23	Barbados	32.4
2	Switzerland	45.1		Belarus	32.4
3	France	42.7	25	Greece	32.3
4	Denmark	42.5	26	Japan	31.2
5	Liechtenstein	42.3	27	Finland	31.1
	Netherlands	42.3	28	Australia	30.6
7	Andorra	42.0	29	Spain	30.4
8	South Korea	40.5	30	Estonia	30.2
9	Norway	40.4	31	Lithuania	29.5
10	Malta	39.9	32	Macau	29.1
11	Germany	39.1	33	Austria	29.0
12	Iceland	38.5	34	Czech Republic	28.9
13	United Kingdom	38.3		Hungary	28.9
14	Belgium	37.6	36	Ireland	28.8
15	Sweden	37.4	37	Slovenia	28.3
16	Canada	36.9	38	Israel	27.6
17	Hong Kong	36.0	39	Uruguay	26.8
18	Luxembourg	35.3	40	Latvia	26.3
19	United States	33.0	41	Italy	26.2
20	Cyprus	32.8	42	Singapore	26.0
	New Zealand	32.8	43	Croatia	24.8
22	Portugal	32.5	44	Slovakia	24.5

Arts and entertainment

Music sales

Total including downloads, $bn, 2016

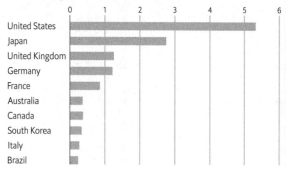

$ per person, 2016

Book publishing
New titles per million population, 2016

1	Japan	10,125	15	Spain	1,109
2	China	7,533	16	Italy[a]	1,078
3	South Korea	7,491	17	Germany	1,044
4	Denmark	4,154	18	United States[a]	1,043
5	Iceland	3,110	19	Norway	1,029
6	United Kingdom[a]	2,710	20	Bosnia & Herz.[a]	731
7	Slovenia	2,640	21	Moldova	704
8	Greece[a]	2,240	22	Turkey	702
9	Serbia	1,686	23	Argentina[a]	687
10	Czech Republic[a]	1,509	24	Australia	572
11	Netherlands[a]	1,482	25	Poland[a]	547
12	Latvia	1,318	26	Georgia[a]	396
13	Finland	1,139	27	Colombia	364
14	France	1,111	28	Sweden	321

a 2015

Cinema attendances
Total visits, m, 2016

India 1,967
China 1,372
United States 1,217
Mexico
South Korea
France
Russia
Brazil
Japan
United Kingdom
Germany
Italy
Indonesia
Spain
Canada
Australia
Malaysia
Colombia
Turkey
Poland
Argentina
South Africa

Visits per person, 2016

Iceland
South Korea
Singapore
Australia
United States
Hong Kong
Ireland
New Zealand
France
Canada
Mexico
United Kingdom
Estonia
Norway
Denmark

Cinema prices
Average cost of a cinema ticket, $, 2015

1	Switzerland	16.2	**17**	Lebanon	8.8
2	Norway	12.7	**18**	New Zealand	8.7
	Sweden	12.7	**19**	Iceland	8.4
4	Macau	12.0		United States	8.4
5	United Arab Emirates	11.6	**21**	Cyprus	8.0
	United Kingdom	11.6	**22**	Belgium	7.8
7	Qatar	11.5	**23**	France	7.2
8	Finland	11.4		Greece	7.2
9	Kuwait	11.2	**25**	Italy	7.1
10	Japan	10.8	**26**	Argentina	6.6
11	Hong Kong	10.7		Malta	6.6
12	Australia	10.2		Spain	6.6
13	Denmark	10.1	**29**	South Korea	6.5
	Israel	10.1	**30**	Bolivia	5.7
15	Austria	9.5		Portugal	5.7
16	Netherlands	9.3		Slovakia	5.7

The press

Press freedom[a]
Scores, 1 = best, 100 = worst, 2016

Most free

1	Norway	7.6
2	Sweden	8.3
3	Finland	8.9
4	Denmark	10.4
5	Netherlands	11.3
6	Costa Rica	11.9
7	Switzerland	12.1
8	Jamaica	12.7
9	Belgium	12.8
10	Iceland	13.0
11	Austria	13.5
12	Estonia	13.6
13	New Zealand	14.0
14	Ireland	14.1
15	Luxembourg	14.7
16	Germany	15.0
17	Slovakia	15.5
18	Portugal	15.8

Least free

1	North Korea	85.0
2	Eritrea	84.2
	Turkmenistan	84.2
4	Syria	81.5
5	China	77.7
6	Vietnam	74.0
7	Sudan	73.6
8	Cuba	71.8
9	Equatorial Guinea	66.5
10	Laos	66.4
11	Uzbekistan	66.1
12	Saudi Arabia	66.0
	Somalia	66.0
14	Yemen	65.8
15	Iran	65.1
16	Bahrain	58.9
17	Libya	56.8
18	Azerbaijan	56.4

Index of abuse against journalists[b]
2016, 100=worst

1	China	89.2
2	Syria	82.8
3	Eritrea	71.7
4	Iran	70.8
5	Mexico	68.2
	Vietnam	68.2
7	Afghanistan	68.1
	Egypt	68.1
9	Turkey	67.1
10	Iraq	65.3
11	Uzbekistan	64.9
12	Yemen	63.4
13	Bahrain	62.7
14	Saudi Arabia	61.6
15	Azerbaijan	61.1
16	Libya	61.0
17	Ethiopia	59.7
18	Brazil	58.9
19	India	57.0
20	Laos	56.7

Number of journalists in prison
As of December 1st 2016

1	Turkey	81
2	China	38
3	Egypt	25
4	Eritrea	17
5	Ethiopia	16
6	Iran	8
	Vietnam	8
8	Bahrain	7
	Israel[c]	7
	Syria	7
11	Saudi Arabia	6
12	Azerbaijan	5
	Uzbekistan	5
14	Gambia, The	3
	Kazakhstan	3
16	Bangladesh	2
	Cuba	2
	Myanmar	2
	Nigeria	2
	Russia	2
	Singapore	2

a Based on 87 questions on topics such as media independence, censorship and transparency.   b Based on the intensity of abuse and violence against the media.
c Includes West Bank & Gaza.

Nobel prize winners: 1901–2017

Peace

1	United States	19
2	United Kingdom	12
3	France	9
4	Sweden	5
5	Belgium	4
	Germany	4

Medicine

1	United States	57
2	United Kingdom	25
3	Germany	15
4	France	8
5	Sweden	7

Literature

1	France	16
2	United States	13
3	United Kingdom	11
4	Germany	8
5	Sweden	7

Economics[a]

1	United States	40
2	United Kingdom	9
3	France	2
	Norway	2
	Sweden	2

Physics

1	United States	55
2	United Kingdom	21
3	Germany	19
4	France	10
5	Japan	7

Chemistry

1	United States	51
2	United Kingdom	25
3	Germany	16
4	France	8
5	Switzerland	7

Nobel prize winners: 1901–2017

By country of birth

1	United States	265		Egypt	6
2	United Kingdom	100		Israel	6
3	Germany	82	26	Finland	5
4	France	54		Ireland	5
5	Sweden	29		Ukraine	5
6	Poland	26	29	Argentina	4
	Russia	26		Belarus	4
8	Japan	25		Romania	4
9	Italy	19	32	Lithuania	3
10	Canada	18		Mexico	3
	Netherlands	18		New Zealand	3
12	Austria	17		Pakistan	3
	Switzerland	17	36	Algeria	2
14	China	12		Bosnia & Herz.	2
	Norway	12		Chile	2
16	Denmark	11		Colombia	2
17	Australia	10		Guatemala	2
18	Belgium	9		Iran	2
	Hungary	9		Liberia	2
	South Africa	9		Luxembourg	2
21	India	8		Portugal	2
22	Spain	7		South Korea	2
23	Czech Republic	6		Turkey	2

Notes: Prizes by country of residence at time awarded. When prizes have been shared in the same field, one credit given to each country.   a Since 1969.

Sports champions and cheats

World Cup winners and finalists

Men's football (since 1930)	Winner	Runner-up
1 Brazil	5	2
2 Germany[a]	4	4
3 Italy	4	2
4 Argentina	2	3
5 Uruguay	2	0
6 France	1	1
7 England	1	0
Spain	1	0
9 Netherlands	0	3
10 Czechoslovakia[b]	0	2
Hungary	0	2
12 Sweden	0	1

Women's football (since 1991)	Winner	Runner-up
1 United States	3	1
2 Germany	2	1
3 Japan	1	1
Norway	1	1
5 Brazil	0	1
China	0	1
Sweden	0	1

Men's cricket (since 1975)	Winner	Runner-up
1 Australia	5	2
2 India	2	1
West Indies	2	1
4 Sri Lanka	1	2
5 Pakistan	1	1
6 England	0	3
7 New Zealand	0	1

Women's cricket (since 1973)	Winner	Runner-up
1 Australia	6	2
2 England	4	3
3 New Zealand	1	3
4 India	0	2
5 West Indies	0	1

Davis Cup, tennis (since 1900)[c]	Winner	Runner-up
1 United States	32	29
2 Australia	28	19
3 Great Britain	10	8
France	10	8
5 Sweden	7	5
6 Spain	5	4
7 Czech Republic[d]	3	2
Germany[a]	3	2
9 Russia	2	3
10 Italy	1	6

Note: Data as of May 2018.   a Including West Germany.   b Until 1993.
c Excludes finalists who have never won.   d Including Czechoslovakia.

Olympic games

Winter games 1924–2018

● Gold ● Silver ● Bronze

Norway
United States
Germany
Soviet Union/
Unified team[a]
Canada
Austria
Sweden
Switzerland
Russia
Netherlands
Finland
Italy
East Germany[b]
France
South Korea
Japan
China
West Germany[b]
United Kingdom
Czech Republic
Belarus
Poland
Australia
Croatia
Estonia
Slovenia

Doping

Anti-doping rule violations, 2016

1 Italy	147	
2 France	86	
3 United States	76	
4 Australia	75	
5 Belgium	73	

6 India	69	
Russia	69	
8 Brazil	55	
Iran	55	
10 South Africa	50	

a Unified team 1952–92.   b 1968–88

Vices

Beer drinkers
Consumption, litres per person, 2016

1	Czech Republic	143.3
2	Namibia	108.0
3	Austria	106.0
4	Germany	104.2
5	Poland	100.8
6	Ireland	98.2
7	Romania	94.1
8	Estonia	89.5
9	Lithuania	88.7
10	Spain	84.8
11	Slovenia	80.3
12	Slovakia	80.1
13	Croatia	78.7
14	Gabon	77.8
15	Finland	76.9
16	Bulgaria	76.3
17	Iceland	75.0
	Panama	75.0

Smokers
Av. ann. consumption of cigarettes per person per day, 2016

1	Belarus	6.5
2	Moldova	6.2
3	Macedonia	6.0
4	Georgia	5.7
5	Czech Republic	5.3
	Russia	5.3
7	Lebanon	5.0
8	Slovenia	4.9
9	China	4.8
10	Bulgaria	4.5
11	Ukraine	4.4
12	Syria	4.2
13	Armenia	4.1
	South Korea	4.1
	Taiwan	4.1

Gambling losses[a]
Total, $bn, 2017

$ per adult

Country	$ per adult
United States	451
China[b]	53
Japan	452
Italy	478
United Kingdom	372
Australia	1,068
Germany	235
Canada	455
France	238
South Korea	132
Spain	275
Singapore	753
Netherlands	221
South Africa	88
Sweden	330
Brazil	14
Ireland	35
Philippines	590
Finland	538
Greece	248

a Data according to H2 Gambling Capital.
b Includes Hong Kong and Macau.

Tourism

Most tourist arrivals
Number of arrivals, '000, 2016

1	France	82,570		21	Netherlands	15,828
2	United States	75,608		22	Macau	15,704
3	Spain	75,315		23	India	14,569
4	China	59,270		24	Croatia	13,809
5	Italy	52,372		25	Ukraine	13,333
6	United Kingdom	35,814		26	Singapore	12,914
7	Germany	35,555		27	Indonesia	11,519
8	Mexico	35,079		28	Portugal	11,223
9	Thailand	32,530		29	Denmark	10,781
10	Turkey	30,289		30	Taiwan	10,690
11	Austria	28,121		31	Morocco	10,332
12	Malaysia	26,757		32	Romania	10,223
13	Hong Kong	26,553		33	Bahrain	10,158
14	Greece	24,799		34	Ireland	10,100
15	Russia	24,571		35	South Africa	10,044
16	Japan	24,040		36	Vietnam	10,013
17	Canada	19,824		37	Belarus	9,424
18	Saudi Arabia	18,049		38	Czech Republic	9,321
19	Poland	17,471		39	Switzerland	9,205
20	South Korea	17,242		40	Australia	8,263

Biggest tourist spenders
$bn, 2016

1	China	261.1		13	Singapore	22.1
2	United States	160.8		14	Belgium	21.6
3	Germany	87.4		15	Netherlands	20.3
4	United Kingdom	79.4		16	Saudi Arabia	19.7
5	France	49.0		17	Spain	19.3
6	Australia	29.8		18	India	19.2
7	Canada	29.1		19	Switzerland	18.8
	South Korea	29.1		20	Brazil	17.1
9	Russia	27.7			United Arab Emirates	17.1
10	Japan	25.8		22	Norway	16.7
11	Italy	25.0		23	Sweden	14.5
12	Hong Kong	24.2				

Largest tourist receipts
$bn, 2016

1	United States	244.7		13	Turkey	26.7
2	Spain	60.6		14	India	23.1
3	United Kingdom	55.6		15	South Korea	21.1
4	Thailand	52.5		16	Mexico	20.6
5	Germany	52.1		17	United Arab Emirates	19.5
6	France	50.9		18	Austria	19.2
7	China	44.4			Switzerland	19.2
8	Italy	40.4		20	Singapore	18.4
9	Hong Kong	38.0		21	Canada	18.3
10	Australia	34.5			Netherlands	18.3
11	Japan	33.4		23	Malaysia	18.1
12	Macau	30.6		24	Portugal	17.2

Country profiles

ALGERIA

Area, sq km	2,381,740	Capital	Algiers
Arable as % of total land	3.1	Currency	Algerian dinar (AD)

People

Population, m	40.6	Life expectancy: men	75.2 yrs
Pop. per sq km	17.0	women	77.7 yrs
Average annual growth		Adult literacy	79.6
in pop. 2015–20, %	1.7	Fertility rate (per woman)	2.7
Pop. aged 0–19, %	36.2	Urban population, %	71.5
Pop. aged 65 and over, %	5.9		per 1,000 pop.
No. of men per 100 women	102.0	Crude birth rate	21.6
Human Development Index	74.5	Crude death rate	4.8

The economy

GDP	$159bn	GDP per head	$3,917
GDP	AD17,407bn	GDP per head in purchasing	
Av. ann. growth in real		power parity (USA=100)	26
GDP 2011–16	3.4%	Economic freedom index	44.7

Origins of GDP		**Components of GDP**	
	% of total		% of total
Agriculture	13	Private consumption	43
Industry, of which:	38	Public consumption	21
manufacturing	6	Investment	51
Services	49	Exports	21
		Imports	-35

Structure of employment

	% of total		% of labour force
Agriculture	12.7	Unemployed 2016	10.0
Industry	47.1	Av. ann. rate 2006–16	11.1
Services	40.2		

Energy

	m TOE		
Total output	168.8	Net energy imports as %	
Total consumption	58.9	of energy use	-177
Consumption per head			
kg oil equivalent	1,321		

Inflation and finance

			% change 2016–17
Consumer price			
inflation 2017	5.6%	Monetary base	14.4
Av. ann. inflation 2012–17	4.6%	Broad money	10.0
Treasury bill rate, Dec. 2017	2.17%		

Exchange rates

	end 2017		December 2017
AD per $	114.9	Effective rates	2005 = 100
AD per sdr	163.1	– nominal	77.9
AD per €	138.5	– real	95.9

Trade

Principal exports		**Principal imports**	
	$bn fob		*$bn cif*
Hydrocarbons	27.9	Capital goods	15.4
Semi-finished goods	1.3	Intermediate goods	11.4
Raw materials	0.1	Consumer goods	8.3
		Food	8.2
Total incl. others	**29.7**	Total	**52.0**

Main export destinations		**Main origins of imports**	
	% of total		*% of total*
Italy	17.6	China	16.2
Spain	13.4	France	9.1
France	11.3	Italy	8.9
United States	11.2	Spain	6.9

Balance of payments, reserves and debt, $bn

Visible exports fob	29.4	Change in reserves	-29.8
Visible imports fob	-49.3	Level of reserves	
Trade balance	-20.0	end Dec.	120.8
Invisibles inflows	5.8	No. months of import cover	22.6
Invisibles outflows	-14.9	Official gold holdings, m oz	5.6
Net transfers	2.8	Foreign debt	5.5
Current account balance	-26.2	– as % of GDP	3.4
– as % of GDP	-16.5	– as % of total exports	14.7
Capital balance	0.3	Debt service ratio	0.9
Overall balance	-26.1		

Health and education

Health spending, % of GDP	7.1	Education spending, % of GDP	...
Doctors per 1,000 pop.	1.2	Enrolment, %: primary	114
Hospital beds per 1,000 pop.	1.9	secondary	...
Improved-water source access,		tertiary	43
% of pop.	83.6		

Society

No. of households, m	7.3	Cost of living, Dec. 2017	
Av. no. per household	5.6	New York = 100	46
Marriages per 1,000 pop.	...	Cars per 1,000 pop.	91
Divorces per 1,000 pop.	...	Colour TV households, % with:	
Religion, % of pop.		cable	...
Muslim	97.9	satellite	93.1
Non-religious	1.8	Telephone lines per 100 pop.	8.4
Christian	0.2	Mobile telephone subscribers	
Hindu	<0.1	per 100 pop.	115.8
Jewish	<0.1	Broadband subs per 100 pop.	7.0
Other	<0.1	Internet users, % of pop.	42.9

ARGENTINA

Area, sq km	2,780,400	Capital	Buenos Aires
Arable as % of total land	14.3	Currency	Peso (P)

People

Population, m	43.8	Life expectancy: men	73.1 yrs
Pop. per sq km	15.8	women	80.5 yrs
Average annual growth		Adult literacy	98.1
in pop. 2015–20, %	0.9	Fertility rate (per woman)	2.3
Pop. aged 0–19, %	33.1	Urban population, %	91.6
Pop. aged 65 and over, %	10.9		per 1,000 pop.
No. of men per 100 women	95.8	Crude birth rate	16.9
Human Development Index	82.7	Crude death rate	7.6

The economy

GDP	$554bn	GDP per head	$12,651
GDP	P8,189bn	GDP per head in purchasing	
Av. ann. growth in real		power parity (USA=100)	34.7
GDP 2011–16	-0.2%	Economic freedom index	52.3

Origins of GDP		**Components of GDP**	
	% of total		% of total
Agriculture	8	Private consumption	66
Industry, of which:	27	Public consumption	18
manufacturing	16	Investment	16
Services	66	Exports	13
		Imports	-13

Structure of employment

	% of total		% of labour force
Agriculture	0.6	Unemployed 2016	8.4
Industry	23.6	Av. ann. rate 2006–16	7.1
Services	75.8		

Energy

	m TOE		
Total output	77.5	Net energy imports as %	
Total consumption	96.9	of energy use	13
Consumption per head			
kg oil equivalent	2,015		

Inflation and finance

			% change 2016–17
Consumer price			
inflation 2017	25.7%	Monetary base	30.0
Av. ann. inflation 2012–17	21.9%	Broad money	16.2
Money market rate, Dec. 2017	29.0%		

Exchange rates

	end 2017		December 2017
P per $	18.6	Effective rates	2005 = 100
P per sdr	25.1	– nominal	...
P per €	22.4	– real	...

Trade

Principal exports		Principal imports	
	$bn fob		*$bn cif*
Processed agricultural products	23.3	Intermediate goods	15.5
Manufactures	16.8	Capital goods	12.1
Primary products	15.7	Consumer goods	7.4
Fuels & energy	2.0	Fuels	4.9
Total	**57.9**	Total incl. others	**55.9**

Main export destinations		Main origins of imports	
	% of total		*% of total*
Brazil	15.9	Brazil	25.3
United States	7.6	China	19.3
China	7.1	United States	12.3
Chile	4.1	Germany	5.3

Balance of payments, reserves and debt, $bn

Visible exports fob	57.9	Change in reserves	12.9
Visible imports fob	-53.5	Level of reserves	
Trade balance	4.4	end Dec.	38.4
Invisibles inflows	15.7	No. months of import cover	5.1
Invisibles outflows	-36.0	Official gold holdings, m oz	1.8
Net transfers	1.2	Foreign debt	190.5
Current account balance	-14.7	– as % of GDP	34.9
– as % of GDP	-2.7	– as % of total exports	256.8
Capital balance	29.2	Debt service ratio	34.6
Overall balance	14.3		

Health and education

Health spending, % of GDP	6.8	Education spending, % of GDP	5.9
Doctors per 1,000 pop.	...	Enrolment, %: primary	110
Hospital beds per 1,000 pop.	5.0	secondary	107
Improved-water source access,		tertiary	86
% of pop.	99.1		

Society

No. of households, m	13.5	Cost of living, Dec. 2017	
Av. no. per household	3.2	New York = 100	69
Marriages per 1,000 pop.	2.8	Cars per 1,000 pop.	238
Divorces per 1,000 pop.	...	Colour TV households, % with:	
Religion, % of pop.		cable	64.8
Christian	85.2	satellite	14.4
Non-religious	12.2	Telephone lines per 100 pop.	22.7
Other	1.1	Mobile telephone subscribers	
Muslim	1.0	per 100 pop.	145.3
Jewish	0.5	Broadband subs per 100 pop.	16.5
Hindu	<0.1	Internet users, % of pop.	71.0

AUSTRALIA

Area, sq km	7,741,220	Capital	Canberra
Arable as % of total land	6.0	Currency	Australian dollar (A$)

People

Population, m	24.1	Life expectancy: men	81.3 yrs
Pop. per sq km	3.1	women	85.0 yrs
Average annual growth		Adult literacy	...
in pop. 2015–20, %	1.3	Fertility rate (per woman)	1.8
Pop. aged 0–19, %	25.1	Urban population, %	85.8
Pop. aged 65 and over, %	15.0		per 1,000 pop.
No. of men per 100 women	99.4	Crude birth rate	12.8
Human Development Index	93.9	Crude death rate	6.7

The economy

GDP	$1,265bn	GDP per head	$52,487
GDP	A$ 1,700bn	GDP per head in purchasing	
Av. ann. growth in real		power parity (USA=100)	85.9
GDP 2011–16	2.8%	Economic freedom index	80.9

Origins of GDP

Components of GDP

	% of total		% of total
Agriculture	3	Private consumption	58
Industry, of which:	24	Public consumption	19
manufacturing	7	Investment	26
Services	73	Exports	19
		Imports	-21

Structure of employment

	% of total		% of labour force
Agriculture	2.6	Unemployed 2016	5.7
Industry	19.4	Av. ann. rate 2006–16	5.3
Services	77.9		

Energy

	m TOE		
Total output	364.5	Net energy imports as %	
Total consumption	141.6	of energy use	-190
Consumption per head			
kg oil equivalent	5,476		

Inflation and finance

			% change 2016–17
Consumer price			
inflation 2017	2.0%	Monetary base	3.0
Av. ann. inflation 2012–17	1.9%	Broad money	4.5
Money Market Rate, Dec. 2017	1.50%		

Exchange rates

	end 2017		December 2017
A$ per $	1.28	Effective rates	2005 = 100
A$ per sdr	1.85	– nominal	92.2
A$ per €	1.54	– real	93.9

Trade

Principal exports		Principal imports	
	$bn fob		*$bn cif*
Crude materials	61.7	Machinery & transport equipment	76.9
Fuels	48.4		
Food	24.2	Mineral fuels	30.0
Machinery & transport equipment	14.0	Manufactured goods	21.0
		Miscellaneous manufactured articles	21.0
Total incl. others	**192.5**	Total incl. others	**189.3**

Main export destinations		Main origins of imports	
	% of total		*% of total*
China	24.9	China	24.9
Japan	8.3	United States	12.2
United States	6.4	Japan	8.3
South Korea	6.1	Thailand	6.0

Balance of payments, reserves and aid, $bn

Visible exports fob	193.0	Overall balance	7.9
Visible imports fob	-198.7	Change in reserves	7.8
Trade balance	-5.7	Level of reserves	
Invisibles inflows	97.1	end Dec.	53.6
Invisibles outflows	-127.8	No. months of import cover	2.0
Net transfers	-0.6	Official gold holdings, m oz	2.3
Current account balance	-37.0	Aid given	3.3
– as % of GDP	-2.9	– as % of GDP	0.3
Capital balance	44.0		

Health and education

Health spending, % of GDP	9.4	Education spending, % of GDP	5.2
Doctors per 1,000 pop.	3.5	Enrolment, %: primary	101
Hospital beds per 1,000 pop.	3.8	secondary	154
Improved-water source access, % of pop.	100	tertiary	122

Society

No. of households, m	8.9	Cost of living, Dec. 2017	
Av. no. per household	2.7	New York = 100	102
Marriages per 1,000 pop.	4.8	Cars per 1,000 pop.	562
Divorces per 1,000 pop.	1.7	Colour TV households, % with:	
Religion, % of pop.		cable	24.9
Christian	67.3	satellite	33.7
Non-religious	24.2	Telephone lines per 100 pop.	33.9
Other	4.2	Mobile telephone subscribers	
Muslim	2.4	per 100 pop.	110.1
Hindu	1.4	Broadband subs per 100 pop.	30.6
Jewish	0.5	Internet users, % of pop.	88.2

AUSTRIA

Area, sq km	83,879	Capital	Vienna
Arable as % of total land	16.3	Currency	Euro (€)

People

Population, m	8.7	Life expectancy: men	79.5 yrs
Pop. per sq km	103.7	women	84.2 yrs
Average annual growth		Adult literacy	...
in pop. 2015–20, %	0.2	Fertility rate (per woman)	1.5
Pop. aged 0–19, %	19.4	Urban population, %	57.9
Pop. aged 65 and over, %	18.8		per 1,000 pop.
No. of men per 100 women	95.9	Crude birth rate	9.7
Human Development Index	89.3	Crude death rate	9.7

The economy

GDP	$391bn	GDP per head	$44,938
GDP	€353bn	GDP per head in purchasing	
Av. ann. growth in real		power parity (USA=100)	83.4
GDP 2011–16	0.8%	Economic freedom index	71.8

Origins of GDP

	% of total
Agriculture	1
Industry, of which:	28
manufacturing	18
Services	71

Components of GDP

	% of total
Private consumption	53
Public consumption	20
Investment	24
Exports	52
Imports	-48

Structure of employment

	% of total		% of labour force
Agriculture	4.3	Unemployed 2016	6.0
Industry	25.6	Av. ann. rate 2006–16	5.1
Services	70.1		

Energy

	m TOE		
Total output	12.8	Net energy imports as %	
Total consumption	35.4	of energy use	64
Consumption per head			
kg oil equivalent	3,804		

Inflation and finance

			% change 2016–17
Consumer price			
inflation 2017	2.2%	Monetary base	24.7
Av. ann. inflation 2012–17	1.5%	Broad money	4.1
Deposit rate, Oct. 2017	0.36%		

Exchange rates

	end 2017		December 2017
€ per $	0.83	Effective rates	2005 = 100
€ per sdr	1.20	– nominal	100.9
		– real	103.4

Trade

Principal exports

	$bn fob
Machinery & transport equip.	62.4
Chemicals & related products	20.0
Food, drink & tobacco	11.4
Raw materials	4.9
Total incl. others	**152.1**

Principal imports

	$bn cif
Machinery & transport equip.	58.4
Chemicals & related products	21.0
Food, drink & tobacco	11.9
Mineral fuels & lubricants	9.9
Total incl. others	**157.7**

Main export destinations

	% of total
Germany	29.9
United States	6.3
Italy	6.2
Switzerland	5.7
EU28	70.6

Main origins of imports

	% of total
Germany	42.5
Italy	6.0
Switzerland	5.6
Czech Republic	4.4
EU28	78.0

Balance of payments, reserves and aid, $bn

Visible exports fob	142.7	Overall balance	0.5
Visible imports fob	-142.3	Change in reserves	1.0
Trade balance	0.4	Level of reserves	
Invisibles inflows	91.1	end Dec.	23.3
Invisibles outflows	-79.1	No. months of import cover	1.3
Net transfers	-4.1	Official gold holdings, m oz	9.0
Current account balance	8.3	Aid given	1.6
– as % of GDP	2.1	– as % of GDP	0.4
Capital balance	-11.2		

Health and education

Health spending, % of GDP	10.3	Education spending, % of GDP	5.4
Doctors per 1,000 pop.	5.2	Enrolment, %: primary	102
Hospital beds per 1,000 pop.	7.5	secondary	101
Improved-water source access,		tertiary	83
% of pop.	100		

Society

No. of households, m	3.9	Cost of living, Dec. 2017	
Av. no. per household	2.2	New York = 100	96
Marriages per 1,000 pop.	5.2	Cars per 1,000 pop.	546
Divorces per 1,000 pop.	1.9	Colour TV households, % with:	
Religion, % of pop.		cable	38.6
Christian	80.4	satellite	54.3
Non-religious	13.5	Telephone lines per 100 pop.	40.9
Muslim	5.4	Mobile telephone subscribers	
Other	0.5	per 100 pop.	163.8
Jewish	0.2	Broadband subs per 100 pop.	29.0
Hindu	<0.1	Internet users, % of pop.	84.3

BANGLADESH

Area, sq km	147,630	Capital	Dhaka
Arable as % of total land	59.6	Currency	Taka (Tk)

People

Population, m	163.0	Life expectancy: men	71.3 yrs
Pop. per sq km	1,104.1	women	74.7 yrs
Average annual growth		Adult literacy	72.8
in pop. 2015–20, %	1.0	Fertility rate (per woman)	2.1
Pop. aged 0–19, %	39.4	Urban population, %	35.1
Pop. aged 65 and over, %	5.0		per 1,000 pop.
No. of men per 100 women	101.9	Crude birth rate	18.5
Human Development Index	57.9	Crude death rate	5.3

The economy

GDP	$236bn	GDP per head	$1,446
GDP	Tk18,543bn	GDP per head in purchasing	
Av. ann. growth in real		power parity (USA=100)	6.7
GDP 2011–16	6.5%	Economic freedom index	55.1

Origins of GDP		Components of GDP	
	% of total		% of total
Agriculture	15	Private consumption	69
Industry, of which:	29	Public consumption	6
manufacturing	18	Investment	30
Services	56	Exports	17
		Imports	-21

Structure of employment

	% of total		% of labour force
Agriculture	41.1	Unemployed 2016	4.2
Industry	20.8	Av. ann. rate 2006–16	3.9
Services	38.0		

Energy

	m TOE		
Total output	25.7	Net energy imports as %	
Total consumption	31.7	of energy use	17
Consumption per head			
kg oil equivalent	222		

Inflation and finance

			% change 2016–17
Consumer price			
inflation 2017	5.7%	Monetary base	13.4
Av. ann. inflation 2012–17	6.4%	Broad money	13.7
Treasury bill rate, Dec. 2017	3.46%		

Exchange rates

	end 2017		December 2017
Tk per $	82.7	Effective rates	2005 = 100
Tk per sdr	116.8	– nominal	...
Tk per €	99.6	– real	...

Trade

Principal exports		Principal imports	
	$bn fob		*$bn cif*
Clothing	21.0	Textiles & yarns	4.2
Jute goods	0.7	Capital machinery	3.6
Fish & fish products	0.4	Iron & steel	3.0
Leather	0.2	Fuels	2.6
Total incl. others	**30.2**	Total incl. others	**41.3**

Main export destinations		Main origins of imports	
	% of total		*% of total*
United States	13.1	China	24.3
Germany	12.7	India	13.4
United Kingdom	8.6	Singapore	5.1
France	5.1	Japan	4.4

Balance of payments, reserves and debt, $bn

Visible exports fob	34.0	Change in reserves	4.8
Visible imports fob	-40.3	Level of reserves	
Trade balance	-6.2	end Dec.	32.3
Invisibles inflows	3.6	No. months of import cover	7.6
Invisibles outflows	-10.6	Official gold holdings, m oz	0.4
Net transfers	14.1	Foreign debt	41.1
Current account balance	0.9	– as % of GDP	18.6
– as % of GDP	0.4	– as % of total exports	80.3
Capital balance	5.4	Debt service ratio	3.5
Overall balance	5.1		

Health and education

Health spending, % of GDP	2.6	Education spending, % of GDP	2.5
Doctors per 1,000 pop.	0.5	Enrolment, %: primary	119
Hospital beds per 1,000 pop.	0.8	secondary	69
Improved-water source access,		tertiary	17
% of pop.	86.9		

Society

No. of households, m	37.1	Cost of living, Dec. 2017	
Av. no. per household	4.4	New York = 100	71
Marriages per 1,000 pop.	...	Cars per 1,000 pop.	2
Divorces per 1,000 pop.	...	Colour TV households, % with:	
Religion, % of pop. of pop.		cable	...
Muslim	89.8	satellite	...
Hindu	9.1	Telephone lines per 100 pop.	0.5
Other	0.9	Mobile telephone subscribers	
Christian	0.2	per 100 pop.	83.4
Jewish	<0.1	Broadband subs per 100 pop.	4.0
Non-religious	<0.1	Internet users, % of pop.	18.2

BELGIUM

Area, sq km	30,530	Capital	Brussels
Arable as % of total land	27.4	Currency	Euro (€)

People

Population, m	11.4	Life expectancy: men	79.0 yrs
Pop. per sq km	373.4	women	83.7 yrs
Average annual growth		Adult literacy	...
in pop. 2015–20, %	0.6	Fertility rate (per woman)	1.8
Pop. aged 0–19, %	22.6	Urban population, %	97.9
Pop. aged 65 and over, %	18.1		per 1,000 pop.
No. of men per 100 women	96.7	Crude birth rate	11.4
Human Development Index	89.6	Crude death rate	9.8

The economy

GDP	$468bn	GDP per head	$41,066
GDP	€423bn	GDP per head in purchasing	
Av. ann. growth in real		power parity (USA=100)	77.5
GDP 2011–16	0.9%	Economic freedom index	67.5

Origins of GDP		**Components of GDP**	
	% of total		% of total
Agriculture	1	Private consumption	51
Industry, of which:	22	Public consumption	24
manufacturing	14	Investment	24
Services	77	Exports	83
		Imports	-82

Structure of employment

	% of total		% of labour force
Agriculture	1.3	Unemployed 2016	7.8
Industry	21.3	Av. ann. rate 2006–16	7.9
Services	77.5		

Energy

	m TOE		
Total output	10.1	Net energy imports as %	
Total consumption	63.7	of energy use	80
Consumption per head			
kg oil equivalent	4,688		

Inflation and finance

			% change 2016–17
Consumer price			
inflation 2017	2.2%	Monetary base	24.7
Av. ann. inflation 2012–17	1.3%	Broad money	4.1
Deposit rate, Sep. 2017	0.12%		

Exchange rates

	end 2017		December 2017
€ per $	0.83	Effective rates	2005 = 100
€ per sdr	1.20	– nominal	100.9
		– real	101.3

Trade

Principal exports		Principal imports	
	$bn fob		*$bn cif*
Chemicals & related products	117.1	Machinery & transport equip.	100.5
Machinery & transport equip.	90.2	Chemicals & related products	95.5
Food, drink & tobacco	38.5	Mineral fuels & lubricants	38.0
Mineral fuels & lubricants	27.6	Food, drink & tobacco	33.0
Total incl. others	**397.9**	Total incl. others	**379.0**

Main export destinations		Main origins of imports	
	% of total		*% of total*
Germany	16.7	Netherlands	15.8
France	15.4	Germany	13.4
Netherlands	11.2	France	9.3
United Kingdom	8.9	United States	8.0
EU28	72.0	EU28	63.8

Balance of payments, reserves and debt, $bn

Visible exports fob	274.6	Overall balance	-1.0
Visible imports fob	-273.4	Change in reserves	-0.6
Trade balance	1.2	Level of reserves	
Invisibles inflows	167.9	end Dec.	23.5
Invisibles outflows	-159.9	No. months of import cover	0.7
Net transfers	-8.7	Official gold holdings, m oz	7.3
Current account balance	0.5	Aid given	2.3
– as % of GDP	0.1	– as % of GDP	0.5
Capital balance	-0.3		

Health and education

Health spending, % of GDP	10.5	Education spending, % of GDP	6.6
Doctors per 1,000 pop.	3.0	Enrolment, %: primary	103
Hospital beds per 1,000 pop.	6.2	secondary	164
Improved-water source access,		tertiary	75
% of pop.	100		

Society

No. of households, m	4.7	Cost of living, Dec. 2017	
Av. no. per household	2.4	New York = 100	84
Marriages per 1,000 pop.	3.5	Cars per 1,000 pop.	490
Divorces per 1,000 pop.	2.2	Colour TV households, % with:	
Religion, % of pop.		cable	74.2
Christian	64.2	satellite	5.9
Non-religious	29.0	Telephone lines per 100 pop.	38.5
Muslim	5.9	Mobile telephone subscribers	
Other	0.6	per 100 pop.	110.5
Jewish	0.3	Broadband subs per 100 pop.	37.6
Hindu	<0.1	Internet users, % of pop.	86.5

BRAZIL

Area, sq km	8,515,770	Capital	Brasília
Arable as % of total land	9.6	Currency	Real (R)

People

Population, m	207.7	Life expectancy: men	72.2 yrs
Pop. per sq km	24.4	women	79.4 yrs
Average annual growth		Adult literacy	92.6
in pop. 2015–20, %	0.8	Fertility rate (per woman)	1.7
Pop. aged 0–19, %	31.0	Urban population, %	86.0
Pop. aged 65 and over, %	8.0		per 1,000 pop.
No. of men per 100 women	96.8	Crude birth rate	13.8
Human Development Index	75.4	Crude death rate	6.3

The economy

GDP	$1,793bn	GDP per head	$8,633
GDP	R6,257bn	GDP per head in purchasing	
Av. ann. growth in real		power parity (USA=100)	26.3
GDP 2011–16	-0.4%	Economic freedom index	51.4

Origins of GDP		**Components of GDP**	
	% of total		% of total
Agriculture	5	Private consumption	64
Industry, of which:	21	Public consumption	20
manufacturing	12	Investment	15
Services	73	Exports	12
		Imports	-12

Structure of employment

	% of total		% of labour force
Agriculture	10.2	Unemployed 2016	11.6
Industry	20.9	Av. ann. rate 2006–16	8.2
Services	68.9		

Energy

	m TOE		
Total output	262.1	Net energy imports as %	
Total consumption	320.0	of energy use	12
Consumption per head			
kg oil equivalent	1,485		

Inflation and finance

			% change 2016–17
Consumer price			
inflation 2017	3.4%	Monetary base	9.6
Av. ann. inflation 2012–17	6.7%	Broad money	4.6
Treasury bill rate, Dec. 2017	6.73%		

Exchange rates

	end 2017		December 2017
R per $	3.31	Effective rates	2005 = 100
R per sdr	4.66	– nominal	66.5
R per €	3.99	– real	82.1

Trade

Principal exports		Principal imports	
	$bn fob		*$bn cif*
Primary products	79.2	Intermediate products & raw	
Manufactured goods	73.9	materials	84.9
Semi-manufactured goods	28.0	Consumer goods	21.7
		Capital goods	18.4
		Fuels & lubricants	12.4
Total incl. others	**185.2**	Total incl. others	**137.6**

Main export destinations		Main origins of imports	
	% of total		*% of total*
China	19.0	United States	18.6
United States	12.6	China	17.9
Argentina	7.2	Germany	7.0
Netherlands	5.6	Argentina	6.9

Balance of payments, reserves and debt, $bn

Visible exports fob	184.5	Change in reserves	8.5
Visible imports fob	-139.4	Level of reserves	
Trade balance	45.0	end Dec.	365.0
Invisibles inflows	44.8	No. months of import cover	17.1
Invisibles outflows	-116.4	Official gold holdings, m oz	2.2
Net transfers	2.9	Foreign debt	543.3
Current account balance	-23.5	– as % of GDP	30.3
– as % of GDP	-1.3	– as % of total exports	234.1
Capital balance	25.9	Debt service ratio	50.6
Overall balance	9.2		

Health and education

Health spending, % of GDP	8.9	Education spending, % of GDP	5.9
Doctors per 1,000 pop.	...	Enrolment, %: primary	115
Hospital beds per 1,000 pop.	2.3	secondary	100
Improved-water source access,		tertiary	51
% of pop.	98.1		

Society

No. of households, m	62.1	Cost of living, Dec. 2017	
Av. no. per household	3.3	New York = 100	67
Marriages per 1,000 pop.	...	Cars per 1,000 pop.	171
Divorces per 1,000 pop.	...	Colour TV households, % with:	
Religion, % of pop.		cable	11.3
Christian	88.9	satellite	16.9
Non-religious	7.9	Telephone lines per 100 pop.	20.2
Other	3.1	Mobile telephone subscribers	
Hindu	<0.1	per 100 pop.	117.5
Jewish	<0.1	Broadband subs per 100 pop.	12.9
Muslim	<0.1	Internet users, % of pop.	60.9

BULGARIA

Area, sq km	111,000	Capital	Sofia
Arable as % of total land	32.3	Currency	Lev (BGL)

People

Population, m	7.1	Life expectancy: men	71.5 yrs
Pop. per sq km	64.0	women	78.4 yrs
Average annual growth		Adult literacy	98.4
in pop. 2015–20, %	-0.7	Fertility rate (per woman)	1.6
Pop. aged 0–19, %	18.3	Urban population, %	74.3
Pop. aged 65 and over, %	20.1		per 1,000 pop.
No. of men per 100 women	94.7	Crude birth rate	9.3
Human Development Index	79.4	Crude death rate	15.3

The economy

GDP	$53bn	GDP per head	$7,498
GDP	BGL94bn	GDP per head in purchasing	
Av. ann. growth in real		power parity (USA=100)	35.4
GDP 2011–16	1.9%	Economic freedom index	68.3

Origins of GDP		**Components of GDP**	
	% of total		% of total
Agriculture	5	Private consumption	61
Industry, of which:	28	Public consumption	16
manufacturing	17	Investment	19
Services	67	Exports	64
		Imports	-60

Structure of employment

	% of total		% of labour force
Agriculture	6.8	Unemployed 2016	7.6
Industry	29.8	Av. ann. rate 2006–16	9.4
Services	63.5		

Energy

	m TOE		
Total output	11.4	Net energy imports as %	
Total consumption	20.9	of energy use	37
Consumption per head			
kg oil equivalent	2,478		

Inflation and finance

Consumer price		av. ann. change 2011–16	
inflation 2017	1.2%	Monetary base	3.0
Av. ann. inflation 2012–17	-0.5%	Broad money	7.7
Deposit rate, Sep. 2017	0.04%		

Exchange rates

	end 2017		December 2017
BGL per $	1.63	Effective rates	2005 = 100
BGL per sdr	2.34	– nominal	112.7
BGL per €	1.96	– real	102.8

Trade

Principal exports		Principal imports	
	$bn fob		*$bn cif*
Raw materials	10.4	Raw materials	10.4
Consumer goods	7.2	Capital goods	7.9
Capital goods	6.4	Consumer goods	6.6
Mineral fuels & lubricants	1.9	Mineral fuels & lubricants	3.0
Total incl. others	**26.7**	Total incl. others	**29.0**

Main export destinations		Main origins of imports	
	% of total		*% of total*
Germany	13.3	Germany	13.1
Italy	9.0	Russia	8.9
Romania	8.6	Italy	7.9
Turkey	7.7	Romania	6.9
EU28	66.3	EU28	66.4

Balance of payments, reserves and debt, $bn

Visible exports fob	25.6	Change in reserves	3.0
Visible imports fob	-26.6	Level of reserves	
Trade balance	-1.1	end Dec.	25.2
Invisibles inflows	9.8	No. months of import cover	8.4
Invisibles outflows	-9.2	Official gold holdings, m oz	1.3
Net transfers	1.8	Foreign debt	39.7
Current account balance	1.2	– as % of GDP	74.5
– as % of GDP	2.3	– as % of total exports	107.6
Capital balance	0.5	Debt service ratio	23.7
Overall balance	3.9		

Health and education

Health spending, % of GDP	8.2	Education spending, % of GDP	4.1
Doctors per 1,000 pop.	4.0	Enrolment, %: primary	95
Hospital beds per 1,000 pop.	...	secondary	100
Improved-water source access,		tertiary	71
% of pop.	99.4		

Society

No. of households, m	2.7	Cost of living, Dec. 2017	
Av. no. per household	2.6	New York = 100	51
Marriages per 1,000 pop.	3.9	Cars per 1,000 pop.	445
Divorces per 1,000 pop.	1.5	Colour TV households, % with:	
Religion, % of pop.		cable	48.2
Christian	82.1	satellite	28.8
Muslim	13.7	Telephone lines per 100 pop.	20.7
Non-religious	4.2	Mobile telephone subscribers	
Hindu	<0.1	per 100 pop.	125.8
Jewish	<0.1	Broadband subs per 100 pop.	23.8
Other	<0.1	Internet users, % of pop.	59.8

CAMEROON

Area, sq km	475,440	Capital	Yaoundé
Arable as % of total land	13.1	Currency	CFA franc (CFAfr)

People

Population, m	23.4	Life expectancy: men	57.8 yrs
Pop. per sq km	49.2	women	59.9 yrs
Average annual growth		Adult literacy	74.9
in pop. 2015–20, %	2.6	Fertility rate (per woman)	4.6
Pop. aged 0–19, %	53.5	Urban population, %	55.2
Pop. aged 65 and over, %	3.2		per 1,000 pop.
No. of men per 100 women	100.1	Crude birth rate	35.5
Human Development Index	51.8	Crude death rate	9.7

The economy

GDP	$32bn	GDP per head	$1,377
GDP	CFAfr19,105bn	GDP per head in purchasing	
Av. ann. growth in real		power parity (USA=100)	6.3
GDP 2011–16	5.2%	Economic freedom index	51.9

Origins of GDP		**Components of GDP**	
	% of total		% of total
Agriculture	17	Private consumption	70
Industry, of which:	27	Public consumption	12
manufacturing	13	Investment	22
Services	57	Exports	19
		Imports	-23

Structure of employment

	% of total		% of labour force
Agriculture	62.0	Unemployed 2016	4.3
Industry	9.3	Av. ann. rate 2006–16	3.8
Services	28.7		

Energy

	m TOE		
Total output	7.2	Net energy imports as %	
Total consumption	4.1	of energy use	-28
Consumption per head			
kg oil equivalent	342		

Inflation and finance

		av. ann. change 2011–16	
Consumer price			
inflation 2017	0.6%	Monetary base	14.1
Av. ann. inflation 2012–17	1.6%	Broad money	5.4
Deposit rate, Mar. 2017	2.45%		

Exchange rates

	end 2017		December 2017
CFAfr per $	546.95	Effective rates	2005 = 100
CFAfr per sdr	784.29	– nominal	108.2
CFAfr per €	658.98	– real	100.8

Trade

Principal exports	$bn fob	Principal imports	$bn cif
Fuels	1.3	Manufactured products	3.1
Cocoa beans & products	0.7	Food	1.1
Timber	0.5	Fuels	0.5
Cotton	0.1		
Total incl. others	**3.3**	Total incl. others	**4.8**

Main export destinations	% of total	Main origins of imports	% of total
Netherlands	21.1	China	21.3
Belgium	9.2	France	12.0
France	7.6	Nigeria	4.5
China	7.0	Thailand	4.5

Balance of payments, reserves and debt, $bn

Visible exports fob	4.6	Change in reserves	-1.3
Visible imports fob	-4.8	Level of reserves	
Trade balance	-0.2	end Dec.	2.2
Invisibles inflows	1.9	No. months of import cover	3.4
Invisibles outflows	-3.0	Official gold holdings, m oz	0.0
Net transfers	0.3	Foreign debt	7.3
Current account balance	-1.0	– as % of GDP	22.6
– as % of GDP	-3.2	– as % of total exports	108.9
Capital balance	-0.2	Debt service ratio	12.2
Overall balance	-1.2		

Health and education

Health spending, % of GDP	5.1	Education spending, % of GDP	2.8
Doctors per 1,000 pop.	...	Enrolment, %: primary	119
Hospital beds per 1,000 pop.	...	secondary	62
Improved-water source access,		tertiary	17
% of pop.	75.6		

Society

No. of households, m	4.4	Cost of living, Dec. 2017	
Av. no. per household	5.3	New York = 100	...
Marriages per 1,000 pop.	...	Cars per 1,000 pop.	11
Divorces per 1,000 pop.	...	Colour TV households, % with:	
Religion, % of pop.		cable	...
Christian	70.3	satellite	2.4
Muslim	18.3	Telephone lines per 100 pop.	4.5
Other	6.0	Mobile telephone subscribers	
Non-religious	5.3	per 100 pop.	79.9
Hindu	<0.1	Broadband subs per 100 pop.	0.2
Jewish	<0.1	Internet users, % of pop.	25.0

CANADA

Area, sq km[a]	9,984,670	Capital	Ottawa
Arable as % of total land	4.8	Currency	Canadian dollar (C$)

People

Population, m	36.3	Life expectancy: men	80.7 yrs
Pop. per sq km	3.6	women	84.4 yrs
Average annual growth		Adult literacy	...
in pop. 2015–20, %	0.9	Fertility rate (per woman)	1.6
Pop. aged 0–19, %	21.9	Urban population, %	81.3
Pop. aged 65 and over, %	16.1		per 1,000 pop.
No. of men per 100 women	98.4	Crude birth rate	10.5
Human Development Index	92.0	Crude death rate	7.5

The economy

GDP	$1,536bn	GDP per head	$42,308
GDP	C$2,036bn	GDP per head in purchasing	
Av. ann. growth in real		power parity (USA=100)	80.4
GDP 2011–16	1.8%	Economic freedom index	77.7

Origins of GDP		Components of GDP	
	% of total		% of total
Agriculture	2	Private consumption	58
Industry, of which:	28	Public consumption	21
manufacturing	...	Investment	23
Services	70	Exports	31
		Imports	-33

Structure of employment

	% of total		% of labour force
Agriculture	1.9	Unemployed 2016	7.0
Industry	19.5	Av. ann. rate 2006–16	7.0
Services	78.5		

Energy

	m TOE		
Total output	518.2	Net energy imports as %	
Total consumption	362.2	of energy use	-73
Consumption per head			
kg oil equivalent	7,604		

Inflation and finance

			% change 2016–17
Consumer price			
inflation 2017	1.6%	Monetary base	6.6
Av. ann. inflation 2012–17	1.4%	Broad money	...
Treasury bill rate, Mar. 2017	0.48%		

Exchange rates

	end 2017		December 2017
C$ per $	1.26	Effective rates	2005 = 100
C$ per sdr	1.81	– nominal	84.6
C$ per €	1.52	– real	83.8

Trade

Principal exports		Principal imports	
	$bn fob		*$bn cif*
Motor vehicles & parts	72.2	Consumer goods	89.7
Consumer goods	55.8	Motor vehicles & parts	80.5
Energy products	54.0	Electronic & electrical equip.	47.8
Metal & mineral products	43.4	Industrial machinery & equip.	40.1
Total incl. others	**393.4**	Total incl. others	**412.9**

Main export destinations		Main origins of imports	
	% of total		*% of total*
United States	76.4	United States	52.2
China	4.1	China	12.1
United Kingdom	3.3	Mexico	6.2
Japan	2.1	Germany	3.2
EU28	7.7	EU28	11.4

Balance of payments, reserves and aid, $bn

Visible exports fob	393.6	Overall balance	5.6
Visible imports fob	-413.4	Change in reserves	3.0
Trade balance	-19.8	Level of reserves	
Invisibles inflows	156.3	end Dec.	82.7
Invisibles outflows	-183.3	No. months of import cover	1.7
Net transfers	-2.6	Official gold holdings, m oz	0.0
Current account balance	-49.4	Aid given	3.9
– as % of GDP	-3.2	– as % of GDP	0.3
Capital balance	57.0		

Health and education

Health spending, % of GDP	10.4	Education spending, % of GDP	...
Doctors per 1,000 pop.	2.5	Enrolment, %: primary	101
Hospital beds per 1,000 pop.	2.6	secondary	113
Improved-water source access,		tertiary	...
% of pop.	99.8		

Society

No. of households, m	14.1	Cost of living, Dec. 2017	
Av. no. per household	2.6	New York = 100	83
Marriages per 1,000 pop.	...	Cars per 1,000 pop.	608
Divorces per 1,000 pop.	...	Colour TV households, % with:	
Religion, % of pop.		cable	66.4
Christian	69.0	satellite	22.2
Non-religious	23.7	Telephone lines per 100 pop.	41.8
Other	2.8	Mobile telephone subscribers	
Muslim	2.1	per 100 pop.	84.7
Hindu	1.4	Broadband subs per 100 pop.	36.9
Jewish	1.0	Internet users, % of pop.	89.8

a Including freshwater.

CHILE

Area, sq km	756,096	Capital	Santiago
Arable as % of total land	1.8	Currency	Chilean peso (Ps)

People

Population, m	17.9	Life expectancy: men	77.3 yrs
Pop. per sq km	23.7	women	82.2 yrs
Average annual growth		Adult literacy	96.3
in pop. 2015–20, %	0.8	Fertility rate (per woman)	1.8
Pop. aged 0–19, %	28.3	Urban population, %	87.4
Pop. aged 65 and over, %	10.4		per 1,000 pop.
No. of men per 100 women	98.1	Crude birth rate	13.1
Human Development Index	84.7	Crude death rate	6.2

The economy

GDP	$250bn	GDP per head	$13,967
GDP	169trn peso	GDP per head in purchasing	
Av. ann. growth in real		power parity (USA=100)	42.2
GDP 2011–16	3.0%	Economic freedom index	75.2

Origins of GDP

Components of GDP

	% of total		% of total
Agriculture	4	Private consumption	64
Industry, of which:	31	Public consumption	14
manufacturing	12	Investment	22
Services	64	Exports	28
		Imports	-28

Structure of employment

	% of total		% of labour force
Agriculture	9.5	Unemployed 2016	6.7
Industry	23.0	Av. ann. rate 2006–16	6.9
Services	67.5		

Energy

	m TOE		
Total output	10.0	Net energy imports as %	
Total consumption	33.7	of energy use	65
Consumption per head			
kg oil equivalent	2,029		

Inflation and finance

			% change 2016–17
Consumer price			
inflation 2017	2.2%	Monetary base	7.4
Av. ann. inflation 2012–17	3.3%	Broad money	0.6
Deposit rate, Nov. 2017	2.67%		

Exchange rates

	end 2017		December 2017
Ps per $	615.22	Effective rates	2005 = 100
Ps per sdr	901.34	– nominal	98.1
Ps per €	741.23	– real	100.4

Trade

Principal exports		Principal imports	
	$bn fob		*$bn cif*
Copper	26.3	Intermediate goods	28.7
Fresh fruit	5.2	Consumer goods	17.8
Cellulose & paper products	2.9	Capital goods	12.2
Total incl. others	**60.8**	Total incl. others	**59.5**

Main export destinations		Main origins of imports	
	% of total		*% of total*
China	28.6	China	23.8
United States	13.9	United States	17.2
Japan	8.5	Brazil	7.9
South Korea	6.9	Argentina	4.1

Balance of payments, reserves and debt, $bn

Visible exports fob	60.7	Change in reserves	1.9
Visible imports fob	-55.3	Level of reserves	
Trade balance	5.4	end Dec.	40.5
Invisibles inflows	17.3	No. months of import cover	5.9
Invisibles outflows	-27.6	Official gold holdings, m oz	0.0
Net transfers	1.4	Foreign debt	163.8
Current account balance	-3.5	– as % of GDP	66.3
– as % of GDP	-1.4	– as % of total exports	218.0
Capital balance	4.4	Debt service ratio	36.8
Overall balance	1.7		

Health and education

Health spending, % of GDP	8.1	Education spending, % of GDP	4.9
Doctors per 1,000 pop.	...	Enrolment, %: primary	100
Hospital beds per 1,000 pop.	2.1	secondary	100
Improved-water source access,		tertiary	90
% of pop.	99.0		

Society

No. of households, m	6.2	Cost of living, Dec. 2017	
Av. no. per household	2.9	New York = 100	72
Marriages per 1,000 pop.	3.6	Cars per 1,000 pop.	175
Divorces per 1,000 pop.	...	Colour TV households, % with:	
Religion, % of pop.		cable	34.2
Christian	89.4	satellite	5.2
Non-religious	8.6	Telephone lines per 100 pop.	18.8
Other	1.9	Mobile telephone subscribers	
Jewish	0.1	per 100 pop.	130.1
Hindu	<0.1	Broadband subs per 100 pop.	16.2
Muslim	<0.1	Internet users, % of pop.	66.0

CHINA

Area, sq km	9,562,911	Capital	Beijing
Arable as % of total land	12.7	Currency	Yuan

People

Population, m	1,403.5	Life expectancy: men	75.0 yrs
Pop. per sq km	146.8	women	78.1 yrs
Average annual growth		Adult literacy	96.4
in pop. 2015–20, %	0.4	Fertility rate (per woman)	1.6
Pop. aged 0–19, %	23.5	Urban population, %	56.7
Pop. aged 65 and over, %	9.7		per 1,000 pop.
No. of men per 100 women	106.3	Crude birth rate	11.6
Human Development Index	73.8	Crude death rate	7.5

The economy

GDP	$11,222bn	GDP per head	$7,996
GDP	Yuan 74,563bn	GDP per head in purchasing	
Av. ann. growth in real		power parity (USA=100)	26.2
GDP 2011–16	7.3%	Economic freedom index	57.8

Origins of GDP		**Components of GDP**	
	% of total		% of total
Agriculture	9	Private consumption	39
Industry, of which:	40	Public consumption	14
manufacturing	29	Investment	44
Services	52	Exports	20
		Imports	-17

Structure of employment

	% of total		% of labour force
Agriculture	18.4	Unemployed 2016	4.7
Industry	26.8	Av. ann. rate 2006–16	4.3
Services	54.9		

Energy

	m TOE		
Total output	2,600.9	Net energy imports as %	
Total consumption	3,016.5	of energy use	15
Consumption per head			
kg oil equivalent	2,237		

Inflation and finance

			% change 2016–17
Consumer price			
inflation 2017	1.6%	Monetary base	9.1
Av. ann. inflation 2012–17	1.9%	Broad money	5.2
Deposit rate, Dec. 2017	1.50%		

Exchange rates

	end 2017		December 2017
			2005 = 100
Yuan per $	6.51	Effective rates	
Yuan per sdr	9.33	– nominal	114.8
Yuan per €	7.84	– real	121.6

Trade

Principal exports		Principal imports	
	$bn fob		*$bn cif*
Telecoms equipment	280.7	Electrical machinery	342.1
Electrical goods	268.9	Petroleum products	137.3
Office machinery	172.2	Metal ores & scrap	103.9
Clothing & apparel	161.4	Professional instruments	74.2
Total incl. others	**2,097.6**	Total incl. others	**1,588.0**

Main export destinations		Main origins of imports	
	% of total		*% of total*
United States	18.6	South Korea	10.0
Hong Kong	14.0	Japan	9.2
Japan	6.2	Taiwan	8.8
South Korea	4.6	United States	8.5
EU28	16.1	EU28	13.1

Balance of payments, reserves and debt, $bn

Visible exports fob	1,989.5	Change in reserves	-307.6
Visible imports fob	-1,500.6	Level of reserves	
Trade balance	488.9	end Dec.	3,097.7
Invisibles inflows	434.2	No. months of import cover	16.8
Invisibles outflows	-711.4	Official gold holdings, m oz	59.2
Net transfers	-9.5	Foreign debt	1,429.5
Current account balance	202.2	– as % of GDP	12.7
– as % of GDP	1.8	– as % of total exports	58.1
Capital balance	-416.4	Debt service ratio	5.2
Overall balance	-443.6		

Health and education

Health spending, % of GDP	5.3	Education spending, % of GDP	...
Doctors per 1,000 pop.	3.6	Enrolment, %: primary	101
Hospital beds per 1,000 pop.	3.9	secondary	95
Improved-water source access,		tertiary	48
% of pop.	95.5		

Society

No. of households, m	452.8	Cost of living, Dec. 2017	
Av. no. per household	3.1	New York = 100	80
Marriages per 1,000 pop.	9.6	Cars per 1,000 pop.	97
Divorces per 1,000 pop.	1.8	Colour TV households, % with:	
Religion, % of pop.		cable	50.0
Non-religious	52.2	satellite	...
Other	22.7	Telephone lines per 100 pop.	14.7
Buddhist	18.2	Mobile telephone subscribers	
Christian	5.1	per 100 pop.	97.3
Muslim	1.8	Broadband subs per 100 pop.	23.0
Jewish	<0.1	Internet users, % of pop.	53.2

Note: Data exclude Special Administrative Regions, ie, Hong Kong and Macau.

COLOMBIA

| Area, sq km | 1,141,749 | Capital | Bogotá |
| Arable as % of total land | 1.5 | Currency | Colombian peso (peso) |

People

Population, m	48.7	Life expectancy: men	71.1 yrs
Pop. per sq km	42.7	women	78.3 yrs
Average annual growth		Adult literacy	94.2
in pop. 2015–20, %	0.8	Fertility rate (per woman)	1.8
Pop. aged 0–19, %	32.7	Urban population, %	80.1
Pop. aged 65 and over, %	7.0		per 1,000 pop.
No. of men per 100 women	97.0	Crude birth rate	14.8
Human Development Index	72.7	Crude death rate	6.1

The economy

GDP	$280bn	GDP per head	$5,749
GDP	855trn peso	GDP per head in purchasing	
Av. ann. growth in real		power parity (USA=100)	24.5
GDP 2011–16	3.7%	Economic freedom index	68.9

Origins of GDP		**Components of GDP**	
	% of total		% of total
Agriculture	7	Private consumption	63
Industry, of which:	33	Public consumption	18
manufacturing	13	Investment	25
Services	60	Exports	14
		Imports	-21

Structure of employment

	% of total		% of labour force
Agriculture	16.1	Unemployed 2016	8.7
Industry	19.3	Av. ann. rate 2006–16	10.0
Services	64.6		

Energy

	m TOE		
Total output	124.5	Net energy imports as %	
Total consumption	40.0	of energy use	-274
Consumption per head			
kg oil equivalent	712		

Inflation and finance

			% change 2016–17
Consumer price			
inflation 2017	4.3%	Monetary base	5.0
Av. ann. inflation 2012–17	4.3%	Broad money	5.4
Deposit rate, Dec. 2017	5.28%		

Exchange rates

	end 2017		December 2017
			2005 = 100
Peso per $	2,971.63	Effective rates	2005 = 100
Peso per sdr	4,233.88	– nominal	81.2
Peso per €	3,580.28	– real	61.3

Trade

Principal exports		Principal imports	
	$bn fob		*$bn cif*
Petroleum & products	10.8	Intermediate goods & raw	
Coal	4.6	materials	20.3
Coffee	2.4	Capital goods	13.5
Nickel	0.3	Consumer goods	11.0
Total incl. others	**31.8**	Total	**44.9**

Main export destinations		Main origins of imports	
	% of total		*% of total*
United States	32.6	United States	26.6
Panama	6.3	China	19.2
Ecuador	3.8	Mexico	7.6
China	3.7	Brazil	4.7

Balance of payments, reserves and debt, $bn

Visible exports fob	34.1	Change in reserves	0.0
Visible imports fob	-43.2	Level of reserves	
Trade balance	-9.2	end Dec.	46.2
Invisibles inflows	12.7	No. months of import cover	8.6
Invisibles outflows	-21.5	Official gold holdings, m oz	0.2
Net transfers	5.9	Foreign debt	120.3
Current account balance	-12.1	– as % of GDP	43.0
– as % of GDP	-4.3	– as % of total exports	235.0
Capital balance	12.8	Debt service ratio	26.2
Overall balance	0.2		

Health and education

Health spending, % of GDP	6.2	Education spending, % of GDP	4.5
Doctors per 1,000 pop.	1.8	Enrolment, %: primary	114
Hospital beds per 1,000 pop.	1.5	secondary	98
Improved-water source access,		tertiary	59
% of pop.	91.4		

Society

No. of households, m	13.3	Cost of living, Dec. 2017	
Av. no. per household	3.7	New York = 100	63
Marriages per 1,000 pop.	...	Cars per 1,000 pop.	64
Divorces per 1,000 pop.	...	Colour TV households, % with:	
Religion, % of pop.		cable	57.0
Christian	92.5	satellite	7.4
Non-religious	6.6	Telephone lines per 100 pop.	14.6
Other	0.8	Mobile telephone subscribers	
Hindu	<0.1	per 100 pop.	120.6
Jewish	<0.1	Broadband subs per 100 pop.	12.2
Muslim	<0.1	Internet users, % of pop.	58.1

CZECH REPUBLIC

Area, sq km	78,870	Capital	Prague
Arable as % of total land	40.6	Currency	Koruna (Kc)

People

Population, m	10.6	Life expectancy: men	76.0 yrs
Pop. per sq km	134.4	women	81.8 yrs
Average annual growth		Adult literacy	...
in pop. 2015–20, %	0.1	Fertility rate (per woman)	1.6
Pop. aged 0–19, %	19.4	Urban population, %	73.6
Pop. aged 65 and over, %	18.0		per 1,000 pop.
No. of men per 100 women	96.6	Crude birth rate	10.1
Human Development Index	87.8	Crude death rate	10.7

The economy

GDP	$195bn	GDP per head	$18,425
GDP	Kc4,773bn	GDP per head in purchasing	
Av. ann. growth in real		power parity (USA=100)	57.8
GDP 2011–16	1.8%	Economic freedom index	74.2

Origins of GDP

	% of total
Agriculture	2
Industry, of which:	38
manufacturing	27
Services	60

Components of GDP

	% of total
Private consumption	47
Public consumption	19
Investment	26
Exports	80
Imports	-72

Structure of employment

	% of total		% of labour force
Agriculture	2.9	Unemployed 2016	4.0
Industry	38.1	Av. ann. rate 2006–16	6.1
Services	59.0		

Energy

	m TOE		
Total output	28.1	Net energy imports as %	
Total consumption	40.3	of energy use	32
Consumption per head			
kg oil equivalent	3,860		

Inflation and finance

			% change 2016–17
Consumer price			
inflation 2017	2.4%	Monetary base	56.3
Av. ann. inflation 2012–17	1.0%	Broad money	10.4
Deposit rate, Jun. 2017	0.28%		

Exchange rates

	end 2017		December 2017
Kc per $	21.29	Effective rates	2005 = 100
Kc per sdr	30.66	– nominal	100.0
Kc per €	25.65	– real	99.1

Trade

Principal exports		Principal imports	
	$bn fob		*$bn cif*
Machinery & transport equip.	91.6	Machinery & transport equip.	65.5
Semi-manufactures	25.1	Semi-manufactures	24.2
Miscellaneous manufactured		Miscellaneous manufactured	
goods	21.6	goods	17.7
Chemicals	9.8	Chemicals	16.4
Total incl. others	**162.7**	Total incl. others	**143.0**

Main export destinations		Main origins of imports	
	% of total		*% of total*
Germany	32.4	Germany	30.6
Slovakia	8.3	Poland	9.7
Poland	5.8	China	7.4
United Kingdom	5.2	Slovakia	6.3
EU28	83.7	EU28	79.2

Balance of payments, reserves and debt, $bn

Visible exports fob	130.6	Change in reserves	21.2
Visible imports fob	-120.5	Level of reserves	
Trade balance	10.1	end Dec.	85.7
Invisibles inflows	32.6	No. months of import cover	6.5
Invisibles outflows	-38.5	Official gold holdings, m oz	0.3
Net transfers	-1.1	Foreign debt	138.0
Current account balance	3.0	– as % of GDP	70.7
– as % of GDP	1.5	– as % of total exports	83.1
Capital balance	20.5	Debt service ratio	10.0
Overall balance	23.0		

Health and education

Health spending, % of GDP	7.3	Education spending, % of GDP	4.0
Doctors per 1,000 pop.	3.6	Enrolment, %: primary	...
Hospital beds per 1,000 pop.	6.5	secondary	...
Improved-water source access,		tertiary	64
% of pop.	100		

Society

No. of households, m	4.7	Cost of living, Dec. 2017	
Av. no. per household	2.3	New York = 100	67
Marriages per 1,000 pop.	4.6	Cars per 1,000 pop.	487
Divorces per 1,000 pop.	2.5	Colour TV households, % with:	
Religion, % of pop.		cable	24.5
Non-religious	76.4	satellite	27.0
Christian	23.3	Telephone lines per 100 pop.	16.6
Other	0.2	Mobile telephone subscribers	
Hindu	<0.1	per 100 pop.	117.7
Jewish	<0.1	Broadband subs per 100 pop.	28.9
Muslim	<0.1	Internet users, % of pop.	76.5

DENMARK

Area, sq km	42,922	Capital	Copenhagen
Arable as % of total land	56.0	Currency	Danish krone (DKr)

People

Population, m	5.7	Life expectancy: men	79.0 yrs
Pop. per sq km	132.8	women	82.8 yrs
Average annual growth		Adult literacy	...
in pop. 2015–20, %	0.4	Fertility rate (per woman)	1.8
Pop. aged 0–19, %	23.2	Urban population, %	87.6
Pop. aged 65 and over, %	19.0		per 1,000 pop.
No. of men per 100 women	98.9	Crude birth rate	10.7
Human Development Index	92.5	Crude death rate	9.6

The economy

GDP	$307bn	GDP per head	$53,842
GDP	DKr2,066bn	GDP per head in purchasing	
Av. ann. growth in real		power parity (USA=100)	83.7
GDP 2011–16	1.3%	Economic freedom index	76.6

Origins of GDP

Components of GDP

	% of total		% of total
Agriculture	1	Private consumption	47
Industry, of which:	23	Public consumption	25
manufacturing	15	Investment	21
Services	76	Exports	54
		Imports	-47

Structure of employment

	% of total		% of labour force
Agriculture	2.5	Unemployed 2016	6.2
Industry	18.6	Av. ann. rate 2006–16	6.0
Services	78.8		

Energy

	m TOE		
Total output	17.4	Net energy imports as %	
Total consumption	18.0	of energy use	2
Consumption per head			
kg oil equivalent	2,817		

Inflation and finance

			% change 2016–17
Consumer price			
inflation 2017	1.1%	Monetary base	0.1
Av. ann. inflation 2012–17	0.6%	Broad money	5.1
Money market rate, Dec. 2016	1.50%		

Exchange rates

	end 2017		December 2017
DKr per $	6.21	Effective rates	2005 = 100
DKr per sdr	8.90	– nominal	101.5
DKr per €	7.48	– real	98.2

Trade

Principal exports		Principal imports	
	$bn fob		*$bn cif*
Machinery & transport equip.	25.1	Machinery & transport equip.	28.6
Chemicals & related products	19.8	Food, drink & tobacco	11.9
Food, drink & tobacco	17.9	Chemicals & related products	10.7
Mineral fuels & lubricants	4.4	Mineral fuels & lubricants	4.5
Total incl. others	**95.2**	Total incl. others	**85.3**

Main export destinations		Main origins of imports	
	% of total		*% of total*
Germany	16.3	Germany	21.6
Sweden	11.8	Sweden	12.1
United States	8.2	Netherlands	8.1
United Kingdom	6.5	China	7.3
EU28	61.7	EU28	71.3

Balance of payments, reserves and aid, $bn

Visible exports fob	104.1	Overall balance	2.3
Visible imports fob	-86.8	Change in reserves	-1.0
Trade balance	17.3	Level of reserves	
Invisibles inflows	87.0	end Dec.	64.2
Invisibles outflows	-77.5	No. months of import cover	4.7
Net transfers	-4.3	Official gold holdings, m oz	2.1
Current account balance	22.5	Aid given	2.4
– as % of GDP	7.3	– as % of GDP	0.8
Capital balance	-12.4		

Health and education

Health spending, % of GDP	10.3	Education spending, % of GDP	7.6
Doctors per 1,000 pop.	3.7	Enrolment, %: primary	102
Hospital beds per 1,000 pop.	2.5	secondary	129
Improved-water source access,		tertiary	81
% of pop.	100		

Society

No. of households, m	2.4	Cost of living, Dec. 2017	
Av. no. per household	2.4	New York = 100	105
Marriages per 1,000 pop.	5.4	Cars per 1,000 pop.	420
Divorces per 1,000 pop.	3.0	Colour TV households, % with:	
Religion, % of pop.		cable	65.3
Christian	83.5	satellite	11.8
Non-religious	11.8	Telephone lines per 100 pop.	27.3
Muslim	4.1	Mobile telephone subscribers	
Hindu	0.4	per 100 pop.	122.3
Other	0.2	Broadband subs per 100 pop.	42.5
Jewish	<0.1	Internet users, % of pop.	97.0

EGYPT

Area, sq km	1,001,450	Capital	Cairo
Arable as % of total land	2.9	Currency	Egyptian pound (£E)

People

Population, m	95.7	Life expectancy: men	69.5 yrs
Pop. per sq km	95.6	women	74.1 yrs
Average annual growth		Adult literacy	75.8
in pop. 2015–20, %	1.9	Fertility rate (per woman)	3.2
Pop. aged 0–19, %	41.8	Urban population, %	42.7
Pop. aged 65 and over, %	5.1		per 1,000 pop.
No. of men per 100 women	102.2	Crude birth rate	25.0
Human Development Index	69.1	Crude death rate	5.8

The economy

GDP	$332bn	GDP per head	$3,474
GDP	£E2,709bn	GDP per head in purchasing	
Av. ann. growth in real		power parity (USA=100)	20.5
GDP 2011–16	3.2%	Economic freedom index	53.4

Origins of GDP

	% of total
Agriculture	12
Industry, of which:	33
manufacturing	17
Services	55

Components of GDP

	% of total
Private consumption	83
Public consumption	11
Investment	15
Exports	10
Imports	-20

Structure of employment

	% of total		% of labour force
Agriculture	25.6	Unemployed 2016	12.4
Industry	25.5	Av. ann. rate 2006–16	11.1
Services	48.9		

Energy

	m TOE		
Total output	83.4	Net energy imports as %	
Total consumption	89.2	of energy use	-7
Consumption per head			
kg oil equivalent	815		

Inflation and finance

			% change 2016–17
Consumer price			
inflation 2017	25.2%	Monetary base	40.9
Av. ann. inflation 2012–17	12.2%	Broad money	20.5
Treasury bill rate, Dec. 2017	18.77%		

Exchange rates

	end 2017		December 2017
£E per $	17.68	Effective rates	2005 = 100
£E per sdr	25.11	– nominal	...
£E per €	21.30	– real	...

Trade

Principal exports		**Principal imports**	
	$bn fob		*$bn cif*
Petroleum & products	5.7	Machinery & equip.	9.4
Food	2.8	Petroleum & products	9.3
Chemicals	1.8	Chemicals	5.9
Finished goods incl. textiles	1.8	Vehicles	3.9
Total incl. others	**20.0**	Total incl. others	**57.8**

Main export destinations		**Main origins of imports**	
	% of total		*% of total*
United Arab Emirates	14.9	China	8.0
Italy	7.2	United Arab Emirates	5.7
United States	7.0	Germany	5.1
United Kingdom	6.5	Saudi Arabia	4.6

Balance of payments, reserves and debt, $bn

Visible exports fob	20.0	Change in reserves	7.8
Visible imports fob	-49.6	Level of reserves	
Trade balance	-29.6	end Dec.	23.6
Invisibles inflows	14.7	No. months of import cover	4.0
Invisibles outflows	-21.7	Official gold holdings, m oz	2.4
Net transfers	16.5	Foreign debt	67.2
Current account balance	-20.1	– as % of GDP	29.0
– as % of GDP	-6.1	– as % of total exports	131.0
Capital balance	32.4	Debt service ratio	12.8
Overall balance	4.7		

Health and education

Health spending, % of GDP	4.2	Education spending, % of GDP	...
Doctors per 1,000 pop.	0.8	Enrolment, %: primary	104
Hospital beds per 1,000 pop.	1.6	secondary	86
Improved-water source access,		tertiary	...
% of pop.	99.4		

Society

No. of households, m	23.4	Cost of living, Dec. 2017	
Av. no. per household	4.1	New York = 100	49
Marriages per 1,000 pop.	11.0	Cars per 1,000 pop.	46
Divorces per 1,000 pop.	2.1	Colour TV households, % with:	
Religion, % of pop.		cable	...
Muslim	94.9	satellite	71.6
Christian	5.1	Telephone lines per 100 pop.	6.4
Hindu	<0.1	Mobile telephone subscribers	
Jewish	<0.1	per 100 pop.	102.2
Non-religious	<0.1	Broadband subs per 100 pop.	4.7
Other	<0.1	Internet users, % of pop.	41.2

FINLAND

Area, sq km	338,420	Capital	Helsinki
Arable as % of total land	7.4	Currency	Euro (€)

People

Population, m	5.5	Life expectancy: men	78.8 yrs
Pop. per sq km	16.3	women	84.4 yrs
Average annual growth		Adult literacy	...
in pop. 2015–20, %	0.4	Fertility rate (per woman)	1.8
Pop. aged 0–19, %	21.9	Urban population, %	85.3
Pop. aged 65 and over, %	20.3		per 1,000 pop.
No. of men per 100 women	96.9	Crude birth rate	10.8
Human Development Index	89.5	Crude death rate	9.8

The economy

GDP	$239bn	GDP per head	$43,414
GDP	€216bn	GDP per head in purchasing	
Av. ann. growth in real		power parity (USA=100)	73.2
GDP 2011–16	-0.2%	Economic freedom index	74.1

Origins of GDP		**Components of GDP**	
	% of total		% of total
Agriculture	3	Private consumption	55
Industry, of which:	27	Public consumption	24
manufacturing	17	Investment	22
Services	70	Exports	35
		Imports	-36

Structure of employment

	% of total		% of labour force
Agriculture	3.9	Unemployed 2016	8.8
Industry	22.2	Av. ann. rate 2006–16	8.0
Services	74.0		

Energy

	m TOE		
Total output	13.0	Net energy imports as %	
Total consumption	29.5	of energy use	45
Consumption per head			
kg oil equivalent	5,925		

Inflation and finance

			% change 2016–17
Consumer price			
inflation 2017	0.8%	Monetary base	24.7
Av. ann. inflation 2012–17	0.9%	Broad money	4.1
Deposit rate, Sep. 2017	0.37%		

Exchange rates

	end 2017		December 2017
€ per $	0.83	Effective rates	2005 = 100
€ per sdr	1.20	– nominal	103.5
		– real	99.0

Trade

Principal exports		Principal imports	
	$bn fob		*$bn cif*
Machinery & transport equip.	17.6	Machinery & transport equip.	21.8
Chemicals & related products	6.0	Mineral fuels & lubricants	7.9
Raw materials	5.2	Chemicals & related products	7.4
Mineral fuels & lubricants	4.6	Food, drink & tobacco	4.8
Total incl. others	**59.1**	**Total incl. others**	**58.2**

Main export destinations		Main origins of imports	
	% of total		*% of total*
Germany	12.8	Germany	17.7
Sweden	10.3	Sweden	16.8
United States	7.4	Russia	11.6
Netherlands	6.5	Netherlands	9.0
EU28	58.9	EU28	73.0

Balance of payments, reserves and aid, $bn

Visible exports fob	59.0	Overall balance	0.9
Visible imports fob	-58.2	Change in reserves	0.4
Trade balance	0.9	Level of reserves	
Invisibles inflows	46.9	end Dec.	10.5
Invisibles outflows	-45.9	No. months of import cover	1.2
Net transfers	-2.8	Official gold holdings, m oz	1.6
Current account balance	-0.8	Aid given	1.1
– as % of GDP	-0.4	– as % of GDP	1.0
Capital balance	26.2		

Health and education

Health spending, % of GDP	9.4	Education spending, % of GDP	7.2
Doctors per 1,000 pop.	3.2	Enrolment, %: primary	100
Hospital beds per 1,000 pop.	4.3	secondary	152
Improved-water source access,		tertiary	87
% of pop.	100		

Society

No. of households, m	2.6	Cost of living, Dec. 2017	
Av. no. per household	2.1	New York = 100	95
Marriages per 1,000 pop.	4.5	Cars per 1,000 pop.	475
Divorces per 1,000 pop.	2.5	Colour TV households, % with:	
Religion, % of pop.		cable	68.5
Christian	81.6	satellite	11.1
Non-religious	17.6	Telephone lines per 100 pop.	8.3
Muslim	0.8	Mobile telephone subscribers	
Hindu	<0.1	per 100 pop.	133.9
Jewish	<0.1	Broadband subs per 100 pop.	31.1
Other	<0.1	Internet users, % of pop.	87.7

FRANCE

Area, sq km	549,087	Capital	Paris
Arable as % of total land	33.7	Currency	Euro (€)

People

Population, m	64.7	Life expectancy: men	79.9 yrs
Pop. per sq km	117.8	women	85.7 yrs
Average annual growth		Adult literacy	...
in pop. 2015–20, %	0.4	Fertility rate (per woman)	2.0
Pop. aged 0–19, %	24.2	Urban population, %	79.9
Pop. aged 65 and over, %	18.9		*per 1,000 pop.*
No. of men per 100 women	96.6	Crude birth rate	11.7
Human Development Index	89.7	Crude death rate	9.0

The economy

GDP	$2,466bn	GDP per head	$38,122
GDP	€2,229bn	GDP per head in purchasing	
Av. ann. growth in real		power parity (USA=100)	73.1
GDP 2011–16	0.8%	Economic freedom index	63.9

Origins of GDP		**Components of GDP**	
	% of total		*% of total*
Agriculture	2	Private consumption	55
Industry, of which:	20	Public consumption	24
manufacturing	11	Investment	23
Services	79	Exports	29
		Imports	-31

Structure of employment

	% of total		*% of labour force*
Agriculture	2.9	Unemployed 2016	10.1
Industry	20.3	Av. ann. rate 2006–16	9.1
Services	76.8		

Energy

	m TOE		
Total output	132.0	Net energy imports as %	
Total consumption	258.8	of energy use	44
Consumption per head			
kg oil equivalent	3,688		

Inflation and finance

Consumer price			*% change 2016–17*
inflation 2017	1.2%	Monetary base	24.7
Av. ann. inflation 2012–17	0.6%	Broad money	4.1
Deposit rate, Sep. 2017	1.00%		

Exchange rates

	end 2017		*December 2017*
€ per $	0.83	Effective rates	*2005 = 100*
€ per sdr	1.20	– nominal	99.7
		– real	95.4

Trade

Principal exports		Principal imports	
	$bn fob		*$bn cif*
Machinery & transport equip.	200.1	Machinery & transport equip.	215.6
Chemicals & related products	92.9	Chemicals & related products	78.1
Food, drink and tobacco	60.0	Food, drink and tobacco	52.5
Mineral fuels & lubricants	12.4	Mineral fuels & lubricants	47.3
Total incl. others	**501.1**	Total incl. others	**554.6**

Main export destinations		Main origins of imports	
	% of total		*% of total*
Germany	16.0	Germany	19.9
Spain	7.6	Belgium	11.0
United States	7.3	Netherlands	8.2
Italy	7.2	Italy	8.1
EU28	59.5	EU28	69.1

Balance of payments, reserves and aid, $bn

Visible exports fob	507.0	Overall balance	2.3
Visible imports fob	-536.7	Change in reserves	7.7
Trade balance	-29.7	Level of reserves	
Invisibles inflows	414.3	end Dec.	145.9
Invisibles outflows	-356.1	No. months of import cover	2.0
Net transfers	-49.6	Official gold holdings, m oz	78.3
Current account balance	-21.1	Aid given	9.6
– as % of GDP	-0.9	– as % of GDP	0.4
Capital balance	35.0		

Health and education

Health spending, % of GDP	11.1	Education spending, % of GDP	5.5
Doctors per 1,000 pop.	3.2	Enrolment, %: primary	107
Hospital beds per 1,000 pop.	6.1	secondary	111
Improved-water source access,		tertiary	65
% of pop.	100		

Society

No. of households, m	29.1	Cost of living, Dec. 2017	
Av. no. per household	2.2	New York = 100	112
Marriages per 1,000 pop.	3.6	Cars per 1,000 pop.	495
Divorces per 1,000 pop.	1.9	Colour TV households, % with:	
Religion, % of pop.		cable	13.1
Christian	63.0	satellite	34.1
Non-religious	28.0	Telephone lines per 100 pop.	60.3
Muslim	7.5	Mobile telephone subscribers	
Other	1.0	per 100 pop.	104.4
Jewish	0.5	Broadband subs per 100 pop.	42.7
Hindu	<0.1	Internet users, % of pop.	85.6

GERMANY

Area, sq km	357,380	Capital	Berlin
Arable as % of total land	34.0	Currency	Euro (€)

People

Population, m	81.9	Life expectancy: men	79.0 yrs
Pop. per sq km	229.2	women	83.6 yrs
Average annual growth		Adult literacy	...
in pop. 2015–20, %	0.2	Fertility rate (per woman)	1.5
Pop. aged 0–19, %	18.1	Urban population, %	77.2
Pop. aged 65 and over, %	21.1		per 1,000 pop.
No. of men per 100 women	96.8	Crude birth rate	8.9
Human Development Index	92.6	Crude death rate	11.3

The economy

GDP	$3,479bn	GDP per head	$42,481
GDP	€3,144bn	GDP per head in purchasing	
Av. ann. growth in real		power parity (USA=100)	84.4
GDP 2011–16	1.3%	Economic freedom index	74.2

Origins of GDP

Components of GDP

	% of total		% of total
Agriculture	1	Private consumption	53
Industry, of which:	30	Public consumption	20
manufacturing	23	Investment	19
Services	69	Exports	46
		Imports	-38

Structure of employment

	% of total		% of labour force
Agriculture	1.3	Unemployed 2016	4.1
Industry	27.4	Av. ann. rate 2006–16	6.5
Services	71.3		

Energy

	m TOE		
Total output	114.1	Net energy imports as %	
Total consumption	333.0	of energy use	61
Consumption per head			
kg oil equivalent	3,818		

Inflation and finance

			% change 2016–17
Consumer price			
inflation 2017	1.7%	Monetary base	24.7
Av. ann. inflation 2012–17	0.9%	Broad money	4.1
Deposit rate, Jun. 2017	0.22%		

Exchange rates

	end 2017		December 2017
€ per $	0.83	Effective rates	2005 = 100
€ per sdr	1.20	– nominal	100.7
		– real	97.9

Trade

Principal exports		Principal imports	
	$bn fob		*$bn cif*
Machinery & transport equip.	667.2	Machinery & transport equip.	402.4
Chemicals & related products	211.9	Chemicals & related products	148.0
Food, drink and tobacco	72.8	Food, drink and tobacco	82.1
Mineral fuels & lubricants	25.5	Mineral fuels & lubricants	78.0
Total incl. others	**1,326.1**	Total incl. others	**1,054.0**

Main export destinations		Main origins of imports	
	% of total		*% of total*
United States	8.9	Netherlands	13.3
France	8.4	China	7.3
United Kingdom	7.2	France	7.3
Netherlands	6.5	Belgium	6.1
EU28	58.5	EU28	66.3

Balance of payments, reserves and aid, $bn

Visible exports fob	1,319.1	Overall balance	1.9
Visible imports fob	-1,022.1	Change in reserves	10.3
Trade balance	296.9	Level of reserves	
Invisibles inflows	501.7	end Dec.	184.0
Invisibles outflows	-457.4	No. months of import cover	1.5
Net transfers	-43.9	Official gold holdings, m oz	108.6
Current account balance	297.3	Aid given	24.7
– as % of GDP	8.5	– as % of GDP	0.7
Capital balance	-278.6		

Health and education

Health spending, % of GDP	11.2	Education spending, % of GDP	4.9
Doctors per 1,000 pop.	4.2	Enrolment, %: primary	102
Hospital beds per 1,000 pop.	8.1	secondary	101
Improved-water source access,		tertiary	66
% of pop.	100		

Society

No. of households, m	40.5	Cost of living, Dec. 2017	
Av. no. per household	2.0	New York = 100	80
Marriages per 1,000 pop.	4.9	Cars per 1,000 pop.	550
Divorces per 1,000 pop.	2.0	Colour TV households, % with:	
Religion, % of pop.		cable	46.0
Christian	68.7	satellite	45.1
Non-religious	24.7	Telephone lines per 100 pop.	53.8
Muslim	5.8	Mobile telephone subscribers	
Other	0.5	per 100 pop.	126.3
Jewish	0.3	Broadband subs per 100 pop.	39.1
Hindu	<0.1	Internet users, % of pop.	89.6

GREECE

Area, sq km	131,960	Capital	Athens
Arable as % of total land	17.3	Currency	Euro (€)

People

Population, m	11.2	Life expectancy: men	79.0 yrs
Pop. per sq km	84.9	women	84.0 yrs
Average annual growth		Adult literacy	...
in pop. 2015–20, %	-0.2	Fertility rate (per woman)	1.3
Pop. aged 0–19, %	19.5	Urban population, %	78.4
Pop. aged 65 and over, %	19.9		*per 1,000 pop.*
No. of men per 100 women	97.0	Crude birth rate	7.9
Human Development Index	86.6	Crude death rate	10.9

The economy

GDP	$193bn	GDP per head	$17,212
GDP	€174bn	GDP per head in purchasing	
Av. ann. growth in real		power parity (USA=100)	44.7
GDP 2011–16	-2.1%	Economic freedom index	57.3

Origins of GDP		**Components of GDP**	
	% of total		*% of total*
Agriculture	4	Private consumption	70
Industry, of which:	16	Public consumption	20
manufacturing	10	Investment	11
Services	80	Exports	30
		Imports	-31

Structure of employment

	% of total		*% of labour force*
Agriculture	12.4	Unemployed 2016	23.5
Industry	15.2	Av. ann. rate 2006–16	17.5
Services	72.4		

Energy

	m TOE		
Total output	8.6	Net energy imports as %	
Total consumption	27.6	of energy use	64
Consumption per head			
kg oil equivalent	2,182		

Inflation and finance

Consumer price			*% change 2016–17*
inflation 2017	1.1%	Monetary base	24.7
Av. ann. inflation 2012–17	-0.4%	Broad money	4.1
Deposit rate, Sep. 2017	0.62%		

Exchange rates

	end 2017		*December 2017*
€ per $	0.83	Effective rates	*2005 = 100*
€ per sdr	1.20	– nominal	101.3
		– real	90.8

Trade

Principal exports		Principal imports	
	$bn fob		*$bn cif*
Mineral fuels & lubricants	7.6	Machinery & transport equip.	10.8
Food, drink and tobacco	5.6	Mineral fuels & lubricants	10.8
Chemicals & related products	3.0	Chemicals & related products	7.6
Machinery & transport equip.	2.9	Food, drink and tobacco	6.7
Total incl. others	**28.2**	Total incl. others	**48.9**

Main export destinations		Main origins of imports	
	% of total		*% of total*
Germany	11.1	Germany	11.1
Italy	7.7	Italy	8.8
Cyprus	6.4	China	6.6
Turkey	5.3	Russia	6.4
EU28	56.3	EU28	54.8

Balance of payments, reserves and debt, $bn

Visible exports fob	27.1	Overall balance	4.3
Visible imports fob	-45.4	Change in reserves	0.8
Trade balance	-18.3	Level of reserves	
Invisibles inflows	34.3	end Dec.	6.9
Invisibles outflows	-17.3	No. months of import cover	1.3
Net transfers	-0.7	Official gold holdings, m oz	3.6
Current account balance	-2.0	Aid given	0.4
– as % of GDP	-1.0	– as % of GDP	0.3
Capital balance	6.3		

Health and education

Health spending, % of GDP	8.4	Education spending, % of GDP	...
Doctors per 1,000 pop.	6.3	Enrolment, %: primary	95
Hospital beds per 1,000 pop.	4.3	secondary	99
Improved-water source access,		tertiary	117
% of pop.	100		

Society

No. of households, m	4.4	Cost of living, Dec. 2017	
Av. no. per household	2.5	New York = 100	66
Marriages per 1,000 pop.	4.6	Cars per 1,000 pop.	456
Divorces per 1,000 pop.	1.3	Colour TV households, % with:	
Religion, % of pop.		cable	0.9
Christian	88.1	satellite	13.5
Non-religious	6.1	Telephone lines per 100 pop.	46.5
Muslim	5.3	Mobile telephone subscribers	
Other	0.3	per 100 pop.	112.1
Hindu	0.1	Broadband subs per 100 pop.	32.3
Jewish	<0.1	Internet users, % of pop.	69.1

HONG KONG

Area, sq km	1,105	Capital	...
Arable as % of total land	2.9	Currency	Hong Kong dollar (HK$)

People

Population, m	7.3	Life expectancy: men	81.2 yrs
Pop. per sq km	6,606.3	women	87.2 yrs
Average annual growth		Adult literacy	...
in pop. 2015–20, %	0.8	Fertility rate (per woman)	1.3
Pop. aged 0–19, %	16.1	Urban population, %	100.0
Pop. aged 65 and over, %	15.2		per 1,000 pop.
No. of men per 100 women	85.9	Crude birth rate	11.1
Human Development Index	91.7	Crude death rate	6.9

The economy

GDP	$321bn	GDP per head	$43,956
GDP	HK$2,491bn	GDP per head in purchasing	
Av. ann. growth in real		power parity (USA=100)	102
GDP 2011–16	2.4%	Economic freedom index	90.2

Origins of GDP

	% of total
Agriculture	0
Industry, of which:	8
manufacturing	1
Services	92

Components of GDP

	% of total
Private consumption	66
Public consumption	10
Investment	22
Exports	187
Imports	-185

Structure of employment

	% of total		% of labour force
Agriculture	0.2	Unemployed 2016	3.4
Industry	13.2	Av. ann. rate 2006–16	3.8
Services	86.6		

Energy

	m TOE		
Total output	-	Net energy imports as %	
Total consumption	30.7	of energy use	99
Consumption per head			
kg oil equivalent	1,970		

Inflation and finance

			% change 2016–17
Consumer price			
inflation 2017	1.5%	Monetary base	9.9
Av. ann. inflation 2012–17	3.1%	Broad money	3.2
Treasury bill rate, Dec. 2017	1.02%		

Exchange rates

	end 2017		December 2017
HK$ per $	7.81	Effective rates	2005 = 100
HK$ per sdr	11.06	– nominal	103.4
HK$ per €	9.41	– real	...

Trade

Principal exports[a]		**Principal imports**[a]	
	$bn fob		*$bn cif*
Capital goods	186.4	Capital goods & raw materials	191.4
Semi-finished goods	167.7	Raw materials & semi-	
Consumer goods	93.5	manufactures	184.7
Foodstuffs	7.6	Consumer goods	105.8
		Foodstuffs	23.9
Total incl. others	**462.5**	Total incl. others	**517.0**

Main export destinations		**Main origins of imports**	
	% of total		*% of total*
China	54.1	China	47.8
United States	9.0	Taiwan	7.3
India	3.3	Singapore	6.5
Japan	3.3	Japan	6.1

Balance of payments, reserves and debt, $bn

Visible exports fob	501.5	Change in reserves	27.5
Visible imports fob	-518.3	Level of reserves	
Trade balance	-16.7	end Dec.	386.3
Invisibles inflows	262.6	No. months of import cover	6.2
Invisibles outflows	-230.5	Official gold holdings, m oz	0.1
Net transfers	-2.7	Foreign debt	537.3
Current account balance	12.7	– as % of GDP	167.4
– as % of GDP	4.0	– as % of total exports	70.1
Capital balance	-11.9	Debt service ratio	6.8
Overall balance	1.1		

Health and education

Health spending, % of GDP	...	Education spending, % of GDP	3.3
Doctors per 1,000 pop.	...	Enrolment, %: primary	107
Hospital beds per 1,000 pop.	...	secondary	103
Improved-water source access,		tertiary	72
% of pop.	...		

Society

No. of households, m	2.5	Cost of living, Dec. 2017	
Av. no. per household	2.9	New York = 100	111
Marriages per 1,000 pop.	6.8	Cars per 1,000 pop.	74
Divorces per 1,000 pop.	...	Colour TV households, % with:	
Religion, % of pop.		cable	94.4
Non-religious	56.1	satellite	0.1
Christian	14.3	Telephone lines per 100 pop.	59.1
Other	14.2	Mobile telephone subscribers	
Buddhist	13.2	per 100 pop.	240.8
Muslim	1.8	Broadband subs per 100 pop.	36.0
Hindu	0.4	Internet users, % of pop.	87.5

a Including re-exports.
Note: Hong Kong became a Special Administrative Region of China on July 1 1997.

HUNGARY

Area, sq km	93,030	Capital	Budapest
Arable as % of total land	48.7	Currency	Forint (Ft)

People

Population, m	9.8	Life expectancy: men	72.5 yrs
Pop. per sq km	105.3	women	79.5 yrs
Average annual growth		Adult literacy	...
in pop. 2015–20, %	-0.3	Fertility rate (per woman)	1.4
Pop. aged 0–19, %	19.7	Urban population, %	70.8
Pop. aged 65 and over, %	17.5		per 1,000 pop.
No. of men per 100 women	90.6	Crude birth rate	9.0
Human Development Index	83.6	Crude death rate	13.0

The economy

GDP	$129bn	GDP per head	$13,178
GDP	Ft35,420bn	GDP per head in purchasing	
Av. ann. growth in real		power parity (USA=100)	48.2
GDP 2011–16	2.0%	Economic freedom index	66.7

Origins of GDP

Components of GDP

	% of total		% of total
Agriculture	4	Private consumption	50
Industry, of which:	31	Public consumption	20
manufacturing	24	Investment	20
Services	65	Exports	90
		Imports	-79

Structure of employment

	% of total		% of labour force
Agriculture	5.0	Unemployed 2016	5.1
Industry	30.4	Av. ann. rate 2006–16	8.7
Services	64.5		

Energy

	m TOE		
Total output	8.4	Net energy imports as %	
Total consumption	25.1	of energy use	58
Consumption per head			
kg oil equivalent	2,433		

Inflation and finance

			% change 2016–17
Consumer price			
inflation 2017	2.4%	Monetary base	0.7
Av. ann. inflation 2012–17	0.8%	Broad money	7.8
Deposit rate, Oct. 2017	0.24%		

Exchange rates

	end 2017		December 2017
Ft per $	258.82	Effective rates	2005 = 100
Ft per sdr	374.60	– nominal	89.4
Ft per €	311.83	– real	91.4

Trade

Trade

Principal exports

	$bn fob
Machinery & equipment	59.6
Manufactured goods	32.2
Food, drink & tobacco	7.3
Raw materials	2.3
Total incl. others	**102.9**

Principal imports

	$bn cif
Machinery & equipment	45.8
Manufactured goods	33.6
Fuels & energy	5.9
Food, drink & tobacco	5.0
Total incl. others	**92.1**

Main export destinations

	% of total
Germany	27.9
Romania	5.2
Slovakia	5.0
Austria	4.9
EU28	81.4

Main origins of imports

	% of total
Germany	27.4
Austria	6.6
China	6.4
Poland	5.6
EU28	77.7

Balance of payments, reserves and debt, $bn

Visible exports fob	88.6	Change in reserves	-7.3
Visible imports fob	-83.5	Level of reserves	
Trade balance	5.1	end Dec.	25.8
Invisibles inflows	39.5	No. months of import cover	2.6
Invisibles outflows	-35.2	Official gold holdings, m oz	0.0
Net transfers	-1.8	Foreign debt	136.1
Current account balance	7.6	– as % of GDP	108.3
– as % of GDP	5.9	– as % of total exports	106.4
Capital balance	-11.1	Debt service ratio	26.9
Overall balance	-6.8		

Health and education

Health spending, % of GDP	7.2	Education spending, % of GDP	4.6
Doctors per 1,000 pop.	3.1	Enrolment, %: primary	102
Hospital beds per 1,000 pop.	7.0	secondary	102
Improved-water source access,		tertiary	48
% of pop.	100		

Society

No. of households, m	4.1	Cost of living, Dec. 2017	
Av. no. per household	2.4	New York = 100	59
Marriages per 1,000 pop.	5.3	Cars per 1,000 pop.	326
Divorces per 1,000 pop.	2.0	Colour TV households, % with:	
Religion, % of pop.		cable	56.4
Christian	81.0	satellite	28.5
Non-religious	18.6	Telephone lines per 100 pop.	32.0
Other	0.2	Mobile telephone subscribers	
Jewish	0.1	per 100 pop.	120.8
Hindu	<0.1	Broadband subs per 100 pop.	28.9
Muslim	<0.1	Internet users, % of pop.	79.3

INDIA

| Area, sq km | 3,287,259 | Capital | New Delhi |
| Arable as % of total land | 52.6 | Currency | Indian rupee (Rs) |

People

Population, m	1,324.2	Life expectancy: men	67.4 yrs
Pop. per sq km	402.8	women	70.5 yrs
Average annual growth		Adult literacy	72.2
in pop. 2015–20, %	1.1	Fertility rate (per woman)	2.3
Pop. aged 0–19, %	38.1	Urban population, %	33.2
Pop. aged 65 and over, %	5.6		per 1,000 pop.
No. of men per 100 women	107.6	Crude birth rate	18.7
Human Development Index	62.4	Crude death rate	7.4

The economy

GDP	$2,274bn	GDP per head	$1,717
GDP	Rs153trn	GDP per head in purchasing	
Av. ann. growth in real		power parity (USA=100)	11.4
GDP 2011–16	6.9%	Economic freedom index	54.5

Origins of GDP

Components of GDP

	% of total		% of total
Agriculture	17	Private consumption	59
Industry, of which:	29	Public consumption	12
manufacturing	17	Investment	30
Services	54	Exports	19
		Imports	-21

Structure of employment

	% of total		% of labour force
Agriculture	43.4	Unemployed 2016	3.5
Industry	23.7	Av. ann. rate 2006–16	2.6
Services	32.8		

Energy

	m TOE		
Total output	359.0	Net energy imports as %	
Total consumption	637.3	of energy use	34
Consumption per head			
kg oil equivalent	637		

Inflation and finance

			% change 2016–17
Consumer price			
inflation 2017	3.6%	Monetary base	9.9
Av. ann. inflation 2012–17	5.6%	Broad money	55.4
Discount rate, Jul. 2017	6.50%		

Exchange rates

	end 2017		December 2017
			2005 = 100
Rs per $	63.93	Effective rates	
Rs per sdr	90.91	– nominal	...
Rs per €	77.02	– real	...

Trade

Principal exports		Principal imports	
	$bn fob		*$bn cif*
Engineering products	67.1	Petroleum & products	86.9
Gems & jewellery	43.5	Electronic goods	41.9
Petroleum & products	31.6	Gold & silver	29.3
Agricultural products	28.4	Machinery	28.7
Total incl. others	**276.5**	Total incl. others	**382.7**

Main export destinations		Main origins of imports	
	% of total		*% of total*
United States	15.2	China	15.8
United Arab Emirates	11.1	United States	5.4
Hong Kong	4.8	United Arab Emirates	5.0
United Kingdom	3.3	Saudi Arabia	4.8

Balance of payments, reserves and debt, $bn

Visible exports fob	268.6	Change in reserves	8.4
Visible imports fob	-376.1	Level of reserves	
Trade balance	-107.5	end Dec.	361.7
Invisibles inflows	177.3	No. months of import cover	8.4
Invisibles outflows	-138.8	Official gold holdings, m oz	17.9
Net transfers	56.8	Foreign debt	456.1
Current account balance	-12.1	– as % of GDP	20.2
– as % of GDP	-0.5	– as % of total exports	89.7
Capital balance	29.5	Debt service ratio	15.2
Overall balance	15.7		

Health and education

Health spending, % of GDP	3.9	Education spending, % of GDP	3.8
Doctors per 1,000 pop.	0.8	Enrolment, %: primary	115
Hospital beds per 1,000 pop.	0.7	secondary	75
Improved-water source access,		tertiary	27
% of pop.	94.1		

Society

No. of households, m	286.6	Cost of living, Dec. 2017	
Av. no. per household	4.6	New York = 100	48
Marriages per 1,000 pop.	...	Cars per 1,000 pop.	17
Divorces per 1,000 pop.	...	Colour TV households, % with:	
Religion, % of pop.		cable	62.5
Hindu	79.5	satellite	17.1
Muslim	14.4	Telephone lines per 100 pop.	1.8
Other	3.6	Mobile telephone subscribers	
Christian	2.5	per 100 pop.	85.2
Jewish	<0.1	Broadband subs per 100 pop.	1.4
Non-religious	<0.1	Internet users, % of pop.	29.5

INDONESIA

Area, sq km	1,910,931	Capital	Jakarta
Arable as % of total land	13.0	Currency	Rupiah (Rp)

People

Population, m	261.1	Life expectancy: men	67.4 yrs
Pop. per sq km	136.6	women	71.7 yrs
Average annual growth		Adult literacy	95.4
in pop. 2015–20, %	1.1	Fertility rate (per woman)	2.3
Pop. aged 0–19, %	36.6	Urban population, %	54.0
Pop. aged 65 and over, %	5.1		per 1,000 pop.
No. of men per 100 women	101.5	Crude birth rate	18.4
Human Development Index	68.9	Crude death rate	7.2

The economy

GDP	$932bn	GDP per head	$3,571
GDP	Rs12,407trn	GDP per head in purchasing	
Av. ann. growth in real		power parity (USA=100)	20.1
GDP 2011–16	5.3%	Economic freedom index	64.2

Origins of GDP		**Components of GDP**	
	% of total		% of total
Agriculture	14	Private consumption	55
Industry, of which:	41	Public consumption	9
manufacturing	21	Investment	34
Services	45	Exports	19
		Imports	-18

Structure of employment

	% of total		% of labour force
Agriculture	31.8	Unemployed 2016	4.3
Industry	21.7	Av. ann. rate 2006–16	5.6
Services	46.5		

Energy

	m TOE		
Total output	330.3	Net energy imports as %	
Total consumption	173.0	of energy use	-103
Consumption per head			
kg oil equivalent	884		

Inflation and finance

			% change 2016–17
Consumer price			
inflation 2017	3.8%	Monetary base	8.6
Av. ann. inflation 2012–17	5.3%	Broad money	9.3
Deposit rate, Nov. 2017	6.17%		

Exchange rates

	end 2017		December 2017
Rp per $	13,548.00	Effective rates	2005 = 100
Rp per sdr	19,184.67	– nominal	...
Rp per €	16,322.89	– real	...

Trade

Principal exports

	$bn fob
Manufactured goods	106.7
Mining & other sector products	29.8
Agricultural goods	5.5
Unclassified exports	1.2
Total incl. others	**145.2**

Principal imports

	$bn cif
Raw materials & auxiliary materials	95.1
Capital goods	22.4
Consumer goods	17.0
Total incl. others	**135.7**

Main export destinations

	% of total
China	11.6
Japan	11.1
United States	11.1
Singapore	8.2

Main origins of imports

	% of total
China	22.7
Singapore	10.7
Japan	9.6
Thailand	6.4

Balance of payments, reserves and debt, $bn

Visible exports fob	144.5	Change in reserves	10.4
Visible imports fob	-129.2	Level of reserves end Dec.	116.4
Trade balance	15.3		
Invisibles inflows	27.4	No. months of import cover	7.2
Invisibles outflows	-64.1	Official gold holdings, m oz	2.5
Net transfers	4.5	Foreign debt	316.4
Current account balance	-17.0	– as % of GDP	33.9
– as % of GDP	-1.8	– as % of total exports	175.0
Capital balance	29.3	Debt service ratio	37.6
Overall balance	12.1		

Health and education

Health spending, % of GDP	3.3	Education spending, % of GDP	3.6
Doctors per 1,000 pop.	0.2	Enrolment, %: primary	103
Hospital beds per 1,000 pop.	1.2	secondary	86
Improved-water source access, % of pop.	87.4	tertiary	28

Society

No. of households, m	65.3	Cost of living, Dec. 2017	
Av. no. per household	4.0	New York = 100	65
Marriages per 1,000 pop.	...	Cars per 1,000 pop.	52
Divorces per 1,000 pop.	...	Colour TV households, % with:	
Religion, % of pop.		cable	6.0
Muslim	87.2	satellite	25.5
Christian	9.9	Telephone lines per 100 pop.	4.1
Hindu	1.7	Mobile telephone subscribers	
Other	1.1	per 100 pop.	147.7
Jewish	<0.1	Broadband subs per 100 pop.	2.0
Non-religious	<0.1	Internet users, % of pop.	25.4

IRAN

Area, sq km	1,745,150	Capital	Tehran
Arable as % of total land	9.0	Currency	Rial (IR)

People

Population, m	80.3	Life expectancy: men	75.1 yrs
Pop. per sq km	46.0	women	77.4 yrs
Average annual growth		Adult literacy	87.2
in pop. 2015–20, %	1.0	Fertility rate (per woman)	1.6
Pop. aged 0–19, %	30.6	Urban population, %	73.9
Pop. aged 65 and over, %	5.0		per 1,000 pop.
No. of men per 100 women	101.3	Crude birth rate	15.6
Human Development Index	77.4	Crude death rate	4.5

The economy

GDP	$404bn	GDP per head	$5,037
GDP	IR12,722trn	GDP per head in purchasing	
Av. ann. growth in real		power parity (USA=100)	33.4
GDP 2011–16	1.6%	Economic freedom index	50.9

Origins of GDP

	% of total
Agriculture	10
Industry, of which:	35
manufacturing	12
Services	55

Components of GDP

	% of total
Private consumption	49
Public consumption	13
Investment	36
Exports	22
Imports	-21

Structure of employment

	% of total		% of labour force
Agriculture	18.0	Unemployed 2016	12.4
Industry	31.9	Av. ann. rate 2006–16	11.5
Services	50.1		

Energy

	m TOE		
Total output	363.6	Net energy imports as %	
Total consumption	273.4	of energy use	-33
Consumption per head			
kg oil equivalent	3,023		

Inflation and finance

			% change 2016–17
Consumer price			
inflation 2017	9.9%	Monetary base	...
Av. ann. inflation 2012–17	15.9%	Broad money	...
Deposit rate, Dec. 2016	12.80%		

Exchange rates

	end 2017		December 2017
			2005 = 100
IR per $	36,074.00	Effective rates	
IR per sdr	50,477.67	– nominal	33.7
IR per €	43,462.65	– real	99.7

Trade

Principal exports[a]		Principal imports[a]	
	$bn fob		*$bn fob*
Oil & gas	55.8	Machinery & transport equip.	17.7
Petrochemicals	8.9	Intermediate goods	7.0
Fresh & dry fruits	2.3	Foodstuffs	6.3
Carpets	0.4	Chemicals	6.0
Total incl. others	**84.0**	Total incl. others	**63.1**

Main export destinations		Main origins of imports	
	% of total		*% of total*
China	30.1	United Arab Emirates	25.6
India	16.7	China	13.8
South Korea	9.6	Turkey	8.1
Turkey	9.5	South Korea	4.6

Balance of payments[a], reserves and debt, $bn

Visible exports fob	84.0	Change in reserves	...
Visible imports fob	-63.1	Level of reserves	
Trade balance	20.8	end Dec.	...
Invisibles inflows	12.6	No. months of import cover	...
Invisibles outflows	-17.6	Official gold holdings, m oz	...
Net transfers	0.6	Foreign debt	5.4
Current account balance	16.4	– as % of GDP	1.3
– as % of GDP	4.1	– as % of total exports	5.5
Capital balance	9.2	Debt service ratio	2.2
Overall balance	19.8		

Health and education

Health spending, % of GDP	7.6	Education spending, % of GDP	3.4
Doctors per 1,000 pop.	1.5	Enrolment, %: primary	109
Hospital beds per 1,000 pop.	0.1	secondary	89
Improved-water source access,		tertiary	...
% of pop.	96.2		

Society

No. of households, m	24.1	Cost of living, Dec. 2017	
Av. no. per household	3.3	New York = 100	49
Marriages per 1,000 pop.	8.7	Cars per 1,000 pop.	158
Divorces per 1,000 pop.	2.1	Colour TV households, % with:	
Religion, % of pop.		cable	...
Muslim	99.5	satellite	37.0
Christian	0.2	Telephone lines per 100 pop.	38.2
Other	0.2	Mobile telephone subscribers	
Non-religious	0.1	per 100 pop.	100.3
Hindu	<0.1	Broadband subs per 100 pop.	11.6
Jewish	<0.1	Internet users, % of pop.	53.2

a Iranian year ending March 20 2017.

IRELAND

Area, sq km	70,280	Capital	Dublin
Arable as % of total land	14.9	Currency	Euro (€)

People

Population, m	4.7	Life expectancy: men	79.8 yrs
Pop. per sq km	66.9	women	83.7 yrs
Average annual growth		Adult literacy	...
in pop. 2015–20, %	0.8	Fertility rate (per woman)	2.0
Pop. aged 0–19, %	27.5	Urban population, %	62.7
Pop. aged 65 and over, %	13.2		per 1,000 pop.
No. of men per 100 women	98.4	Crude birth rate	13.5
Human Development Index	92.3	Crude death rate	6.6

The economy

GDP	$304bn	GDP per head	$64,787
GDP	€275bn	GDP per head in purchasing	
Av. ann. growth in real		power parity (USA=100)	119.8
GDP 2011–16	7.8%	Economic freedom index	80.4

Origins of GDP		**Components of GDP**	
	% of total		% of total
Agriculture	1	Private consumption	33
Industry, of which:	39	Public consumption	12
manufacturing	35	Investment	33
Services	60	Exports	122
		Imports	-100

Structure of employment

	% of total		% of labour force
Agriculture	5.6	Unemployed 2016	8.4
Industry	19.6	Av. ann. rate 2006–16	10.7
Services	74.8		

Energy

	m TOE		
Total output	2.0	Net energy imports as %	
Total consumption	14.9	of energy use	86
Consumption per head			
kg oil equivalent	2,853		

Inflation and finance

			% change 2016–17
Consumer price			
inflation 2017	0.3%	Monetary base	24.7
Av. ann. inflation 2012–17	0.2%	Broad money	4.1
Deposit rate, Sep. 2017	0.05%		

Exchange rates

	end 2017		December 2017
€ per $	0.83	Effective rates	2005 = 100
€ per sdr	1.20	– nominal	97.8
		– real	91.7

Trade

Principal exports

	$bn fob
Chemicals & related products	73.3
Machinery & transport equip.	23.1
Food, drink and tobacco	12.6
Raw materials	1.8
Total incl. others	**132.1**

Principal imports

	$bn cif
Machinery & transport equip.	34.7
Chemicals & related products	16.2
Food, drink and tobacco	8.4
Mineral fuels & lubricants	4.2
Total incl. others	**82.0**

Main export destinations

	% of total
United States	26.6
United Kingdom	12.4
Belgium	12.2
Germany	6.5
EU28	50.2

Main origins of imports

	% of total
United Kingdom	27.7
United States	17.7
France	12.5
Germany	9.6
EU28	65.5

Balance of payments, reserves and aid, $bn

Visible exports fob	206.0	Overall balance	1.4
Visible imports fob	-92.1	Change in reserves	1.4
Trade balance	113.9	Level of reserves	
Invisibles inflows	222.1	end Dec.	3.6
Invisibles outflows	-318.6	No. months of import cover	0.1
Net transfers	-3.0	Official gold holdings, m oz	0.2
Current account balance	14.3	Aid given	0.8
– as % of GDP	4.7	– as % of GDP	0.3
Capital balance	-10.9		

Health and education

Health spending, % of GDP	7.8	Education spending, % of GDP	4.9
Doctors per 1,000 pop.	3.0	Enrolment, %: primary	101
Hospital beds per 1,000 pop.	3.0	secondary	126
Improved-water source access,		tertiary	84
% of pop.	97.9		

Society

No. of households, m	1.7	Cost of living, Dec. 2017	
Av. no. per household	2.8	New York = 100	93
Marriages per 1,000 pop.	4.8	Cars per 1,000 pop.	422
Divorces per 1,000 pop.	0.6	Colour TV households, % with:	
Religion, % of pop.		cable	31.7
Christian	92.0	satellite	47.6
Non-religious	6.2	Telephone lines per 100 pop.	40.1
Muslim	1.1	Mobile telephone subscribers	
Other	0.4	per 100 pop.	103.2
Hindu	0.2	Broadband subs per 100 pop.	28.8
Jewish	<0.1	Internet users, % of pop.	85.0

ISRAEL

Area, sq km	22,070	Capital	Jerusalem[a]
Arable as % of total land	13.7	Currency	New Shekel (NIS)

People

Population, m	8.2	Life expectancy: men	81.0 yrs
Pop. per sq km	371.5	women	84.3 yrs
Average annual growth		Adult literacy	...
in pop. 2015–20, %	1.6	Fertility rate (per woman)	2.9
Pop. aged 0–19, %	35.6	Urban population, %	92.3
Pop. aged 65 and over, %	11.2		per 1,000 pop.
No. of men per 100 women	98.4	Crude birth rate	19.6
Human Development Index	89.9	Crude death rate	5.3

The economy

GDP	$318bn	GDP per head	$38,750
GDP	NIS1,220bn	GDP per head in purchasing	
Av. ann. growth in real		power parity (USA=100)	63.5
GDP 2011–16	3.3%	Economic freedom index	72.2

Origins of GDP		Components of GDP	
	% of total		% of total
Agriculture	1	Private consumption	55
Industry, of which:	21	Public consumption	22
manufacturing	13	Investment	20
Services	78	Exports	30
		Imports	-28

Structure of employment

	% of total		% of labour force
Agriculture	1.1	Unemployed 2016	4.8
Industry	17.4	Av. ann. rate 2006–16	7.5
Services	81.6		

Energy

	m TOE		
Total output	8.1	Net energy imports as %	
Total consumption	23.3	of energy use	65
Consumption per head			
kg oil equivalent	2,778		

Inflation and finance

			% change 2016–17
Consumer price			
inflation 2017	0.2%	Monetary base	-2.5
Av. ann. inflation 2012–17	0.2%	Broad money	6.3
Treasury bill rate, Dec. 2017	0.12%		

Exchange rates

	end 2017		December 2017
			2005 = 100
NIS per $	3.47	Effective rates	
NIS per sdr	4.96	– nominal	119.9
NIS per €	4.18	– real	109.5

Trade

Principal exports

	$bn fob
Chemicals & chemical products	12.9
Communications, medical & scientific equipment	8.5
Polished diamonds	7.4
Electronic components & computers	5.0
Total incl. others	**52.2**

Principal imports

	$bn cif
Machinery & equipment	7.5
Diamonds	6.5
Fuel	5.8
Chemicals	4.3
Total incl. others	**65.1**

Main export destinations

	% of total
United States	33.7
Hong Kong	8.5
United Kingdom	7.5
China	6.4

Main origins of imports

	% of total
United States	12.4
China	9.1
Switzerland	6.6
Germany	6.3

Balance of payments, reserves and debt, $bn

Visible exports fob	56.2	Change in reserves	4.9
Visible imports fob	-63.5	Level of reserves	
Trade balance	-7.4	end Dec.	95.4
Invisibles inflows	50.0	No. months of import cover	11.1
Invisibles outflows	-40.0	Official gold holdings, m oz	0.0
Net transfers	9.3	Foreign debt	87.7
Current account balance	11.9	– as % of GDP	27.6
– as % of GDP	3.7	– as % of total exports	81.7
Capital balance	2.5	Debt service ratio	10.5
Overall balance	8.1		

Health and education

Health spending, % of GDP	7.4	Education spending, % of GDP	5.7
Doctors per 1,000 pop.	3.6	Enrolment, %: primary	104
Hospital beds per 1,000 pop.	3.0	secondary	104
Improved-water source access, % of pop.	100	tertiary	64

Society

No. of households, m	2.3	Cost of living, Dec. 2017	
Av. no. per household	3.6	New York = 100	103
Marriages per 1,000 pop.	6.4	Cars per 1,000 pop.	318
Divorces per 1,000 pop.	1.7	Colour TV households, % with:	
Religion, % of pop.		cable	77.8
Jewish	75.6	satellite	19.2
Muslim	18.6	Telephone lines per 100 pop.	40.8
Non-religious	3.1	Mobile telephone subscribers	
Christian	2.0	per 100 pop.	129.0
Other	0.6	Broadband subs per 100 pop.	27.6
Hindu	<0.1	Internet users, % of pop.	79.7

a Sovereignty over the city is disputed.

ITALY

Area, sq km	301,340	Capital	Rome
Arable as % of total land	22.4	Currency	Euro (€)

People

Population, m	59.4	Life expectancy: men	81.1 yrs
Pop. per sq km	197.1	women	85.4 yrs
Average annual growth		Adult literacy	99.0
in pop. 2015–20, %	-0.1	Fertility rate (per woman)	1.5
Pop. aged 0–19, %	18.4	Urban population, %	69.9
Pop. aged 65 and over, %	22.4		per 1,000 pop.
No. of men per 100 women	94.8	Crude birth rate	8.2
Human Development Index	88.7	Crude death rate	10.6

The economy

GDP	$1,860bn	GDP per head	$31,316
GDP	€1,681bn	GDP per head in purchasing	
Av. ann. growth in real		power parity (USA=100)	65.2
GDP 2011–16	-0.5%	Economic freedom index	62.5

Origins of GDP		Components of GDP	
	% of total		% of total
Agriculture	2	Private consumption	61
Industry, of which:	24	Public consumption	19
manufacturing	16	Investment	17
Services	74	Exports	30
		Imports	-26

Structure of employment

	% of total		% of labour force
Agriculture	3.9	Unemployed 2016	11.7
Industry	26.1	Av. ann. rate 2006–16	9.4
Services	70.0		

Energy

	m TOE		
Total output	37.8	Net energy imports as %	
Total consumption	168.2	of energy use	76
Consumption per head			
kg oil equivalent	2,482		

Inflation and finance

Consumer price			% change 2016–17
inflation 2017	1.3%	Monetary base	24.7
Av. ann. inflation 2012–17	0.6%	Broad money	4.1
Treasury bill rate, Dec. 2017	-0.41%		

Exchange rates

	end 2017		December 2017
€ per $	0.83	Effective rates	2005 = 100
€ per sdr	1.20	– nominal	101.4
		– real	97.4

Trade

Principal exports
	$bn fob
Machinery & transport equip.	169.5
Chemicals & related products	58.2
Food, drink and tobacco	38.5
Mineral fuels & lubricants	12.7
Total incl. others	**461.7**

Principal imports
	$bn cif
Machinery & transport equip.	120.1
Chemicals & related products	65.7
Mineral fuels & lubricants	41.7
Food, drink and tobacco	39.6
Total incl. others	**406.8**

Main export destinations
	% of total
Germany	12.6
France	10.5
United States	8.8
United Kingdom	6.1
EU28	55.9

Main origins of imports
	% of total
Germany	16.3
France	8.9
China	7.4
Netherlands	5.5
EU28	60.8

Balance of payments, reserves and aid, $bn

Visible exports fob	453.6	Overall balance	-1.3
Visible imports fob	-389.8	Change in reserves	4.5
Trade balance	63.8	Level of reserves	
Invisibles inflows	171.8	end Dec.	135.1
Invisibles outflows	-169.6	No. months of import cover	2.9
Net transfers	-18.4	Official gold holdings, m oz	78.8
Current account balance	47.7	Aid given	5.1
– as % of GDP	2.6	– as % of GDP	0.3
Capital balance	-77.3		

Health and education

Health spending, % of GDP	9.0	Education spending, % of GDP	4.1
Doctors per 1,000 pop.	4.0	Enrolment, %: primary	101
Hospital beds per 1,000 pop.	3.2	secondary	103
Improved-water source access,		tertiary	63
% of pop.	100		

Society

No. of households, m	25.8	Cost of living, Dec. 2017	
Av. no. per household	2.3	New York = 100	86
Marriages per 1,000 pop.	3.2	Cars per 1,000 pop.	629
Divorces per 1,000 pop.	1.4	Colour TV households, % with:	
Religion, % of pop.		cable	1.1
Christian	83.3	satellite	29.0
Non-religious	12.4	Telephone lines per 100 pop.	34.1
Muslim	3.7	Mobile telephone subscribers	
Other	0.4	per 100 pop.	153.0
Hindu	0.1	Broadband subs per 100 pop.	26.2
Jewish	<0.1	Internet users, % of pop.	61.3

IVORY COAST

Area, sq km	322,460	Capital	Yamoussoukro
Arable as % of total land	9.1	Currency	CFA franc (CFAfr)

People

Population, m	23.7	Life expectancy: men	53.0 yrs
Pop. per sq km	73.5	women	55.9 yrs
Average annual growth		Adult literacy	43.9
in pop. 2015–20, %	2.5	Fertility rate (per woman)	4.8
Pop. aged 0–19, %	53.7	Urban population, %	49.9
Pop. aged 65 and over, %	2.9		per 1,000 pop.
No. of men per 100 women	103.1	Crude birth rate	36.4
Human Development Index	47.4	Crude death rate	11.8

The economy

GDP	$36bn	GDP per head	$1,535
GDP	CFAfr21,562bn	GDP per head in purchasing	
Av. ann. growth in real		power parity (USA=100)	6.4
GDP 2011–16	9.1%	Economic freedom index	62.0

Origins of GDP		**Components of GDP**	
	% of total		% of total
Agriculture	23	Private consumption	56
Industry, of which:	31	Public consumption	11
manufacturing	14	Investment	21
Services	46	Exports	32
		Imports	-20

Structure of employment

	% of total		% of labour force
Agriculture	48.9	Unemployed 2016	2.6
Industry	6.3	Av. ann. rate 2006–16	4.7
Services	44.8		

Energy

	m TOE		
Total output	3.7	Net energy imports as %	
Total consumption	4.4	of energy use	7
Consumption per head			
kg oil equivalent	616		

Inflation and finance

			% change 2016–17
Consumer price			
inflation 2017	0.8%	Monetary base	-3.5
Av. ann. inflation 2012–17	1.2%	Broad money	8.3
Deposit rate, Dec. 2016	6.93%		

Exchange rates

	end 2017		December 2017
CFAfr per $	546.95	Effective rates	2005 = 100
CFAfr per sdr	784.29	– nominal	105.1
CFAfr per €	658.98	– real	100.2

Trade

Principal exports		Principal imports	
	$bn fob		*$bn cif*
Cocoa beans & butter	4.6	Foodstuffs	1.8
Petroleum products	1.5	Capital equip.	1.7
Cashew nuts	0.8	Fuels & lubricants	1.5
Gold	0.8	Raw materials & intermediate goods	1.5
Total incl. others	**10.8**	Total incl. others	**9.1**

Main export destinations		Main origins of imports	
	% of total		*% of total*
Netherlands	11.6	China	16.3
United States	8.9	France	12.8
Belgium	6.1	Nigeria	11.4
France	5.8	India	4.5

Balance of payments, reserves and debt, $bn

Visible exports fob	10.9	Change in reserves	-0.6
Visible imports fob	-7.8	Level of reserves	
Trade balance	3.1	end Dec.	4.9
Invisibles inflows	1.2	No. months of import cover	4.9
Invisibles outflows	-4.3	Official gold holdings, m oz	0.0
Net transfers	-0.4	Foreign debt	11.3
Current account balance	-0.4	– as % of GDP	31.2
– as % of GDP	-1.1	– as % of total exports	91.2
Capital balance	0.3	Debt service ratio	12.5
Overall balance	-0.1		

Health and education

Health spending, % of GDP	5.4	Education spending, % of GDP	4.8
Doctors per 1,000 pop.	...	Enrolment, %: primary	97
Hospital beds per 1,000 pop.	...	secondary	46
Improved-water source access, % of pop.	81.9	tertiary	9

Society

No. of households, m	3.7	Cost of living, Dec. 2017	
Av. no. per household	6.4	New York = 100	61
Marriages per 1,000 pop.	...	Cars per 1,000 pop.	18
Divorces per 1,000 pop.	...	Colour TV households, % with:	
Religion, % of pop.	...	cable	...
		satellite	...
		Telephone lines per 100 pop.	1.2
		Mobile telephone subscribers per 100 pop.	115.8
		Broadband subs per 100 pop.	0.6
		Internet users, % of pop.	26.5

JAPAN

Area, sq km	377,962	Capital	Tokyo
Arable as % of total land	11.5	Currency	Yen (¥)

People

Population, m	127.7	Life expectancy: men	80.7 yrs
Pop. per sq km	337.9	women	87.2 yrs
Average annual growth		Adult literacy	...
in pop. 2015–20, %	-0.2	Fertility rate (per woman)	1.5
Pop. aged 0–19, %	17.7	Urban population, %	91.5
Pop. aged 65 and over, %	26.0		per 1,000 pop.
No. of men per 100 women	95.5	Crude birth rate	8.1
Human Development Index	90.3	Crude death rate	10.8

The economy

GDP	$4,949bn	GDP per head	$38,757
GDP	¥538trn	GDP per head in purchasing	
Av. ann. growth in real		power parity (USA=100)	71.0
GDP 2011–16	1.2%	Economic freedom index	72.3

Origins of GDP		Components of GDP	
	% of total		% of total
Agriculture	1	Private consumption	56
Industry, of which:	30	Public consumption	20
manufacturing	...	Investment	23
Services	69	Exports	16
		Imports	-15

Structure of employment

	% of total		% of labour force
Agriculture	3.5	Unemployed 2016	3.1
Industry	25.6	Av. ann. rate 2006–16	4.1
Services	70.9		

Energy

	m TOE		
Total output	46.1	Net energy imports as %	
Total consumption	472.6	of energy use	93
Consumption per head			
kg oil equivalent	3,429		

Inflation and finance

			% change 2016–17
Consumer price			
inflation 2017	0.5%	Monetary base	12.3
Av. ann. inflation 2012–17	0.8%	Broad money	4.1
Treasury bill rate, Jun. 2017	-0.12%		

Exchange rates

	end 2017		December 2017
¥ per $	112.90	Effective rates	2005 = 100
¥ per sdr	159.84	– nominal	80.8
¥ per €	136.02	– real	73.5

Trade

Principal exports		Principal imports	
	$bn fob		*$bn cif*
Capital equipment	327.0	Industrial supplies	255.2
Industrial supplies	145.5	Capital equipment	180.6
Consumer durable goods	111.4	Food & direct consumer goods	57.7
Consumer non-durable goods	5.7	Consumer durable goods	50.6
Total incl. others	**645.1**	Total incl. others	**607.7**

Main export destinations		Main origins of imports	
	% of total		*% of total*
United States	20.2	China	25.8
China	17.7	United States	11.4
South Korea	7.2	Australia	5.0
Taiwan	6.1	South Korea	4.1

Balance of payments, reserves and aid, $bn

Visible exports fob	635.8	Overall balance	-5.3
Visible imports fob	-584.7	Change in reserves	-16.6
Trade balance	51.2	Level of reserves	
Invisibles inflows	436.5	end Dec.	1,216.5
Invisibles outflows	-274.0	No. months of import cover	17.0
Net transfers	-19.7	Official gold holdings, m oz	24.6
Current account balance	194.0	Aid given	10.4
– as % of GDP	3.9	– as % of GDP	0.2
Capital balance	-273.6		

Health and education

Health spending, % of GDP	10.9	Education spending, % of GDP	3.6
Doctors per 1,000 pop.	2.4	Enrolment, %: primary	99
Hospital beds per 1,000 pop.	13.2	secondary	102
Improved-water source access,		tertiary	63
% of pop.	100		

Society

No. of households, m	53.3	Cost of living, Dec. 2017	
Av. no. per household	2.4	New York = 100	101
Marriages per 1,000 pop.	5.0	Cars per 1,000 pop.	478
Divorces per 1,000 pop.	1.8	Colour TV households, % with:	
Religion, % of pop.		cable	52.7
Non-religious	57.0	satellite	42.3
Buddhist	36.2	Telephone lines per 100 pop.	50.2
Other	5.0	Mobile telephone subscribers	
Christian	1.6	per 100 pop.	130.6
Muslim	0.2	Broadband subs per 100 pop.	31.2
Jewish	<0.1	Internet users, % of pop.	93.2

KENYA

Area, sq km	580,370	Capital	Nairobi
Arable as % of total land	10.2	Currency	Kenyan shilling (KSh)

People

Population, m	48.5	Life expectancy: men	65.0 yrs
Pop. per sq km	83.6	women	69.6 yrs
Average annual growth		Adult literacy	78.7
in pop. 2015–20, %	2.5	Fertility rate (per woman)	3.8
Pop. aged 0–19, %	52.3	Urban population, %	26.1
Pop. aged 65 and over, %	2.6		per 1,000 pop.
No. of men per 100 women	98.8	Crude birth rate	30.7
Human Development Index	55.5	Crude death rate	5.7

The economy

GDP	$71bn	GDP per head	$1,454
GDP	KSh7,159bn	GDP per head in purchasing	
Av. ann. growth in real		power parity (USA=100)	5.5
GDP 2011–16	5.5%	Economic freedom index	54.7

Origins of GDP

Components of GDP

	% of total		% of total
Agriculture	36	Private consumption	78
Industry, of which:	19	Public consumption	14
manufacturing	10	Investment	17
Services	45	Exports	15
		Imports	-23

Structure of employment

	% of total		% of labour force
Agriculture	38.1	Unemployed 2016	11.5
Industry	14.2	Av. ann. rate 2006–16	11.6
Services	47.7		

Energy

	m TOE		
Total output	2.0	Net energy imports as %	
Total consumption	7.5	of energy use	17
Consumption per head			
kg oil equivalent	513		

Inflation and finance

			% change 2016–17
Consumer price			
inflation 2017	8.0%	Monetary base	6.7
Av. ann. inflation 2012–17	6.7%	Broad money	8.9
Treasury bill rate, Mar. 2017	8.63%		

Exchange rates

	end 2017		December 2017
KSh per $	103.23	Effective rates	2005 = 100
KSh per sdr	145.90	– nominal	...
KSh per €	124.37	– real	...

Trade

Principal exports		**Principal imports**	
	$bn fob		*$bn cif*
Tea	1.2	Industrial supplies	5.1
Horticultural products	1.1	Machinery & other capital equip.	3.1
Coffee	0.2	Transport equipment	1.5
		Food & beverages	1.1
Total incl. others	**5.0**	Total incl. others	**13.4**

Main export destinations		**Main origins of imports**	
	% of total		*% of total*
Uganda	10.8	India	23.6
Netherlands	7.5	China	14.4
United States	7.5	United Arab Emirates	6.4
Tanzania	7.0	Saudi Arabia	5.8

Balance of payments, reserves and debt, $bn

Visible exports fob	5.7	Change in reserves	0.1
Visible imports fob	-13.6	Level of reserves	
Trade balance	-7.9	end Dec.	7.6
Invisibles inflows	5.0	No. months of import cover	5.3
Invisibles outflows	-3.6	Official gold holdings, m oz	0.0
Net transfers	3.2	Foreign debt	22.3
Current account balance	-3.3	– as % of GDP	31.7
– as % of GDP	-4.7	– as % of total exports	179.6
Capital balance	4.3	Debt service ratio	8.1
Overall balance	0.4		

Health and education

Health spending, % of GDP	5.2	Education spending, % of GDP	5.3
Doctors per 1,000 pop.	0.2	Enrolment, %: primary	105
Hospital beds per 1,000 pop.	1.4	secondary	...
Improved-water source access,		tertiary	...
% of pop.	63.2		

Society

No. of households, m	10.8	Cost of living, Dec. 2017	
Av. no. per household	4.5	New York = 100	69
Marriages per 1,000 pop.	...	Cars per 1,000 pop.	17
Divorces per 1,000 pop.	...	Colour TV households, % with:	
Religion, % of pop.		cable	2.4
Christian	84.8	satellite	3.4
Muslim	9.7	Telephone lines per 100 pop.	0.2
Other	3.0	Mobile telephone subscribers	
Non-religious	2.5	per 100 pop.	80.4
Hindu	0.1	Broadband subs per 100 pop.	0.3
Jewish	<0.1	Internet users, % of pop.	26.0

MALAYSIA

Area, sq km	330,800	Capital	Kuala Lumpur
Arable as % of total land	2.9	Currency	Malaysian dollar/ringgit (M$)

People

Population, m	31.2	Life expectancy: men	73.4 yrs
Pop. per sq km	94.3	women	77.9 yrs
Average annual growth		Adult literacy	94.6
in pop. 2015–20, %	1.4	Fertility rate (per woman)	2.0
Pop. aged 0–19, %	34.4	Urban population, %	74.8
Pop. aged 65 and over, %	5.9		per 1,000 pop.
No. of men per 100 women	106.9	Crude birth rate	17.0
Human Development Index	78.9	Crude death rate	5.0

The economy

GDP	$297bn	GDP per head	$9,504
GDP	M$1,230bn	GDP per head in purchasing	
Av. ann. growth in real		power parity (USA=100)	47.9
GDP 2011–16	5.1%	Economic freedom index	74.5

Origins of GDP

	% of total
Agriculture	9
Industry, of which:	38
manufacturing	22
Services	53

Components of GDP

	% of total
Private consumption	55
Public consumption	13
Investment	26
Exports	68
Imports	-61

Structure of employment

	% of total		% of labour force
Agriculture	11.4	Unemployed 2016	3.4
Industry	27.5	Av. ann. rate 2006–16	3.2
Services	61.1		

Energy

	m TOE		
Total output	99.9	Net energy imports as %	
Total consumption	79.1	of energy use	-6
Consumption per head			
kg oil equivalent	2,968		

Inflation and finance

			% change 2016–17
Consumer price			
inflation 2017	3.8%	Monetary base	5.1
Av. ann. inflation 2012–17	2.6%	Broad money	5.2
Deposit rate, Sep. 2017	2.93%		

Exchange rates

	end 2017		December 2017
M$ per $	4.06	Effective rates	2005 = 100
M$ per SDR	5.77	– nominal	85.6
M$ per €	4.89	– real	89.9

Trade

Principal exports		Principal imports	
	$bn fob		*$bn cif*
Machinery & transport equip.	81.7	Machinery & transport equip.	76.3
Mineral fuels	26.5	Manufactured goods	21.2
Manufactured goods	16.9	Chemicals	17.7
Chemicals	15.6	Mineral fuels	17.4
Total incl. others	**189.7**	Total incl. others	**168.4**

Main export destinations		Main origins of imports	
	% of total		*% of total*
Singapore	14.5	China	20.4
China	12.5	Singapore	10.4
United States	10.2	Japan	8.2
Japan	8.0	United States	8.0

Balance of payments, reserves and debt, $bn

Visible exports fob	165.3	Change in reserves	-0.8
Visible imports fob	-140.9	Level of reserves	
Trade balance	24.4	end Dec.	94.5
Invisibles inflows	46.7	No. months of import cover	5.7
Invisibles outflows	-59.7	Official gold holdings, m oz	1.2
Net transfers	-4.5	Foreign debt	200.4
Current account balance	6.9	– as % of GDP	67.6
– as % of GDP	2.3	– as % of total exports	93.8
Capital balance	-0.1	Debt service ratio	4.9
Overall balance	3.6		

Health and education

Health spending, % of GDP	4.0	Education spending, % of GDP	4.8
Doctors per 1,000 pop.	1.5	Enrolment, %: primary	103
Hospital beds per 1,000 pop.	1.9	secondary	85
Improved-water source access,		tertiary	44
% of pop.	98.2		

Society

No. of households, m	7.3	Cost of living, Dec. 2017	
Av. no. per household	4.3	New York = 100	60
Marriages per 1,000 pop.	...	Cars per 1,000 pop.	386
Divorces per 1,000 pop.	...	Colour TV households, % with:	
Religion, % of pop.		cable	12.7
Muslim	63.7	satellite	56.2
Buddhist	17.7	Telephone lines per 100 pop.	15.5
Christian	9.4	Mobile telephone subscribers	
Hindu	6.0	per 100 pop.	140.8
Other	2.5	Broadband subs per 100 pop.	8.7
Non-religious	0.7	Internet users, % of pop.	78.8

MEXICO

Area, sq km	1,964,380	Capital	Mexico City
Arable as % of total land	11.8	Currency	Mexican peso (PS)

People

Population, m	127.5	Life expectancy: men	75.0 yrs
Pop. per sq km	64.9	women	79.8 yrs
Average annual growth		Adult literacy	94.5
in pop. 2015–20, %	1.2	Fertility rate (per woman)	2.1
Pop. aged 0–19, %	36.8	Urban population, %	79.6
Pop. aged 65 and over, %	6.5		per 1,000 pop.
No. of men per 100 women	99.2	Crude birth rate	17.6
Human Development Index	76.2	Crude death rate	4.9

The economy

GDP	$1,077bn	GDP per head	$8,446
GDP	PS20,100bn	GDP per head in purchasing	
Av. ann. growth in real		power parity (USA=100)	32.1
GDP 2011–16	2.5%	Economic freedom index	64.8

Origins of GDP		Components of GDP	
	% of total		% of total
Agriculture	4	Private consumption	66
Industry, of which:	33	Public consumption	12
manufacturing	19	Investment	23
Services	63	Exports	38
		Imports	-40

Structure of employment

	% of total		% of labour force
Agriculture	12.9	Unemployed 2016	3.9
Industry	25.7	Av. ann. rate 2006–16	4.5
Services	61.4		

Energy

	m TOE		
Total output	196.0	Net energy imports as %	
Total consumption	192.2	of energy use	-5
Consumption per head			
kg oil equivalent	1,488		

Inflation and finance

			% change 2016–17
Consumer price			
inflation 2017	6.0%	Monetary base	8.8
Av. ann. inflation 2012–17	3.9%	Broad money	11.1
Treasury bill rate, Nov. 2017	7.02%		

Exchange rates

	end 2017		December 2017
PS per $	19.79	Effective rates	2005 = 100
PS per sdr	26.98	– nominal	69.4
PS per €	23.84	– real	81.3

Trade

Principal exports

	$bn fob
Manufactured goods	336.1
Crude oil & products	18.8
Agricultural products	14.7
Mining products	4.4
Total	**373.9**

Principal imports

	$bn cif
Intermediate goods	295.0
Consumer goods	52.0
Capital goods	40.1
Total	**387.1**

Main export destinations

	% of total
United States	80.9
Canada	2.8
China	1.4
Germany	1.1

Main origins of imports

	% of total
United States	49.2
China	19.0
Japan	4.9
Germany	3.8

Balance of payments, reserves and debt, $bn

Visible exports fob	374.3	Change in reserves	0.4
Visible imports fob	-387.4	Level of reserves	
Trade balance	-13.1	end Dec.	178.0
Invisibles inflows	33.4	No. months of import cover	4.7
Invisibles outflows	-69.7	Official gold holdings, m oz	3.9
Net transfers	26.5	Foreign debt	422.7
Current account balance	-22.8	– as % of GDP	39.3
– as % of GDP	-2.1	– as % of total exports	97.2
Capital balance	31.5	Debt service ratio	18.2
Overall balance	-0.1		

Health and education

Health spending, % of GDP	5.9	Education spending, % of GDP	5.3
Doctors per 1,000 pop.	2.2	Enrolment, %: primary	104
Hospital beds per 1,000 pop.	1.5	secondary	97
Improved-water source access,		tertiary	37
% of pop.	96.1		

Society

No. of households, m	32.8	Cost of living, Dec. 2017	
Av. no. per household	3.9	New York = 100	74
Marriages per 1,000 pop.	4.6	Cars per 1,000 pop.	211
Divorces per 1,000 pop.	1.0	Colour TV households, % with:	
Religion, % of pop.		cable	21.4
Christian	95.1	satellite	23.5
Non-religious	4.7	Telephone lines per 100 pop.	16.0
Hindu	<0.1	Mobile telephone subscribers	
Jewish	<0.1	per 100 pop.	87.6
Muslim	<0.1	Broadband subs per 100 pop.	12.6
Other	<0.1	Internet users, % of pop.	59.5

MOROCCO

| Area, sq km | 446,550 | Capital | Rabat |
| Arable as % of total land | 18.2 | Currency | Dirham (Dh) |

People

Population, m	35.3	Life expectancy: men	74.9 yrs
Pop. per sq km	79.1	women	77.3 yrs
Average annual growth		Adult literacy	69.4
in pop. 2015–20, %	1.3	Fertility rate (per woman)	2.4
Pop. aged 0–19, %	36.2	Urban population, %	61.4
Pop. aged 65 and over, %	6.4		per 1,000 pop.
No. of men per 100 women	97.9	Crude birth rate	19.2
Human Development Index	64.7	Crude death rate	5.1

The economy

GDP	$104bn	GDP per head	$2,935
GDP	Dh1,016bn	GDP per head in purchasing	
Av. ann. growth in real		power parity (USA=100)	13.8
GDP 2011–16	3.2%	Economic freedom index	61.9

Origins of GDP		**Components of GDP**	
	% of total		% of total
Agriculture	14	Private consumption	58
Industry, of which:	30	Public consumption	19
manufacturing	18	Investment	33
Services	57	Exports	35
		Imports	-45

Structure of employment

	% of total		% of labour force
Agriculture	37.7	Unemployed 2016	9.4
Industry	19.5	Av. ann. rate 2006–16	9.3
Services	42.8		

Energy

	m TOE		
Total output	1.1	Net energy imports as %	
Total consumption	20.0	of energy use	91
Consumption per head			
kg oil equivalent	553		

Inflation and finance

Consumer price			% change 2016–17
inflation 2017	0.8%	Monetary base	5.3
Av. ann. inflation 2012–17	1.3%	Broad money	5.5
Deposit rate, Oct. 2017	3.11%		

Exchange rates

	end 2017		December 2017
Dh per $	9.33	Effective rates	2005 = 100
Dh per sdr	13.31	– nominal	104.7
Dh per €	11.24	– real	99.8

Trade

Principal exports		Principal imports	
	$bn fob		*$bn cif*
Electric cables & wires	2.4	Capital goods	10.6
Clothing & textiles	2.2	Consumer goods	9.9
Fertilisers & chemicals	2.2	Semi-finished goods	9.4
Phosphoric acid	1.1	Fuel & lubricants	5.6
Total incl. others	**22.9**	Total incl. others	**41.8**

Main export destinations		Main origins of imports	
	% of total		*% of total*
Spain	23.4	Spain	15.7
France	21.1	France	13.2
Italy	4.6	China	9.1
United States	3.5	United States	6.4

Balance of payments, reserves and debt, $bn

Visible exports fob	18.9	Change in reserves	2.1
Visible imports fob	-36.6	Level of reserves	
Trade balance	-17.7	end Dec.	25.1
Invisibles inflows	16.1	No. months of import cover	6.3
Invisibles outflows	-11.1	Official gold holdings, m oz	0.7
Net transfers	8.2	Foreign debt	46.3
Current account balance	-4.5	– as % of GDP	44.5
– as % of GDP	-4.4	– as % of total exports	109.9
Capital balance	6.5	Debt service ratio	9.0
Overall balance	2.9		

Health and education

Health spending, % of GDP	5.5	Education spending, % of GDP	...
Doctors per 1,000 pop.	0.6	Enrolment, %: primary	110
Hospital beds per 1,000 pop.	0.9	secondary	...
Improved-water source access,		tertiary	32
% of pop.	85.4		

Society

No. of households, m	7.5	Cost of living, Dec. 2017	
Av. no. per household	4.7	New York = 100	54
Marriages per 1,000 pop.	...	Cars per 1,000 pop.	72
Divorces per 1,000 pop.	...	Colour TV households, % with:	
Religion, % of pop.		cable	...
Muslim	99.9	satellite	92.0
Christian	<0.1	Telephone lines per 100 pop.	5.9
Hindu	<0.1	Mobile telephone subscribers	
Jewish	<0.1	per 100 pop.	117.7
Non-religious	<0.1	Broadband subs per 100 pop.	3.6
Other	<0.1	Internet users, % of pop.	58.3

NETHERLANDS

Area, sq km[a]	41,540	Capital	Amsterdam
Arable as % of total land	30.7	Currency	Euro (€)

People

Population, m	17.0	Life expectancy: men	80.3 yrs
Pop. per sq km	409.2	women	83.8 yrs
Average annual growth		Adult literacy	...
in pop. 2015–20, %	0.3	Fertility rate (per woman)	1.8
Pop. aged 0–19, %	22.7	Urban population, %	90.6
Pop. aged 65 and over, %	17.9		per 1,000 pop.
No. of men per 100 women	98.9	Crude birth rate	10.6
Human Development Index	92.4	Crude death rate	8.7

The economy

GDP	$778bn	GDP per head	$45,738
GDP	€703bn	GDP per head in purchasing	
Av. ann. growth in real		power parity (USA=100)	88.8
GDP 2011–16	0.9%	Economic freedom index	76.2

Origins of GDP		Components of GDP	
	% of total		% of total
Agriculture	2	Private consumption	44
Industry, of which:	20	Public consumption	25
manufacturing	12	Investment	20
Services	78	Exports	82
		Imports	-71

Structure of employment

	% of total		% of labour force
Agriculture	2.3	Unemployed 2016	6.0
Industry	16.5	Av. ann. rate 2006–16	5.1
Services	81.3		

Energy

	m TOE		
Total output	50.1	Net energy imports as %	
Total consumption	94.8	of energy use	35
Consumption per head			
kg oil equivalent	4,233		

Inflation and finance

			% change 2016–17
Consumer price			
inflation 2017	1.3%	Monetary base	24.7
Av. ann. inflation 2012–17	0.9%	Broad money	4.1
Deposit rate, Oct. 2017	1.27%		

Exchange rates

	end 2017		December 2017
€ per $	0.83	Effective rates	2005 = 100
€ per sdr	1.20	– nominal	100.3
		– real	99.5

Trade

Principal exports

	$bn fob
Machinery & transport equip.	186.6
Chemicals & related products	95.4
Food, drink & tobacco	77.5
Mineral fuels & lubricants	64.8
Total incl. others	**470.2**

Principal imports

	$bn cif
Machinery & transport equip.	173.0
Mineral fuels & lubricants	69.9
Chemicals & related products	67.9
Food, drink & tobacco	52.0
Total incl. others	**412.3**

Main export destinations

	% of total
Germany	24.3
Belgium	10.7
United Kingdom	9.5
France	8.8
EU28	76.0

Main origins of imports

	% of total
Germany	15.3
China	14.1
Belgium	8.5
United States	8.0
EU28	47.1

Balance of payments, reserves and aid, $bn

Visible exports fob	495.4	Overall balance	-3.5
Visible imports fob	-402.9	Change in reserves	-2.3
Trade balance	92.6	Level of reserves	
Invisibles inflows	421.5	end Dec.	35.9
Invisibles outflows	-440.0	No. months of import cover	0.5
Net transfers	-8.5	Official gold holdings, m oz	19.7
Current account balance	65.6	Aid given	5.0
– as % of GDP	8.4	– as % of GDP	0.6
Capital balance	-69.1		

Health and education

Health spending, % of GDP	10.7	Education spending, % of GDP	5.5
Doctors per 1,000 pop.	3.5	Enrolment, %: primary	103
Hospital beds per 1,000 pop.	...	secondary	133
Improved-water source access,		tertiary	80
% of pop.	100		

Society

No. of households, m	7.7	Cost of living, Dec. 2017	
Av. no. per household	2.2	New York = 100	81
Marriages per 1,000 pop.	3.8	Cars per 1,000 pop.	490
Divorces per 1,000 pop.	2.0	Colour TV households, % with:	
Religion, % of pop.		cable	69.3
Christian	50.6	satellite	7.2
Non-religious	42.1	Telephone lines per 100 pop.	39.9
Muslim	6.0	Mobile telephone subscribers	
Other	0.6	per 100 pop.	123.0
Hindu	0.5	Broadband subs per 100 pop.	42.3
Jewish	0.2	Internet users, % of pop.	90.4

a Includes water.

NEW ZEALAND

Area, sq km	267,710	Capital	Wellington
Arable as % of total land	2.2	Currency	New Zealand dollar (NZ$)

People

Population, m	4.7	Life expectancy: men	80.5 yrs
Pop. per sq km	17.6	women	83.7 yrs
Average annual growth		Adult literacy	...
in pop. 2015–20, %	0.9	Fertility rate (per woman)	2.0
Pop. aged 0–19, %	26.9	Urban population, %	86.4
Pop. aged 65 and over, %	14.6		per 1,000 pop.
No. of men per 100 women	96.7	Crude birth rate	13.1
Human Development Index	91.5	Crude death rate	7.0

The economy

GDP	$185bn	GDP per head	$39,443
GDP	NZ$266bn	GDP per head in purchasing	
Av. ann. growth in real		power parity (USA=100)	66.2
GDP 2011–16	2.9%	Economic freedom index	84.2

Origins of GDP

Components of GDP

	% of total		% of total
Agriculture	6	Private consumption	58
Industry, of which:	22	Public consumption	18
manufacturing	...	Investment	23
Services	72	Exports	26
		Imports	-26

Structure of employment

	% of total		% of labour force
Agriculture	6.5	Unemployed 2016	5.1
Industry	20.2	Av. ann. rate 2006–16	5.2
Services	73.3		

Energy

	m TOE		
Total output	16.8	Net energy imports as %	
Total consumption	22.3	of energy use	19
Consumption per head			
kg oil equivalent	4,445		

Inflation and finance

			% change 2016–17
Consumer price			
inflation 2017	1.9%	Monetary base	...
Av. ann. inflation 2012–17	1.0%	Broad money	...
Central bank policy rate, Dec. 2017	1.75%		

Exchange rates

	end 2017		December 2017
NZ$ per $	1.41	Effective rates	2005 = 100
NZ$ per sdr	2.04	– nominal	108.9
NZ$ per €	1.70	– real	106.3

Trade

Principal exports		Principal imports	
	$bn fob		*$bn cif*
Dairy produce	7.8	Machinery & electrical equip.	7.8
Meat	4.1	Transport equipment	6.7
Forestry products	2.9	Mineral fuels	3.0
Wool	0.5	Textiles	1.8
Total incl. others	**33.7**	Total incl. others	**36.1**

Main export destinations		Main origins of imports	
	% of total		*% of total*
China	19.3	China	20.1
Australia	17.0	Australia	12.7
United States	10.9	United States	11.0
Japan	6.2	Japan	7.2

Balance of payments, reserves and aid, $bn

Visible exports fob	33.6	Overall balance	3.1
Visible imports fob	-35.5	Change in reserves	3.1
Trade balance	-1.9	Level of reserves	
Invisibles inflows	20.9	end Dec.	17.8
Invisibles outflows	-23.1	No. months of import cover	3.6
Net transfers	-0.2	Official gold holdings, m oz	0.0
Current account balance	-4.4	Aid given	0.4
– as % of GDP	-2.4	– as % of GDP	0.2
Capital balance	9.5		

Health and education

Health spending, % of GDP	9.3	Education spending, % of GDP	6.3
Doctors per 1,000 pop.	3.1	Enrolment, %: primary	99
Hospital beds per 1,000 pop.	2.7	secondary	114
Improved-water source access,		tertiary	82
% of pop.	100		

Society

No. of households, m	1.5	Cost of living, Dec. 2017	
Av. no. per household	3.1	New York = 100	89
Marriages per 1,000 pop.	4.3	Cars per 1,000 pop.	655
Divorces per 1,000 pop.	1.7	Colour TV households, % with:	
Religion, % of pop.		cable	5.9
Christian	57.0	satellite	40.7
Non-religious	36.6	Telephone lines per 100 pop.	37.8
Other	2.8	Mobile telephone subscribers	
Hindu	2.1	per 100 pop.	124.4
Muslim	1.2	Broadband subs per 100 pop.	32.8
Jewish	0.2	Internet users, % of pop.	88.5

NIGERIA

Area, sq km	923,768	Capital	Abuja
Arable as % of total land	37.3	Currency	Naira (N)

People

Population, m	186.0	Life expectancy: men	53.3 yrs
Pop. per sq km	201.3	women	54.9 yrs
Average annual growth		Adult literacy	59.6
in pop. 2015–20, %	2.6	Fertility rate (per woman)	5.4
Pop. aged 0–19, %	54.4	Urban population, %	48.7
Pop. aged 65 and over, %	2.7		per 1,000 pop.
No. of men per 100 women	102.6	Crude birth rate	38.1
Human Development Index	52.7	Crude death rate	12.0

The economy

GDP	$405bn	GDP per head	$2,180
GDP	N102,575bn	GDP per head in purchasing	
Av. ann. growth in real		power parity (USA=100)	10.1
GDP 2011–16	3.4%	Economic freedom index	58.5

Origins of GDP

Components of GDP

	% of total		% of total
Agriculture	21	Private consumption	78
Industry, of which:	18	Public consumption	6
manufacturing	9	Investment	15
Services	60	Exports	11
		Imports	-10

Structure of employment

	% of total		% of labour force
Agriculture	36.3	Unemployed 2016	7.1
Industry	11.8	Av. ann. rate 2006–16	3.7
Services	51.9		

Energy

	m TOE		
Total output	162.8	Net energy imports as %	
Total consumption	34.5	of energy use	-93
Consumption per head			
kg oil equivalent	763		

Inflation and finance

			% change 2016–17
Consumer price			
inflation 2017	16.5%	Monetary base	10.8
Av. ann. inflation 2012–17	11.5%	Broad money	5.7
Treasury bill rate, Sep. 2017	13.20%		

Exchange rates

	end 2017		December 2017
N per $	306.00	Effective rates	2005 = 100
N per sdr	433.48	– nominal	57.1
N per €	368.67	– real	108.0

Trade

Principal exports		Principal imports	
	$bn fob		*$bn cif*
Crude oil	27.4	Machinery & transport equip.	10.8
Gas	4.7	Mineral fuels	9.9
Food, drink & tobacco	0.5	Food & live animals	4.2
Vegetable products	0.2	Manufactured goods	3.3
Total incl. others	**34.7**	Total incl. others	**38.2**

Main export destinations		Main origins of imports	
	% of total		*% of total*
India	36.1	China	19.8
United States	10.2	United States	8.1
Spain	6.6	Belgium	7.5
China	4.5	United Kingdom	4.3

Balance of payments, reserves and debt, $bn

Visible exports fob	34.6	Change in reserves	-1.3
Visible imports fob	-35.1	Level of reserves	
Trade balance	-0.5	end Dec.	30.0
Invisibles inflows	5.0	No. months of import cover	6.4
Invisibles outflows	-21.6	Official gold holdings, m oz	0.7
Net transfers	19.8	Foreign debt	31.2
Current account balance	2.7	– as % of GDP	7.7
– as % of GDP	0.7	– as % of total exports	53.1
Capital balance	1.9	Debt service ratio	4.3
Overall balance	-1.0		

Health and education

Health spending, % of GDP	3.6	Education spending, % of GDP	...
Doctors per 1,000 pop.	0.4	Enrolment, %: primary	94
Hospital beds per 1,000 pop.	...	secondary	56
Improved-water source access,		tertiary	...
% of pop.	68.5		

Society

No. of households, m	38.3	Cost of living, Dec. 2017	
Av. no. per household	4.9	New York = 100	40
Marriages per 1,000 pop.	...	Cars per 1,000 pop.	16
Divorces per 1,000 pop.	...	Colour TV households, % with:	
Religion, % of pop.		cable	1.9
Christian	49.3	satellite	...
Muslim	48.8	Telephone lines per 100 pop.	0.1
Other	1.4	Mobile telephone subscribers	
Non-religious	0.4	per 100 pop.	83.0
Hindu	<0.1	Broadband subs per 100 pop.	0.1
Jewish	<0.1	Internet users, % of pop.	25.7

NORWAY

Area, sq km	385,178	Capital	Oslo
Arable as % of total land	2.2	Currency	Norwegian krone (Nkr)

People

Population, m	5.3	Life expectancy: men	80.5 yrs
Pop. per sq km	13.8	women	84.3 yrs
Average annual growth		Adult literacy	...
in pop. 2015–20, %	0.9	Fertility rate (per woman)	1.8
Pop. aged 0–19, %	24.2	Urban population, %	81.5
Pop. aged 65 and over, %	16.3		per 1,000 pop.
No. of men per 100 women	101.4	Crude birth rate	12.0
Human Development Index	94.9	Crude death rate	7.9

The economy

GDP	$371bn	GDP per head	$70,014
GDP	Nkr3,117bn	GDP per head in purchasing	
Av. ann. growth in real		power parity (USA=100)	119.7
GDP 2011–16	1.8%	Economic freedom index	74.3

Origins of GDP		**Components of GDP**	
	% of total		% of total
Agriculture	2	Private consumption	46
Industry, of which:	32	Public consumption	24
manufacturing	8	Investment	29
Services	66	Exports	34
		Imports	-33

Structure of employment

	% of total		% of labour force
Agriculture	2.1	Unemployed 2016	4.7
Industry	19.5	Av. ann. rate 2006–16	3.4
Services	78.4		

Energy

	m TOE		
Total output	240.4	Net energy imports as %	
Total consumption	48.2	of energy use	-581
Consumption per head			
kg oil equivalent	5,816		

Inflation and finance

			% change 2016–17
Consumer price			
inflation 2017	1.9%	Monetary base	119.9
Av. ann. inflation 2012–17	2.3%	Broad money	7.3
Central bank policy rate Dec. 2017 0.75%			

Exchange rates

	end 2017		December 2017
Nkr per $	8.21	Effective rates	2005 = 100
Nkr per sdr	11.76	– nominal	81.2
Nkr per €	9.89	– real	84.1

Trade

Principal exports		**Principal imports**	
	$bn fob		*$bn cif*
Mineral fuels & lubricants	47.5	Machinery & transport equip.	30.2
Food & beverages	11.4	Miscellaneous manufactured	
Machinery & transport equip.	10.8	goods	12.4
Manufactured goods	8.6	Manufactured goods	10.6
		Chemicals & mineral products	7.7
Total incl. others	**89.5**	Total incl. others	**75.0**

Main export destinations		**Main origins of imports**	
	% of total		*% of total*
United Kingdom	20.7	Germany	11.6
Germany	14.3	Sweden	11.6
Netherlands	10.6	China	10.7
France	6.9	United States	6.2
EU28	78.2	EU28	62.5

Balance of payments, reserves and aid, $bn

Visible exports fob	88.9	Overall balance	2.8
Visible imports fob	-74.9	Change in reserves	3.0
Trade balance	13.9	Level of reserves	
Invisibles inflows	79.5	end Dec.	60.4
Invisibles outflows	-72.4	No. months of import cover	4.9
Net transfers	-6.7	Official gold holdings, m oz	0.0
Current account balance	14.3	Aid given	4.4
– as % of GDP	3.9	– as % of GDP	1.1
Capital balance	-36.4		

Health and education

Health spending, % of GDP	10.0	Education spending, % of GDP	7.7
Doctors per 1,000 pop.	4.4	Enrolment, %: primary	100
Hospital beds per 1,000 pop.	3.8	secondary	114
Improved-water source access,		tertiary	81
% of pop.	100		

Society

No. of households, m	2.3	Cost of living, Dec. 2017	
Av. no. per household	2.3	New York = 100	107
Marriages per 1,000 pop.	4.5	Cars per 1,000 pop.	489
Divorces per 1,000 pop.	1.9	Colour TV households, % with:	
Religion, % of pop.		cable	44.5
Christian	84.7	satellite	38.5
Non-religious	10.1	Telephone lines per 100 pop.	15.3
Muslim	3.7	Mobile telephone subscribers	
Other	0.9	per 100 pop.	109.0
Hindu	0.5	Broadband subs per 100 pop.	40.4
Jewish	<0.1	Internet users, % of pop.	97.3

PAKISTAN

Area, sq km	796,095	Capital	Islamabad
Arable as % of total land	39.4	Currency	Pakistan rupee (PRs)

People

Population, m	193.2	Life expectancy: men	65.7 yrs
Pop. per sq km	242.7	women	67.8 yrs
Average annual growth		Adult literacy	57.0
in pop. 2015–20, %	1.9	Fertility rate (per woman)	3.4
Pop. aged 0–19, %	45.2	Urban population, %	36.2
Pop. aged 65 and over, %	4.5		per 1,000 pop.
No. of men per 100 women	105.6	Crude birth rate	27.4
Human Development Index	55.0	Crude death rate	7.2

The economy

GDP	$279bn	GDP per head	$1,444
GDP	PRs29,103bn	GDP per head in purchasing	
Av. ann. growth in real		power parity (USA=100)	8.8
GDP 2011–16	4.6%	Economic freedom index	54.4

Origins of GDP		Components of GDP	
	% of total		% of total
Agriculture	25	Private consumption	80
Industry, of which:	19	Public consumption	11
manufacturing	13	Investment	16
Services	56	Exports	9
		Imports	-16

Structure of employment

	% of total		% of labour force
Agriculture	42.3	Unemployed 2016	3.8
Industry	23.6	Av. ann. rate 2006–16	1.3
Services	34.1		

Energy

	m TOE		
Total output	46.0	Net energy imports as %	
Total consumption	70.2	of energy use	24
Consumption per head			
kg oil equivalent	484		

Inflation and finance

Consumer price			% change 2016–17
inflation 2017	4.1%	Monetary base	...
Av. ann. inflation 2012–17	5.5%	Broad money	9.96
Deposit rate, Nov. 2017	4.43%		

Exchange rates

	end 2017		December 2017
PRs per $	110.43	Effective rates	2005 = 100
PRs per sdr	154.34	– nominal	86.7
PRs per €	133.05	– real	119.6

Trade

Principal exports		Principal imports	
	$bn fob		*$bn cif*
Cotton fabrics	2.2	Petroleum products	6.1
Knitwear	2.2	Crude oil	2.4
Rice	1.7	Palm oil	1.8
Cotton yarn & thread	1.0	Telecoms equipment	1.1
Total incl. others	**20.4**	Total incl. others	**46.8**

Main export destinations		Main origins of imports	
	% of total		*% of total*
United States	16.8	China	29.2
China	7.8	United Arab Emirates	13.2
United Kingdom	7.6	Indonesia	4.5
Afghanistan	6.7	United States	4.3

Balance of payments, reserves and debt, $bn

Visible exports fob	21.7	Change in reserves	2.0
Visible imports fob	-42.7	Level of reserves	
Trade balance	-21.0	end Dec.	22.0
Invisibles inflows	5.8	No. months of import cover	4.6
Invisibles outflows	-14.4	Official gold holdings, m oz	2.1
Net transfers	22.7	Foreign debt	72.7
Current account balance	-6.9	– as % of GDP	26.1
– as % of GDP	-2.5	– as % of total exports	153.9
Capital balance	7.5	Debt service ratio	8.9
Overall balance	1.4		

Health and education

Health spending, % of GDP	2.7	Education spending, % of GDP	2.8
Doctors per 1,000 pop.	1.0	Enrolment, %: primary	98
Hospital beds per 1,000 pop.	0.6	secondary	46
Improved-water source access,		tertiary	10
% of pop.	91.4		

Society

No. of households, m	28.1	Cost of living, Dec. 2017	
Av. no. per household	6.9	New York = 100	46
Marriages per 1,000 pop.	...	Cars per 1,000 pop.	14
Divorces per 1,000 pop.	...	Colour TV households, % with:	
Religion, % of pop.		cable	1.3
Muslim	96.4	satellite	15.4
Hindu	1.9	Telephone lines per 100 pop.	1.6
Christian	1.6	Mobile telephone subscribers	
Jewish	<0.1	per 100 pop.	70.6
Non-religious	<0.1	Broadband subs per 100 pop.	0.9
Other	<0.1	Internet users, % of pop.	15.5

PERU

Area, sq km	1,285,216	Capital	Lima
Arable as % of total land	3.2	Currency	Nuevo Sol (new Sol)

People

Population, m	31.8	Life expectancy: men	72.7 yrs
Pop. per sq km	24.7	women	78.0 yrs
Average annual growth		Adult literacy	94.2
in pop. 2015–20, %	1.2	Fertility rate (per woman)	2.4
Pop. aged 0–19, %	36.7	Urban population, %	77.5
Pop. aged 65 and over, %	6.8		per 1,000 pop.
No. of men per 100 women	99.8	Crude birth rate	18.7
Human Development Index	74.0	Crude death rate	5.7

The economy

GDP	$195bn	GDP per head	$6,146
GDP	New Soles 660bn	GDP per head in purchasing	
Av. ann. growth in real		power parity (USA=100)	22.1
GDP 2011–16	4.3%	Economic freedom index	68.7

Origins of GDP		**Components of GDP**	
	% of total		% of total
Agriculture	8	Private consumption	65
Industry, of which:	33	Public consumption	13
manufacturing	14	Investment	22
Services	60	Exports	22
		Imports	-22

Structure of employment

	% of total		% of labour force
Agriculture	28.4	Unemployed 2016	6.6
Industry	16.2	Av. ann. rate 2006–16	7.1
Services	55.4		

Energy

	m TOE		
Total output	26.6	Net energy imports as %	
Total consumption	27.2	of energy use	-15
Consumption per head			
kg oil equivalent	768		

Inflation and finance

			% change 2016–17
Consumer price			
inflation 2017	2.8%	Monetary base	1.6
Av. ann. inflation 2012–17	3.2%	Broad money	-8.6
Deposit rate, Mar. 2017	2.71%		

Exchange rates

	end 2017		December 2017
New Soles per $	3.24	Effective rates	2005 = 100
New Soles per sdr	4.59	– nominal	...
New Soles per €	3.90	– real	...

Trade

Principal exports		**Principal imports**	
	$bn fob		*$bn cif*
Copper	10.2	Intermediate goods	15.1
Gold	7.4	Capital goods	11.1
Zinc	1.5	Consumer goods	8.6
Fishmeal	1.3		
Total incl. others	**37.0**	Total incl. others	**35.1**

Main export destinations		**Main origins of imports**	
	% of total		*% of total*
China	22.9	China	24.5
United States	16.8	United States	20.9
Switzerland	6.9	Brazil	6.3
Canada	4.6	Mexico	5.0

Balance of payments, reserves and debt, $bn

Visible exports fob	37.0	Change in reserves	0.2
Visible imports fob	-34.9	Level of reserves	
Trade balance	2.1	end Dec.	61.8
Invisibles inflows	7.2	No. months of import cover	13.9
Invisibles outflows	-18.6	Official gold holdings, m oz	1.1
Net transfers	4.0	Foreign debt	69.5
Current account balance	-5.3	– as % of GDP	35.6
– as % of GDP	-2.7	– as % of total exports	147.6
Capital balance	6.5	Debt service ratio	12.6
Overall balance	0.2		

Health and education

Health spending, % of GDP	5.3	Education spending, % of GDP	3.8
Doctors per 1,000 pop.	1.1	Enrolment, %: primary	103
Hospital beds per 1,000 pop.	1.6	secondary	98
Improved-water source access,		tertiary	...
% of pop.	86.7		

Society

No. of households, m	7.8	Cost of living, Dec. 2017	
Av. no. per household	4.1	New York = 100	68
Marriages per 1,000 pop.	2.8	Cars per 1,000 pop.	47
Divorces per 1,000 pop.	0.4	Colour TV households, % with:	
Religion, % of pop.		cable	32.5
Christian	95.5	satellite	0.2
Non-religious	3.0	Telephone lines per 100 pop.	9.7
Other	1.5	Mobile telephone subscribers	
Hindu	<0.1	per 100 pop.	116.2
Jewish	<0.1	Broadband subs per 100 pop.	6.7
Muslim	<0.1	Internet users, % of pop.	45.5

PHILIPPINES

Area, sq km	300,000	Capital	Manila
Arable as % of total land	18.7	Currency	Philippine peso (P)

People

Population, m	103.3	Life expectancy: men	66.0 yrs
Pop. per sq km	344.3	women	72.9 yrs
Average annual growth		Adult literacy	96.4
in pop. 2015–20, %	1.5	Fertility rate (per woman)	2.9
Pop. aged 0–19, %	42.3	Urban population, %	46.5
Pop. aged 65 and over, %	4.6		per 1,000 pop.
No. of men per 100 women	101.5	Crude birth rate	22.9
Human Development Index	68.2	Crude death rate	6.5

The economy

GDP	$305bn	GDP per head	$2,952
GDP	P14,481bn	GDP per head in purchasing	
Av. ann. growth in real		power parity (USA=100)	13.5
GDP 2011–16	6.6%	Economic freedom index	65.0

Origins of GDP		**Components of GDP**	
	% of total		% of total
Agriculture	10	Private consumption	74
Industry, of which:	31	Public consumption	11
manufacturing	20	Investment	24
Services	60	Exports	28
		Imports	-37

Structure of employment

	% of total		% of labour force
Agriculture	27.0	Unemployed 2016	2.7
Industry	17.5	Av. ann. rate 2006–16	3.6
Services	55.5		

Energy

	m TOE		
Total output	12.4	Net energy imports as %	
Total consumption	38.9	of energy use	46
Consumption per head			
kg oil equivalent	476		

Inflation and finance

Consumer price			% change 2016–17
inflation 2017	3.2%	Monetary base	13.7
Av. ann. inflation 2012–17	2.7%	Broad money	14.6
Treasury bill rate, Mar. 2017	2.08%		

Exchange rates

	end 2017		December 2017
P per $	49.92	Effective rates	2005 = 100
P per sdr	71.32	– nominal	96.9
P per €	60.14	– real	104.4

Trade

Principal exports

	$bn fob
Electrical & electronic equip.	29.3
Machinery & transport equip.	4.3
Agricultural products	3.1
Mineral products	2.4
Total incl. others	**57.4**

Principal imports

	$bn cif
Raw materials & intermediate goods	31.8
Capital goods	28.6
Consumer goods	14.7
Mineral fuels & lubricants	8.0
Total incl. others	**89.4**

Main export destinations

	% of total
Japan	20.3
United States	15.1
Hong Kong	11.5
China	10.8

Main origins of imports

	% of total
China	17.8
Japan	11.4
United States	8.6
Thailand	7.5

Balance of payments, reserves and debt, $bn

Visible exports fob	42.7	Change in reserves	0.0
Visible imports fob	-78.3	Level of reserves	
Trade balance	-35.5	end Dec.	80.7
Invisibles inflows	40.8	No. months of import cover	8.8
Invisibles outflows	-31.1	Official gold holdings, m oz	6.3
Net transfers	24.7	Foreign debt	77.3
Current account balance	-1.2	– as % of GDP	25.4
– as % of GDP	-0.4	– as % of total exports	67.4
Capital balance	-0.1	Debt service ratio	9.2
Overall balance	-1.0		

Health and education

Health spending, % of GDP	4.4	Education spending, % of GDP	...
Doctors per 1,000 pop.	...	Enrolment, %: primary	113
Hospital beds per 1,000 pop.	...	secondary	88
Improved-water source access,		tertiary	35
% of pop.	91.8		

Society

No. of households, m	22.9	Cost of living, Dec. 2017	
Av. no. per household	4.5	New York = 100	59
Marriages per 1,000 pop.	...	Cars per 1,000 pop.	33
Divorces per 1,000 pop.	...	Colour TV households, % with:	
Religion, % of pop.		cable	52.5
Christian	92.6	satellite	0.6
Muslim	5.5	Telephone lines per 100 pop.	3.7
Other	1.7	Mobile telephone subscribers	
Non-religious	0.1	per 100 pop.	109.4
Hindu	<0.1	Broadband subs per 100 pop.	5.5
Jewish	<0.1	Internet users, % of pop.	55.5

POLAND

Area, sq km	312,680	Capital	Warsaw
Arable as % of total land	35.6	Currency	Zloty (Zl)

People

Population, m	38.2	Life expectancy: men	73.9 yrs
Pop. per sq km	122.2	women	81.7 yrs
Average annual growth		Adult literacy	99.8
in pop. 2015–20, %	-0.2	Fertility rate (per woman)	1.3
Pop. aged 0–19, %	20.2	Urban population, %	60.2
Pop. aged 65 and over, %	15.6		per 1,000 pop.
No. of men per 100 women	93.4	Crude birth rate	9.1
Human Development Index	85.5	Crude death rate	10.5

The economy

GDP	$471bn	GDP per head	$12,336
GDP	Zl1,859bn	GDP per head in purchasing	
Av. ann. growth in real		power parity (USA=100)	47.7
GDP 2011–16	2.6%	Economic freedom index	68.5

Origins of GDP		Components of GDP	
	% of total		% of total
Agriculture	3	Private consumption	59
Industry, of which:	34	Public consumption	18
manufacturing	20	Investment	20
Services	64	Exports	52
		Imports	-48

Structure of employment

	% of total		% of labour force
Agriculture	10.6	Unemployed 2016	6.2
Industry	31.4	Av. ann. rate 2006–16	9.2
Services	58.0		

Energy

	m TOE		
Total output	57.9	Net energy imports as %	
Total consumption	98.0	of energy use	29
Consumption per head			
kg oil equivalent	2,490		

Inflation and finance

			% change 2016–17
Consumer price			
inflation 2017	2.0%	Monetary base	6.8
Av. ann. inflation 2012–17	0.3%	Broad money	4.7
Central bank policy rate, Dec. 2017	1.47%		

Exchange rates

	end 2017		December 2017
			2005 = 100
Zl per $	3.48	Effective rates	99.0
Zl per sdr	5.02	– nominal	99.0
Zl per €	4.19	– real	95.5

Trade

Principal exports	
	$bn fob
Machinery & transport equip.	77.1
Manufactured goods	37.5
Foodstuffs & live animals	22.2
Total incl. others	**203.7**

Principal imports	
	$bn cif
Machinery & transport equip.	70.4
Manufactured goods	35.2
Chemicals & mineral products	29.0
Total incl. others	**198.4**

Main export destinations	
	% of total
Germany	27.2
United Kingdom	6.6
Czech Republic	6.5
France	5.4
EU28	79.6

Main origins of imports	
	% of total
Germany	28.1
China	7.8
Netherlands	5.9
Russia	5.7
EU28	72.1

Balance of payments, reserves and debt, $bn

Visible exports fob	196.3	Change in reserves	19.4
Visible imports fob	-193.1	Level of reserves	
Trade balance	3.3	end Dec.	114.3
Invisibles inflows	62.5	No. months of import cover	5.3
Invisibles outflows	-65.6	Official gold holdings, m oz	3.3
Net transfers	-1.5	Foreign debt	227.4
Current account balance	-1.4	– as % of GDP	48.3
– as % of GDP	-0.3	– as % of total exports	86.2
Capital balance	28.1	Debt service ratio	11.6
Overall balance	22.7		

Health and education

Health spending, % of GDP	6.3	Education spending, % of GDP	4.9
Doctors per 1,000 pop.	2.3	Enrolment, %: primary	110
Hospital beds per 1,000 pop.	6.6	secondary	107
Improved-water source access,		tertiary	67
% of pop.	98.3		

Society

No. of households, m	14.2	Cost of living, Dec. 2017	
Av. no. per household	2.7	New York = 100	62
Marriages per 1,000 pop.	5.1	Cars per 1,000 pop.	542
Divorces per 1,000 pop.	1.7	Colour TV households, % with:	
Religion, % of pop.		cable	33.8
Christian	94.3	satellite	62.8
Non-religious	5.6	Telephone lines per 100 pop.	21.3
Hindu	<0.1	Mobile telephone subscribers	
Jewish	<0.1	per 100 pop.	138.7
Muslim	<0.1	Broadband subs per 100 pop.	19.2
Other	<0.1	Internet users, % of pop.	73.3

PORTUGAL

Area, sq km	92,225	Capital	Lisbon
Arable as % of total land	12.4	Currency	Euro (€)

People

Population, m	10.4	Life expectancy: men	78.6 yrs
Pop. per sq km	112.8	women	84.3 yrs
Average annual growth		Adult literacy	...
in pop. 2015–20, %	-0.4	Fertility rate (per woman)	1.2
Pop. aged 0–19, %	19.3	Urban population, %	64.1
Pop. aged 65 and over, %	20.7		per 1,000 pop.
No. of men per 100 women	90.0	Crude birth rate	7.5
Human Development Index	84.3	Crude death rate	10.8

The economy

GDP	$205bn	GDP per head	$19,737
GDP	€185bn	GDP per head in purchasing	
Av. ann. growth in real		power parity (USA=100)	49.9
GDP 2011–16	-0.2%	Economic freedom index	63.4

Origins of GDP		**Components of GDP**	
	% of total		% of total
Agriculture	2	Private consumption	66
Industry, of which:	22	Public consumption	18
manufacturing	14	Investment	16
Services	76	Exports	40
		Imports	-39

Structure of employment

	% of total		% of labour force
Agriculture	6.9	Unemployed 2016	11.1
Industry	24.5	Av. ann. rate 2006–16	11.4
Services	68.6		

Energy

	m TOE		
Total output	5.7	Net energy imports as %	
Total consumption	25.6	of energy use	77
Consumption per head			
kg oil equivalent	2,132		

Inflation and finance

Consumer price			% change 2016–17
inflation 2017	1.6%	Monetary base	24.7
Av. ann. inflation 2012–17	0.6%	Broad money	4.1
Deposit rate, Oct. 2017	0.22%		

Exchange rates

	end 2017		December 2017
€ per $	0.83	Effective rates	2005 = 100
€ per sdr	1.20	– nominal	100.1
		– real	98.8

Trade

Principal exports		Principal imports	
	$bn fob		*$bn cif*
Machinery & transport equip.	14.8	Machinery & transport equip.	20.7
Food, drink & tobacco	6.2	Chemicals & related products	9.5
Chemicals & related products	5.0	Food, drink & tobacco	9.3
Mineral fuels & lubricants	3.5	Mineral fuels & lubricants	6.8
Total incl. others	**55.4**	Total incl. others	**67.8**

Main export destinations		Main origins of imports	
	% of total		*% of total*
Spain	25.9	Spain	32.9
France	12.6	Germany	13.4
Germany	11.7	France	7.7
United Kingdom	7.1	Italy	5.5
EU28	75.1	EU28	77.8

Balance of payments, reserves and debt, $bn

Visible exports fob	54.3	Overall balance	10.1
Visible imports fob	-65.0	Change in reserves	5.6
Trade balance	-10.7	Level of reserves	
Invisibles inflows	39.0	end Dec.	25.0
Invisibles outflows	-29.0	No. months of import cover	3.2
Net transfers	1.8	Official gold holdings, m oz	12.3
Current account balance	1.2	Aid given	0.3
– as % of GDP	0.6	– as % of GDP	0.2
Capital balance	8.8		

Health and education

Health spending, % of GDP	9.0	Education spending, % of GDP	5.1
Doctors per 1,000 pop.	4.4	Enrolment, %: primary	105
Hospital beds per 1,000 pop.	3.4	secondary	118
Improved-water source access,		tertiary	63
% of pop.	100		

Society

No. of households, m	4.1	Cost of living, Dec. 2017	
Av. no. per household	2.5	New York = 100	66
Marriages per 1,000 pop.	3.1	Cars per 1,000 pop.	442
Divorces per 1,000 pop.	2.2	Colour TV households, % with:	
Religion, % of pop.		cable	56.1
Christian	93.8	satellite	20.1
Non-religious	4.4	Telephone lines per 100 pop.	46.2
Other	1.0	Mobile telephone subscribers	
Muslim	0.6	per 100 pop.	111.6
Hindu	0.1	Broadband subs per 100 pop.	32.5
Jewish	<0.1	Internet users, % of pop.	70.4

ROMANIA

Area, sq km	238,391	Capital	Bucharest
Arable as % of total land	38.1	Currency	Leu (RON)

People

Population, m	19.8	Life expectancy: men	72.2 yrs
Pop. per sq km	83.1	women	79.1 yrs
Average annual growth		Adult literacy	...
in pop. 2015–20, %	-0.5	Fertility rate (per woman)	1.5
Pop. aged 0–19, %	20.9	Urban population, %	53.9
Pop. aged 65 and over, %	17.0		per 1,000 pop.
No. of men per 100 women	94.0	Crude birth rate	9.5
Human Development Index	80.2	Crude death rate	13.0

The economy

GDP	$188bn	GDP per head	$9,485
GDP	RON762bn	GDP per head in purchasing	
Av. ann. growth in real		power parity (USA=100)	38.6
GDP 2011–16	3.2%	Economic freedom index	69.4

Origins of GDP		Components of GDP	
	% of total		% of total
Agriculture	4	Private consumption	62
Industry, of which:	32	Public consumption	14
manufacturing	21	Investment	25
Services	63	Exports	41
		Imports	-42

Structure of employment

	% of total		% of labour force
Agriculture	23.1	Unemployed 2016	5.9
Industry	29.9	Av. ann. rate 2006–16	6.7
Services	47.0		

Energy

	m TOE		
Total output	27.9	Net energy imports as %	
Total consumption	32.1	of energy use	17
Consumption per head			
kg oil equivalent	1,592		

Inflation and finance

			% change 2016–17
Consumer price			
inflation 2017	1.3%	Monetary base	14.5
Av. ann. inflation 2012–17	0.8%	Broad money	11.6
Deposit rate, Oct. 2017	0.92%		

Exchange rates

	end 2017		December 2017
			2005 = 100
Lei per $	3.89	Effective rates	
Lei per sdr	5.55	– nominal	94.8
Lei per €	4.69	– real	96.3

Trade

Principal exports		Principal imports	
	$bn fob		*$bn cif*
Machinery & transport equip.	29.9	Machinery & transport equip.	28.5
Basic metals & products	5.0	Chemical products	7.4
Textiles & apparel	4.5	Textiles & products	5.2
Minerals, fuels & lubricants	2.3	Minerals, fuels & lubricants	4.6
Total incl. others	**63.6**	Total incl. others	**74.6**

Main export destinations		Main origins of imports	
	% of total		*% of total*
Germany	21.5	Germany	20.5
Italy	11.6	Italy	10.3
France	7.2	Hungary	7.5
Hungary	5.2	France	5.5
EU28	75.1	EU28	77.1

Balance of payments, reserves and debt, $bn

Visible exports fob	57.7	Change in reserves	1.3
Visible imports fob	-68.0	Level of reserves	
Trade balance	-10.3	end Dec.	40.0
Invisibles inflows	23.0	No. months of import cover	5.5
Invisibles outflows	-19.5	Official gold holdings, m oz	3.3
Net transfers	2.8	Foreign debt	95.9
Current account balance	-4.0	– as % of GDP	51.1
– as % of GDP	-2.1	– as % of total exports	113.8
Capital balance	5.6	Debt service ratio	23.1
Overall balance	2.6		

Health and education

Health spending, % of GDP	5.0	Education spending, % of GDP	3.1
Doctors per 1,000 pop.	2.4	Enrolment, %: primary	89
Hospital beds per 1,000 pop.	6.3	secondary	89
Improved-water source access,		tertiary	48
% of pop.	100		

Society

No. of households, m	7.5	Cost of living, Dec. 2017	
Av. no. per household	2.6	New York = 100	48
Marriages per 1,000 pop.	6.7	Cars per 1,000 pop.	260
Divorces per 1,000 pop.	1.5	Colour TV households, % with:	
Religion, % of pop.		cable	45.9
Christian	99.5	satellite	37.4
Muslim	0.3	Telephone lines per 100 pop.	20.8
Non-religious	0.1	Mobile telephone subscribers	
Hindu	<0.1	per 100 pop.	115.8
Jewish	<0.1	Broadband subs per 100 pop.	22.5
Other	<0.1	Internet users, % of pop.	59.5

RUSSIA

Area, sq km	17,098,246	Capital	Moscow
Arable as % of total land	7.5	Currency	Rouble (Rb)

People

Population, m	144.0	Life expectancy: men	65.6 yrs
Pop. per sq km	8.4	women	76.8 yrs
Average annual growth		Adult literacy	99.7
in pop. 2015–20, %	0.0	Fertility rate (per woman)	...
Pop. aged 0–19, %	21.2	Urban population, %	74.2
Pop. aged 65 and over, %	13.5		per 1,000 pop.
No. of men per 100 women	86.8	Crude birth rate	12.4
Human Development Index	80.4	Crude death rate	13.6

The economy

GDP	$1,281bn	GDP per head	$8,898
GDP	Rb85,918bn	GDP per head in purchasing	
Av. ann. growth in real		power parity (USA=100)	46.6
GDP 2011–16	0.6%	Economic freedom index	58.2

Origins of GDP		**Components of GDP**	
	% of total		% of total
Agriculture	5	Private consumption	53
Industry, of which:	32	Public consumption	18
manufacturing	14	Investment	23
Services	63	Exports	26
		Imports	-21

Structure of employment

	% of total		% of labour force
Agriculture	6.7	Unemployed 2016	5.6
Industry	26.9	Av. ann. rate 2006–16	6.3
Services	66.3		

Energy

	m TOE		
Total output	1,410.7	Net energy imports as %	
Total consumption	747.1	of energy use	-84
Consumption per head			
kg oil equivalent	4,943		

Inflation and finance

Consumer price			% change 2016–17
inflation 2017	3.7%	Monetary base	23.7
Av. ann. inflation 2012–17	8.1%	Broad money	7.4
Money market rate, Jun. 2017	9.11%		

Exchange rates

	end 2017		December 2017
Rb per $	57.60	Effective rates	2005 = 100
Rb per sdr	82.91	– nominal	68.7
Rb per €	69.40	– real	90.5

Trade

Principal exports		Principal imports	
	$bn fob		*$bn cif*
Fuels	169.0	Machinery & equipment	86.3
Ores & metals	38.0	Chemicals	33.8
Machinery & equipment	24.3	Food & agricultural products	24.9
Chemicals	20.8	Metals	11.8
Total incl. others	**285.8**	Total incl. others	**182.3**

Main export destinations		Main origins of imports	
	% of total		*% of total*
Netherlands	10.2	China	20.9
China	9.8	Germany	10.6
Germany	7.4	United States	6.1
Belarus	4.9	Belarus	5.2
EU28	45.8	EU28	38.2

Balance of payments, reserves and debt, $bn

Visible exports fob	281.8	Change in reserves	9.0
Visible imports fob	-191.6	Level of reserves	
Trade balance	90.3	end Dec.	377.1
Invisibles inflows	91.1	No. months of import cover	13.2
Invisibles outflows	-150.6	Official gold holdings, m oz	51.9
Net transfers	-6.3	Foreign debt	524.7
Current account balance	24.4	– as % of GDP	41.0
– as % of GDP	1.9	– as % of total exports	138.2
Capital balance	-11.6	Debt service ratio	18.8
Overall balance	8.2		

Health and education

Health spending, % of GDP	5.6	Education spending, % of GDP	...
Doctors per 1,000 pop.	4.0	Enrolment, %: primary	102
Hospital beds per 1,000 pop.	8.5	secondary	105
Improved-water source access,		tertiary	82
% of pop.	96.9		

Society

No. of households, m	56.5	Cost of living, Dec. 2017	
Av. no. per household	2.5	New York = 100	66
Marriages per 1,000 pop.	8.5	Cars per 1,000 pop.	307
Divorces per 1,000 pop.	4.7	Colour TV households, % with:	
Religion, % of pop.		cable	32.9
Christian	73.3	satellite	24.7
Non-religious	16.2	Telephone lines per 100 pop.	22.4
Muslim	10.0	Mobile telephone subscribers	
Jewish	0.2	per 100 pop.	159.2
Hindu	<0.1	Broadband subs per 100 pop.	19.1
Other	<0.1	Internet users, % of pop.	73.1

SAUDI ARABIA

Area, sq km	2,149,690	Capital	Riyadh
Arable as % of total land	1.6	Currency	Riyal (SR)

People

Population, m	32.3	Life expectancy: men	73.5 yrs
Pop. per sq km	15.0	women	76.6 yrs
Average annual growth		Adult literacy	94.4
in pop. 2015–20, %	1.9	Fertility rate (per woman)	2.5
Pop. aged 0–19, %	33.4	Urban population, %	83.4
Pop. aged 65 and over, %	3.1		per 1,000 pop.
No. of men per 100 women	130.9	Crude birth rate	19.1
Human Development Index	84.7	Crude death rate	3.6

The economy

GDP	$645bn	GDP per head	$19,967
GDP	SR2,419bn	GDP per head in purchasing	
Av. ann. growth in real		power parity (USA=100)	94
GDP 2011–16	3.5%	Economic freedom index	59.6

Origins of GDP		Components of GDP	
	% of total		% of total
Agriculture	3	Private consumption	43
Industry, of which:	43	Public consumption	26
manufacturing	13	Investment	31
Services	54	Exports	31
		Imports	-30

Structure of employment

	% of total		% of labour force
Agriculture	6.0	Unemployed 2016	5.7
Industry	22.5	Av. ann. rate 2006–16	5.6
Services	71.5		

Energy

	m TOE		
Total output	719.9	Net energy imports as %	
Total consumption	268.8	of energy use	-192
Consumption per head			
kg oil equivalent	6,937		

Inflation and finance

			% change 2016–17
Consumer price			
inflation 2017	-0.9%	Monetary base	0.2
Av. ann. inflation 2012–17	1.6%	Broad money	1.4
Treasury bill rate, Nov. 2017	1.37%		

Exchange rates

	end 2017		December 2017
SR per $	3.75	Effective rates	2005 = 100
SR per sdr	5.31	– nominal	116.7
SR per €	4.52	– real	118.5

Trade

Principal exports		Principal imports	
	$bn fob		*$bn cif*
Crude oil	108.7	Machinery & transport equip.	59.5
Refined petroleum products	27.8	Foodstuffs	22.7
		Chemical & metal products	12.9
Total incl. others	**183.6**	Total incl. others	**136.3**

Main export destinations		Main origins of imports	
	% of total		*% of total*
Japan	14.1	United States	14.9
China	13.9	China	14.4
India	10.3	Germany	6.5
South Korea	9.7	United Arab Emirates	5.5

Balance of payments, reserves and aid, $bn

Visible exports fob	183.6	Change in reserves	-79.7
Visible imports fob	-127.8	Level of reserves	
Trade balance	55.8	end Dec.	547.3
Invisibles inflows	41.2	No. months of import cover	31.8
Invisibles outflows	-78.5	Official gold holdings, m oz	10.4
Net transfers	-42.3	Foreign debt	189.3
Current account balance	-23.8	– as % of GDP	29.4
– as % of GDP	-3.7	– as % of total exports	84.2
Capital balance	9.8	Debt service ratio	6.2
Overall balance	-80.3		

Health and education

Health spending, % of GDP	5.8	Education spending, % of GDP	...
Doctors per 1,000 pop.	2.6	Enrolment, %: primary	116
Hospital beds per 1,000 pop.	2.7	secondary	117
Improved-water source access,		tertiary	67
% of pop.	97.0		

Society

No. of households, m	5.0	Cost of living, Dec. 2017	
Av. no. per household	6.5	New York = 100	52
Marriages per 1,000 pop.	...	Cars per 1,000 pop.	136
Divorces per 1,000 pop.	...	Colour TV households, % with:	
Religion, % of pop.		cable	0.3
Muslim	93.0	satellite	99.5
Christian	4.4	Telephone lines per 100 pop.	11.3
Hindu	1.1	Mobile telephone subscribers	
Other	0.9	per 100 pop.	148.5
Non-religious	0.7	Broadband subs per 100 pop.	10.2
Jewish	<0.1	Internet users, % of pop.	73.8

SINGAPORE

Area, sq km	719	Capital	Singapore
Arable as % of total land	0.8	Currency	Singapore dollar (S$)

People

Population, m	5.6	Life expectancy: men	81.3 yrs
Pop. per sq km	7,788.6	women	85.3 yrs
Average annual growth		Adult literacy	97.0
in pop. 2015–20, %	1.4	Fertility rate (per woman)	1.3
Pop. aged 0–19, %	21.9	Urban population, %	100.0
Pop. aged 65 and over, %	11.7		per 1,000 pop.
No. of men per 100 women	97.6	Crude birth rate	8.7
Human Development Index	92.5	Crude death rate	5.1

The economy

GDP	$310bn	GDP per head	$55,313
GDP	S$428bn	GDP per head in purchasing	
Av. ann. growth in real		power parity (USA=100)	154.3
GDP 2011–16	3.3%	Economic freedom index	88.8

Origins of GDP		Components of GDP	
	% of total		% of total
Agriculture	0	Private consumption	38
Industry, of which:	26	Public consumption	11
manufacturing	20	Investment	25
Services	74	Exports	172
		Imports	-146

Structure of employment

	% of total		% of labour force
Agriculture	0.1	Unemployed 2016	4.1
Industry	16.3	Av. ann. rate 2006–16	4.1
Services	83.6		

Energy

	m TOE		
Total output	0.4	Net energy imports as %	
Total consumption	86.8	of energy use	98
Consumption per head			
kg oil equivalent	5,122		

Inflation and finance

		% change 2016–17	
Consumer price			
inflation 2017	0.6%	Monetary base	3.2
Av. ann. inflation 2012–17	0.6%	Broad money	5.4
Money market rate, Nov. 2017	0.86%		

Exchange rates

	end 2017		December 2017
S$ per $	1.34	Effective rates	2005 = 100
S$ per sdr	1.91	– nominal	111.5
S$ per €	1.61	– real	108.3

Trade

Principal exports

	$bn fob
Mineral fuels	50.1
Chemicals & chemical products	46.7
Electronic components & parts	46.5
Manufactured products	31.1
Total incl. others	**337.8**

Principal imports

	$bn cif
Machinery & transport equip.	139.9
Mineral fuels	51.1
Misc. manufactured articles	26.9
Manufactured products	19.2
Total incl. others	**292.0**

Main export destinations

	% of total
China	12.5
Hong Kong	12.2
Malaysia	10.3
Indonesia	8.6

Main origins of imports

	% of total
China	13.8
Malaysia	11.0
United States	10.4
Taiwan	7.9

Balance of payments, reserves and debt, $bn

Visible exports fob	363.0	Change in reserves	-0.8
Visible imports fob	-277.6	Level of reserves	
Trade balance	85.5	end Dec.	251.1
Invisibles inflows	229.9	No. months of import cover	5.7
Invisibles outflows	-250.5	Official gold holdings, m oz	4.1
Net transfers	-6.1	Foreign debt	504.2
Current account balance	58.8	– as % of GDP	162.8
– as % of GDP	19.0	– as % of total exports	85.0
Capital balance	-60.6	Debt service ratio	9.0
Overall balance	-1.8		

Health and education

Health spending, % of GDP	4.3	Education spending, % of GDP	2.9
Doctors per 1,000 pop.	2.3	Enrolment, %: primary	101
Hospital beds per 1,000 pop.	2.4	secondary	108
Improved-water source access,		tertiary	...
% of pop.	100		

Society

No. of households, m	1.6	Cost of living, Dec. 2017	
Av. no. per household	3.5	New York = 100	116
Marriages per 1,000 pop.	7.1	Cars per 1,000 pop.	113
Divorces per 1,000 pop.	1.8	Colour TV households, % with:	
Religion, % of pop.		cable	55.8
Buddhist	33.9	satellite	...
Christian	18.2	Telephone lines per 100 pop.	35.5
Non-religious	16.4	Mobile telephone subscribers	
Muslim	14.3	per 100 pop.	150.5
Other	12.0	Broadband subs per 100 pop.	26.0
Hindu	5.2	Internet users, % of pop.	81.0

SLOVAKIA

Area, sq km	49,035	Capital	Bratislava
Arable as % of total land	28.8	Currency	Euro (€)

People

Population, m	5.4	Life expectancy: men	73.5 yrs
Pop. per sq km	110.1	women	80.4 yrs
Average annual growth		Adult literacy	...
in pop. 2015–20, %	0.0	Fertility rate (per woman)	1.5
Pop. aged 0–19, %	20.6	Urban population, %	53.8
Pop. aged 65 and over, %	14.1		per 1,000 pop.
No. of men per 100 women	94.6	Crude birth rate	10.3
Human Development Index	84.5	Crude death rate	10.1

The economy

GDP	$90bn	GDP per head	$16,631
GDP	€81bn	GDP per head in purchasing	
Av. ann. growth in real		power parity (USA=100)	54.6
GDP 2011–16	2.6%	Economic freedom index	65.3

Origins of GDP		Components of GDP	
	% of total		% of total
Agriculture	4	Private consumption	55
Industry, of which:	35	Public consumption	19
manufacturing	23	Investment	23
Services	62	Exports	95
		Imports	-91

Structure of employment

	% of total		% of labour force
Agriculture	2.9	Unemployed 2016	9.7
Industry	36.5	Av. ann. rate 2006–16	12.4
Services	60.6		

Energy

	m TOE		
Total output	6.1	Net energy imports as %	
Total consumption	17.4	of energy use	61
Consumption per head			
kg oil equivalent	3,004		

Inflation and finance

			% change 2016–17
Consumer price			
inflation 2017	1.3%	Monetary base	24.7
Av. ann. inflation 2012–17	0.4%	Broad money	4.1
Central bank policy rate, Dec. 2017	0.05%		

Exchange rates

	end 2017		December 2017
€ per $	0.83	Effective rates	2005 = 100
€ per sdr	1.20	– nominal	101.7
		– real	99.4

Trade

Principal exports		**Principal imports**	
	$bn fob		*$bn cif*
Machinery & transport equip.	47.0	Machinery & transport equip.	36.3
Chemicals & related products	3.5	Chemicals & related products	6.8
Food, drink & tobacco	2.7	Mineral fuels & lubricants	4.9
Mineral fuels & lubricants	2.5	Food, drink & tobacco	4.2
Total incl. others	**77.5**	Total incl. others	**73.5**

Main export destinations		**Main origins of imports**	
	% of total		*% of total*
Germany	21.9	Germany	20.7
Czech Republic	11.9	Czech Republic	17.4
Poland	7.7	Austria	10.0
France	6.2	Poland	6.7
EU28	85.5	EU28	80.2

Balance of payments, reserves and debt, $bn

Visible exports fob	74.3	Overall balance	-0.1
Visible imports fob	-72.5	Change in reserves	0.0
Trade balance	1.8	Level of reserves	
Invisibles inflows	11.7	end Dec.	2.9
Invisibles outflows	-13.3	No. months of import cover	0.4
Net transfers	-1.5	Official gold holdings, m oz	1.0
Current account balance	-1.3	Aid given	0.1
– as % of GDP	-1.4	– as % of GDP	0.1
Capital balance	2.1		

Health and education

Health spending, % of GDP	6.9	Education spending, % of GDP	4.6
Doctors per 1,000 pop.	3.5	Enrolment, %: primary	99
Hospital beds per 1,000 pop.	5.8	secondary	91
Improved-water source access,		tertiary	53
% of pop.	100		

Society

No. of households, m	1.8	Cost of living, Dec. 2017	
Av. no. per household	3.0	New York = 100	...
Marriages per 1,000 pop.	5.3	Cars per 1,000 pop.	377
Divorces per 1,000 pop.	1.8	Colour TV households, % with:	
Religion, % of pop.		cable	43.0
Christian	85.3	satellite	49.6
Non-religious	14.3	Telephone lines per 100 pop.	15.1
Muslim	0.2	Mobile telephone subscribers	
Other	0.1	per 100 pop.	128.4
Hindu	<0.1	Broadband subs per 100 pop.	24.5
Jewish	<0.1	Internet users, % of pop.	80.5

SLOVENIA

| Area, sq km | 20,273 | Capital | Ljubljana |
| Arable as % of total land | 9.1 | Currency | Euro (€) |

People

Population, m	2.1	Life expectancy: men	78.4 yrs
Pop. per sq km	103.6	women	83.9 yrs
Average annual growth		Adult literacy	...
in pop. 2015–20, %	0.1	Fertility rate (per woman)	1.6
Pop. aged 0–19, %	19.3	Urban population, %	54.0
Pop. aged 65 and over, %	18.0		per 1,000 pop.
No. of men per 100 women	98.5	Crude birth rate	10.0
Human Development Index	89.0	Crude death rate	9.9

The economy

GDP	$45bn	GDP per head	$21,299
GDP	€40bn	GDP per head in purchasing	
Av. ann. growth in real		power parity (USA=100)	54.8
GDP 2011–16	0.9%	Economic freedom index	64.8

Origins of GDP		**Components of GDP**	
	% of total		% of total
Agriculture	2	Private consumption	53
Industry, of which:	32	Public consumption	19
manufacturing	23	Investment	19
Services	66	Exports	78
		Imports	-68

Structure of employment

	% of total		% of labour force
Agriculture	5.0	Unemployed 2016	8.0
Industry	33.2	Av. ann. rate 2006–16	7.5
Services	61.8		

Energy

	m TOE		
Total output	3.1	Net energy imports as %	
Total consumption	6.6	of energy use	49
Consumption per head			
kg oil equivalent	3,175		

Inflation and finance

Consumer price			% change 2016–17
inflation 2017	1.4%	Monetary base	24.7
Av. ann. inflation 2012–17	0.6%	Broad money	4.1
Central bank policy rate, Dec. 2017	0.05%		

Exchange rates

	end 2017		December 2017
€ per $	0.83	Effective rates	2005 = 100
€ per sdr	1.20	– nominal	...
		– real	...

Trade

Principal exports	$bn fob	Principal imports	$bn cif
Machinery & transport equip.	12.8	Machinery & transport equip.	10.7
Manufactures	10.4	Manufactures	8.9
Chemicals	5.1	Chemicals	4.3
Miscellaneous manufactures	4.5	Mineral fuels & lubricants	2.3
Total incl. others	**32.9**	Total incl. others	**30.5**

Main export destinations	% of total	Main origins of imports	% of total
Germany	19.3	Germany	16.8
Italy	10.4	Italy	13.5
Austria	7.5	Austria	9.9
Croatia	7.3	Croatia	5.5
EU28	75.3	EU28	70.9

Balance of payments, reserves and debt, $bn

Visible exports fob	27.7	Overall balance	-0.1
Visible imports fob	-25.9	Change in reserves	-0.1
Trade balance	1.7	Level of reserves	
Invisibles inflows	8.7	end Dec.	0.7
Invisibles outflows	-7.7	No. months of import cover	0.3
Net transfers	-0.3	Official gold holdings, m oz	0.1
Current account balance	2.3	Aid given	0.08
– as % of GDP	5.2	– as % of GDP	0.2
Capital balance	-1.7		

Health and education

Health spending, % of GDP	8.5	Education spending, % of GDP	5.3
Doctors per 1,000 pop.	2.8	Enrolment, %: primary	99
Hospital beds per 1,000 pop.	4.5	secondary	110
Improved-water source access,		tertiary	80
% of pop.	99.5		

Society

No. of households, m	0.9	Cost of living, Dec. 2017	
Av. no. per household	2.3	New York = 100	...
Marriages per 1,000 pop.	3.2	Cars per 1,000 pop.	518
Divorces per 1,000 pop.	1.2	Colour TV households, % with:	
Religion, % of pop.		cable	70.7
Christian	78.4	satellite	9.1
Non-religious	18.0	Telephone lines per 100 pop.	35.2
Muslim	3.6	Mobile telephone subscribers	
Hindu	<0.1	per 100 pop.	114.8
Jewish	<0.1	Broadband subs per 100 pop.	28.3
Other	<0.1	Internet users, % of pop.	75.5

SOUTH AFRICA

Area, sq km	1,219,090	Capital	Pretoria
Arable as % of total land	10.3	Currency	Rand (R)

People

Population, m	56.0	Life expectancy: men	60.2 yrs
Pop. per sq km	45.9	women	67.3 yrs
Average annual growth		Adult literacy	94.4
in pop. 2015–20, %	1.2	Fertility rate (per woman)	2.4
Pop. aged 0–19, %	38.6	Urban population, %	65.3
Pop. aged 65 and over, %	5.1		per 1,000 pop.
No. of men per 100 women	96.5	Crude birth rate	20.5
Human Development Index	66.6	Crude death rate	9.5

The economy

GDP	$296bn	GDP per head	$5,280
GDP	R4,350bn	GDP per head in purchasing	
Av. ann. growth in real		power parity (USA=100)	22.9
GDP 2011–16	1.6%	Economic freedom index	63.0

Origins of GDP

	% of total
Agriculture	2
Industry, of which:	29
manufacturing	13
Services	69

Components of GDP

	% of total
Private consumption	60
Public consumption	21
Investment	19
Exports	30
Imports	-30

Structure of employment

	% of total		% of labour force
Agriculture	5.6	Unemployed 2016	26.6
Industry	23.3	Av. ann. rate 2006–16	24.2
Services	71.1		

Energy

	m TOE		
Total output	119.2	Net energy imports as %	
Total consumption	123.5	of energy use	-14
Consumption per head			
kg oil equivalent	2,696		

Inflation and finance

			% change 2016–17
Consumer price			
inflation 2017	5.3%	Monetary base	7.0
Av. ann. inflation 2012–17	5.6%	Broad money	6.4
Treasury bill rate, Nov. 2017	7.45%		

Exchange rates

	end 2017		December 2017
R per $	12.34	Effective rates	2005 = 100
R per sdr	18.75	– nominal	62.0
R per €	14.87	– real	80.7

Trade

Principal exports

	$bn fob
Mineral products	15.4
Precious metals	12.4
Vehicles, aircraft & vessels	10.1
Iron & steel products	9.1
Total incl. others	**76.4**

Principal imports

	$bn cif
Machinery & equipment	18.3
Mineral products	10.4
Chemicals	7.8
Vehicles, aircraft & vessels	7.4
Total incl. others	**75.1**

Main export destinations

	% of total
China	9.0
Germany	7.4
United States	7.2
Botswana	4.9

Main origins of imports

	% of total
China	19.2
Germany	12.5
United States	7.1
India	4.4

Balance of payments, reserves and debt, $bn

Visible exports fob	76.8	Change in reserves	1.3
Visible imports fob	-74.3	Level of reserves	
Trade balance	2.5	end Dec.	47.2
Invisibles inflows	20.4	No. months of import cover	5.5
Invisibles outflows	-29.1	Official gold holdings, m oz	4.0
Net transfers	-1.9	Foreign debt	146.0
Current account balance	-8.1	– as % of GDP	49.4
– as % of GDP	-2.7	– as % of total exports	151.7
Capital balance	11.7	Debt service ratio	13.1
Overall balance	2.9		

Health and education

Health spending, % of GDP	8.2	Education spending, % of GDP	5.9
Doctors per 1,000 pop.	0.8	Enrolment, %: primary	103
Hospital beds per 1,000 pop.	...	secondary	103
Improved-water source access,		tertiary	20
% of pop.	93.2		

Society

No. of households, m	15.3	Cost of living, Dec. 2017	
Av. no. per household	3.7	New York = 100	58
Marriages per 1,000 pop.	...	Cars per 1,000 pop.	114
Divorces per 1,000 pop.	...	Colour TV households, % with:	
Religion, % of pop.		cable	...
Christian	81.2	satellite	8.9
Non-religious	14.9	Telephone lines per 100 pop.	8.1
Muslim	1.7	Mobile telephone subscribers	
Hindu	1.1	per 100 pop.	147.1
Other	0.9	Broadband subs per 100 pop.	2.1
Jewish	0.1	Internet users, % of pop.	54.0

SOUTH KOREA

Area, sq km	100,280	Capital	Seoul
Arable as % of total land	15.0	Currency	Won (W)

People

Population, m	50.8	Life expectancy: men	79.3 yrs
Pop. per sq km	506.6	women	85.4 yrs
Average annual growth		Adult literacy	...
in pop. 2015–20, %	0.4	Fertility rate (per woman)	1.3
Pop. aged 0–19, %	20.2	Urban population, %	81.6
Pop. aged 65 and over, %	13.0		per 1,000 pop.
No. of men per 100 women	100.2	Crude birth rate	8.9
Human Development Index	90.1	Crude death rate	6.1

The economy

GDP	$1,411bn	GDP per head	$27,776
GDP	W1,637trn	GDP per head in purchasing	
Av. ann. growth in real		power parity (USA=100)	65.8
GDP 2011–16	2.8%	Economic freedom index	73.8

Origins of GDP

Components of GDP

	% of total		% of total
Agriculture	2	Private consumption	49
Industry, of which:	39	Public consumption	15
manufacturing	29	Investment	29
Services	59	Exports	42
		Imports	-35

Structure of employment

	% of total		% of labour force
Agriculture	4.9	Unemployed 2016	3.7
Industry	24.9	Av. ann. rate 2006–16	3.4
Services	70.2		

Energy

	m TOE		
Total output	42.2	Net energy imports as %	
Total consumption	287.5	of energy use	81
Consumption per head			
kg oil equivalent	5,413		

Inflation and finance

			% change 2016–17
Consumer price			
inflation 2017	1.9%	Monetary base	8.7
Av. ann. inflation 2012–17	1.2%	Broad money	5.1
Central bank policy rate, Dec. 2017	1.50%		

Exchange rates

	end 2017		December 2017
W per $	1,070.50	Effective rates	2005 = 100
W per sdr	1,536.78	– nominal	...
W per €	1,289.76	– real	...

Trade

Principal exports

	$bn fob
Machinery & transport equip.	278.0
Manufactured goods	63.5
Chemicals & related products	52.8
Miscellaneous manufactured articles	33.7
Total incl. others	**495.1**

Principal imports

	$bn cif
Machinery & transport equip.	132.0
Mineral fuels & lubricants	80.6
Manufactured goods	44.9
Chemicals & related products	40.3
Total incl. others	**405.8**

Main export destinations

	% of total
China	25.1
United States	13.5
Hong Kong	6.6
Vietnam	6.6

Main origins of imports

	% of total
China	21.4
Japan	11.7
United States	10.7
Germany	4.7

Balance of payments, reserves and debt, $bn

Visible exports fob	511.9	Change in reserves	3.4
Visible imports fob	-393.1	Level of reserves	
Trade balance	118.9	end Dec.	370.2
Invisibles inflows	120.3	No. months of import cover	8.4
Invisibles outflows	-134.2	Official gold holdings, m oz	3.4
Net transfers	-5.8	Foreign debt	358.7
Current account balance	99.2	– as % of GDP	25.4
– as % of GDP	7.0	– as % of total exports	56.7
Capital balance	-95.0	Debt service ratio	6.1
Overall balance	7.6		

Health and education

Health spending, % of GDP	7.4	Education spending, % of GDP	5.1
Doctors per 1,000 pop.	2.1	Enrolment, %: primary	98
Hospital beds per 1,000 pop.	11.5	secondary	100
Improved-water source access, % of pop.	97.6	tertiary	93

Society

No. of households, m	19.1	Cost of living, Dec. 2017	
Av. no. per household	2.7	New York = 100	106
Marriages per 1,000 pop.	5.5	Cars per 1,000 pop.	326
Divorces per 1,000 pop.	2.1	Colour TV households, % with:	
Religion, % of pop.		cable	81.8
Non-religious	46.4	satellite	13.5
Christian	29.4	Telephone lines per 100 pop.	55.2
Buddhist	22.9	Mobile telephone subscribers	
Other	1.0	per 100 pop.	120.7
Muslim	0.2	Broadband subs per 100 pop.	40.5
Jewish	<0.1	Internet users, % of pop.	92.8

SPAIN

| Area, sq km | 505,940 | Capital | Madrid |
| Arable as % of total land | 24.6 | Currency | Euro (€) |

People

Population, m	46.3	Life expectancy: men	80.6 yrs
Pop. per sq km	91.5	women	86.1 yrs
Average annual growth		Adult literacy	98.3
in pop. 2015–20, %	0.0	Fertility rate (per woman)	1.4
Pop. aged 0–19, %	19.4	Urban population, %	79.8
Pop. aged 65 and over, %	18.9		per 1,000 pop.
No. of men per 100 women	96.4	Crude birth rate	8.5
Human Development Index	88.4	Crude death rate	9.1

The economy

GDP	$1,238bn	GDP per head	$26,734
GDP	€1,119bn	GDP per head in purchasing	
Av. ann. growth in real		power parity (USA=100)	63.2
GDP 2011–16	0.7%	Economic freedom index	65.1

Origins of GDP		**Components of GDP**	
	% of total		% of total
Agriculture	3	Private consumption	58
Industry, of which:	23	Public consumption	19
manufacturing	14	Investment	20
Services	74	Exports	33
		Imports	-30

Structure of employment

	% of total		% of labour force
Agriculture	4.2	Unemployed 2016	19.6
Industry	19.6	Av. ann. rate 2006–16	18.6
Services	76.2		

Energy

	m TOE		
Total output	37.6	Net energy imports as %	
Total consumption	139.9	of energy use	71
Consumption per head			
kg oil equivalent	2,571		

Inflation and finance

Consumer price			% change 2016–17
inflation 2017	2.0%	Monetary base	24.7
Av. ann. inflation 2012–17	0.5%	Broad money	4.1
Treasury bill rate, Nov. 2017	-0.38%		

Exchange rates

	end 2017		December 2017
€ per $	0.83	Effective rates	2005 = 100
€ per sdr	1.20	– nominal	100.7
		– real	97.8

Trade

Principal exports

	$bn fob
Machinery & transport equip.	102.5
Food, drink & tobacco	44.3
Chemicals & related products	38.2
Mineral fuels & lubricants	15.3
Total incl. others	**283.8**

Principal imports

	$bn cif
Machinery & transport equip.	103.3
Chemicals & related products	45.6
Mineral fuels & lubricants	33.8
Food, drink & tobacco	32.1
Total incl. others	**303.0**

Main export destinations

	% of total
France	15.7
Germany	11.7
United Kingdom	8.1
Italy	7.9
EU28	66.8

Main origins of imports

	% of total
Germany	15.1
France	12.5
China	7.3
Italy	6.9
EU28	61.9

Balance of payments, reserves and aid, $bn

Visible exports fob	280.9	Overall balance	9.3
Visible imports fob	-300.2	Change in reserves	9.1
Trade balance	-19.2	Level of reserves	
Invisibles inflows	185.3	end Dec.	63.0
Invisibles outflows	-129.0	No. months of import cover	1.8
Net transfers	-13.3	Official gold holdings, m oz	9.1
Current account balance	23.8	Aid given	4.3
– as % of GDP	1.9	– as % of GDP	0.3
Capital balance	-17.2		

Health and education

Health spending, % of GDP	9.2	Education spending, % of GDP	4.3
Doctors per 1,000 pop.	3.9	Enrolment, %: primary	104
Hospital beds per 1,000 pop.	3.0	secondary	128
Improved-water source access,		tertiary	91
% of pop.	100		

Society

No. of households, m	18.4	Cost of living, Dec. 2017	
Av. no. per household	2.5	New York = 100	85
Marriages per 1,000 pop.	3.6	Cars per 1,000 pop.	483
Divorces per 1,000 pop.	2.1	Colour TV households, % with:	
Religion, % of pop.		cable	13.9
Christian	78.6	satellite	12.7
Non-religious	19.0	Telephone lines per 100 pop.	42.4
Muslim	2.1	Mobile telephone subscribers	
Jewish	0.1	per 100 pop.	111.2
Other	0.1	Broadband subs per 100 pop.	30.4
Hindu	<0.1	Internet users, % of pop.	80.6

SWEDEN

Area, sq km	447,420	Capital	Stockholm
Arable as % of total land	6.3	Currency	Swedish krona (Skr)

People

Population, m	9.8	Life expectancy: men	81.0 yrs
Pop. per sq km	21.9	women	84.4 yrs
Average annual growth		Adult literacy	...
in pop. 2015–20, %	0.7	Fertility rate (per woman)	1.9
Pop. aged 0–19, %	22.5	Urban population, %	86.9
Pop. aged 65 and over, %	19.6		per 1,000 pop.
No. of men per 100 women	99.9	Crude birth rate	12.3
Human Development Index	91.3	Crude death rate	9.1

The economy

GDP	$514bn	GDP per head	$52,496
GDP	Skr4,405bn	GDP per head in purchasing	
Av. ann. growth in real		power parity (USA=100)	88.2
GDP 2011–16	2.2%	Economic freedom index	76.3

Origins of GDP		Components of GDP	
	% of total		% of total
Agriculture	1	Private consumption	44
Industry, of which:	25	Public consumption	26
manufacturing	15	Investment	25
Services	74	Exports	44
		Imports	-39

Structure of employment

	% of total		% of labour force
Agriculture	1.9	Unemployed 2016	7.0
Industry	18.2	Av. ann. rate 2006–16	7.5
Services	79.9		

Energy

	m TOE		
Total output	38.1	Net energy imports as %	
Total consumption	54.3	of energy use	25
Consumption per head			
kg oil equivalent	5,103		

Inflation and finance

			% change 2016–17
Consumer price			
inflation 2017	1.9%	Monetary base	24.7
Av. ann. inflation 2012–17	0.9%	Broad money	4.1
Treasury bill rate, Mar. 2017	-0.63%		

Exchange rates

	end 2017		December 2017
			2005 = 100
Skr per $	8.21	Effective rates	
Skr per sdr	11.88	– nominal	97.5
Skr per €	9.89	– real	92.5

Trade

Principal exports

	$bn fob
Machinery & transport equip.	55.7
Chemicals & related products	17.4
Raw materials	8.7
Mineral fuels & lubricants	8.4
Total incl. others	**139.3**

Principal imports

	$bn cif
Machinery & transport equip.	55.3
Chemicals & related products	15.8
Food, drink & tobacco	15.8
Mineral fuels & lubricants	12.5
Total incl. others	**141.0**

Main export destinations

	% of total
Germany	10.6
Norway	10.4
United States	7.3
Denmark	7.0
EU28	59.2

Main origins of imports

	% of total
Germany	18.8
Netherlands	8.1
Norway	7.8
Denmark	7.6
EU28	71.2

Balance of payments, reserves and aid, $bn

Visible exports fob	152.2	Overall balance	4.4
Visible imports fob	-140.2	Change in reserves	1.3
Trade balance	12.0	Level of reserves	
Invisibles inflows	120.1	end Dec.	59.4
Invisibles outflows	-103.4	No. months of import cover	2.9
Net transfers	-6.9	Official gold holdings, m oz	4.0
Current account balance	21.7	Aid given	4.9
– as % of GDP	4.2	– as % of GDP	0.9
Capital balance	21.4		

Health and education

Health spending, % of GDP	11.0	Education spending, % of GDP	7.7
Doctors per 1,000 pop.	4.2	Enrolment, %: primary	123
Hospital beds per 1,000 pop.	2.4	secondary	140
Improved-water source access,		tertiary	62
% of pop.	100		

Society

No. of households, m	4.8	Cost of living, Dec. 2017	
Av. no. per household	2.0	New York = 100	84
Marriages per 1,000 pop.	5.5	Cars per 1,000 pop.	476
Divorces per 1,000 pop.	2.5	Colour TV households, % with:	
Religion, % of pop.		cable	57.5
Christian	67.2	satellite	20.1
Non-religious	27.0	Telephone lines per 100 pop.	31.6
Muslim	4.6	Mobile telephone subscribers	
Other	0.8	per 100 pop.	127.5
Hindu	0.2	Broadband subs per 100 pop.	37.4
Jewish	0.1	Internet users, % of pop.	89.7

SWITZERLAND

Area, sq km	41,285	Capital	Berne
Arable as % of total land	10.1	Currency	Swiss franc (SFr)

People

Population, m	8.4	Life expectancy: men	81.6 yrs
Pop. per sq km	203.5	women	85.4 yrs
Average annual growth		Adult literacy	...
in pop. 2015–20, %	0.8	Fertility rate (per woman)	1.6
Pop. aged 0–19, %	20.0	Urban population, %	73.7
Pop. aged 65 and over, %	18.0		per 1,000 pop.
No. of men per 100 women	98.0	Crude birth rate	10.4
Human Development Index	93.9	Crude death rate	8.0

The economy

GDP	$669bn	GDP per head	$79,613
GDP	SFr659bn	GDP per head in purchasing	
Av. ann. growth in real		power parity (USA=100)	103.5
GDP 2011–16	1.6%	Economic freedom index	81.7

Origins of GDP		**Components of GDP**	
	% of total		% of total
Agriculture	1	Private consumption	54
Industry, of which:	26	Public consumption	12
manufacturing	18	Investment	23
Services	74	Exports	66
		Imports	-55

Structure of employment

	% of total		% of labour force
Agriculture	3.4	Unemployed 2016	4.9
Industry	20.6	Av. ann. rate 2006–16	4.4
Services	76.0		

Energy

	m TOE		
Total output	15.6	Net energy imports as %	
Total consumption	30.5	of energy use	50
Consumption per head			
kg oil equivalent	2,960		

Inflation and finance

			% change 2016–17
Consumer price			
inflation 2017	0.5%	Monetary base	4.1
Av. ann. inflation 2012–17	-0.3%	Broad money	11.5
Treasury bill rate, Mar. 2017	-0.93%		

Exchange rates

	end 2017		December 2017
			2005 = 100
SFr per $	0.98	Effective rates	117.9
SFr per sdr	1.40	– nominal	117.9
SFr per €	1.18	– real	104.1

Trade

Principal exports

	$bn fob
Chemicals	95.7
Precision instruments, watches & jewellery	46.0
Machinery, equipment & electronics	31.5
Metals & metal manufactures	12.3
Total incl. others	**213.8**

Principal imports

	$bn cif
Chemicals	44.3
Machinery, equipment & electronics	29.1
Precision instruments, watches & jewellery	21.3
Motor vehicles	19.4
Total incl. others	**176.3**

Main export destinations

	% of total
Germany	20.4
United States	17.3
United Kingdom	15.3
China	12.8
EU28	48.4

Main origins of imports

	% of total
Germany	29.5
United States	13.6
Italy	11.2
United Kingdom	10.8
EU28	56.0

Balance of payments, reserves and aid, $bn

Visible exports fob	315.8	Overall balance	78.2
Visible imports fob	-266.3	Change in reserves	76.5
Trade balance	49.5	Level of reserves	
Invisibles inflows	262.0	end Dec.	678.9
Invisibles outflows	-238.2	No. months of import cover	16.1
Net transfers	-10.0	Official gold holdings, m oz	33.4
Current account balance	63.2	Aid given	3.6
– as % of GDP	9.5	– as % of GDP	0.5
Capital balance	5.6		

Health and education

Health spending, % of GDP	12.1	Education spending, % of GDP	5.1
Doctors per 1,000 pop.	4.2	Enrolment, %: primary	104
Hospital beds per 1,000 pop.	4.6	secondary	102
Improved-water source access, % of pop.	100	tertiary	58

Society

No. of households, m	3.7	Cost of living, Dec. 2017	
Av. no. per household	2.3	New York = 100	106
Marriages per 1,000 pop.	5.0	Cars per 1,000 pop.	536
Divorces per 1,000 pop.	...	Colour TV households, % with:	
Religion, % of pop.		cable	82.4
Christian	81.3	satellite	16.0
Non-religious	11.9	Telephone lines per 100 pop.	47.2
Muslim	5.5	Mobile telephone subscribers	
Other	0.6	per 100 pop.	133.8
Hindu	0.4	Broadband subs per 100 pop.	45.1
Jewish	0.3	Internet users, % of pop.	89.1

TAIWAN

Area, sq km	36,179	Capital	Taipei
Arable as % of total land	...	Currency	Taiwan dollar (T$)

People

Population, m	23.6	Life expectancy: men	77.5 yrs
Pop. per sq km	652.3	women	83.0 yrs
Average annual growth		Adult literacy	...
in pop. 2015–20, %	0.3	Fertility rate (per woman)	1.2
Pop. aged 0–19, %	20.2	Urban population, %	77.3
Pop. aged 65 and over, %	12.3		per 1,000 pop.
No. of men per 100 women	100.1	Crude birth rate	9.0
Human Development Index	...	Crude death rate	7.4

The economy

GDP	$531bn	GDP per head	$22,483
GDP	T$17,152bn	GDP per head in purchasing	
Av. ann. growth in real		power parity (USA=100)	83.0
GDP 2011–16	2.1%	Economic freedom index	76.6

Origins of GDP		Components of GDP	
	% of total		% of total
Agriculture	2	Private consumption	51
Industry, of which:	35	Public consumption	14
manufacturing	30	Investment	20
Services	63	Exports	61
		Imports	-49

Structure of employment

	% of total		% of labour force
Agriculture	...	Unemployed 2016	3.9
Industry	...	Av. ann. rate 2006–16	4.3
Services	...		
Energy			

Energy

	m TOE		
Total output	11.5	Net energy imports as %	
Total consumption	113.8	of energy use	...
Consumption per head			
kg oil equivalent	...		

Inflation and finance

			% change 2016–17
Consumer price			
inflation 2017	0.6%	Monetary base	...
Av. ann. inflation 2012–17	0.7%	Broad money	...
Treasury bill rate, Dec. 2017	...		

Exchange rates

	end 2017		December 2017
			2005 = 100
T$ per $	29.85	Effective rates	2005 = 100
T$ per sdr	42.43	– nominal	...
T$ per €	35.96	– real	...

Trade

Principal exports		Principal imports	
	$bn fob		*$bn cif*
Machinery & electrical equip.	154.2	Machinery & electrical equip.	92.0
Basic metals & articles	24.5	Minerals	35.0
Plastic & rubber articles	19.9	Chemicals & related products	25.0
Chemicals	17.2	Basic metals & articles	16.8
Total incl. others	**256.9**	Total incl. others	**229.8**

Main export destinations		Main origins of imports	
	% of total		*% of total*
China	28.8	China	19.1
Hong Kong	14.9	Japan	17.7
United States	13.1	United States	12.4
Japan	7.6	South Korea	6.4

Balance of payments, reserves and debt, $bn

Visible exports fob	310.4	Change in reserves	9.3
Visible imports fob	-239.7	Level of reserves	
Trade balance	70.6	end Dec.	449.8
Invisibles inflows	71.0	No. months of import cover	17.6
Invisibles outflows	-66.3	Official gold holdings, m oz	13.6
Net transfers	-3.1	Foreign debt	172.2
Current account balance	72.3	– as % of GDP	32.5
– as % of GDP	13.6	– as % of total exports	45.2
Capital balance	-54.6	Debt service ratio	2.8
Overall balance	10.7		

Health and education

Health spending, % of GDP	...	Education spending, % of GDP	...
Doctors per 1,000 pop.	...	Enrolment, %: primary	...
Hospital beds per 1,000 pop.	...	secondary	...
Improved-water source access,		tertiary	...
% of pop.	...		

Society

No. of households, m	7.8	Cost of living, Dec. 2017	
Av. no. per household	3.0	New York = 100	77
Marriages per 1,000 pop.	...	Cars per 1,000 pop.	279
Divorces per 1,000 pop.	...	Colour TV households, % with:	
Religion, % of pop.		cable	84.6
Other	60.5	satellite	0.4
Buddhist	21.3	Telephone lines per 100 pop.	58.5
Non-religious	12.7	Mobile telephone subscribers	
Christian	5.5	per 100 pop.	124.1
Hindu	<0.1	Broadband subs per 100 pop.	24.1
Jewish	<0.1	Internet users, % of pop.	79.7

THAILAND

Area, sq km	513,120	Capital	Bangkok
Arable as % of total land	32.9	Currency	Baht (Bt)

People

Population, m	68.9	Life expectancy: men	71.9 yrs
Pop. per sq km	134.3	women	79.3 yrs
Average annual growth		Adult literacy	92.9
in pop. 2015–20, %	0.2	Fertility rate (per woman)	1.5
Pop. aged 0–19, %	25.0	Urban population, %	48.4
Pop. aged 65 and over, %	10.6		per 1,000 pop.
No. of men per 100 women	95.4	Crude birth rate	10.0
Human Development Index	74.0	Crude death rate	8.1

The economy

GDP	$412bn	GDP per head	$5,977
GDP	Bt14,533bn	GDP per head in purchasing	
Av. ann. growth in real		power parity (USA=100)	29.3
GDP 2011–16	3.4%	Economic freedom index	67.1

Origins of GDP		Components of GDP	
	% of total		% of total
Agriculture	8	Private consumption	48
Industry, of which:	36	Public consumption	17
manufacturing	27	Investment	22
Services	56	Exports	69
		Imports	-54

Structure of employment

	% of total		% of labour force
Agriculture	33.3	Unemployed 2016	0.7
Industry	22.8	Av. ann. rate 2006–16	0.9
Services	44.0		

Energy

	m TOE		
Total output	65.1	Net energy imports as %	
Total consumption	127.9	of energy use	42
Consumption per head			
kg oil equivalent	1,970		

Inflation and finance

Consumer price			% change 2016–17
inflation 2017	0.7%	Monetary base	6.6
Av. ann. inflation 2012–17	0.8%	Broad money	5.1
Treasury bill rate, Dec. 2017	1.22%		

Exchange rates

	end 2017		December 2017
Bt per $	32.68	Effective rates	2005 = 100
Bt per sdr	46.23	– nominal	...
Bt per €	39.37	– real	...

Trade

Principal exports

	$bn fob
Machinery, equip. & supplies	96.5
Food	26.8
Manufactured goods	26.3
Chemicals	19.7
Total incl. others	**214.3**

Principal imports

	$bn cif
Machinery, equip. & supplies	76.2
Manufactured goods	34.4
Fuel & lubricants	24.1
Chemicals	21.5
Total incl. others	**195.2**

Main export destinations

	% of total
United States	11.4
China	11.0
Japan	9.5
Hong Kong	5.3

Main origins of imports

	% of total
China	21.6
Japan	15.8
United States	6.2
Malaysia	5.6

Balance of payments, reserves and debt, $bn

Visible exports fob	214.3	Change in reserves	15.3
Visible imports fob	-177.7	Level of reserves	
Trade balance	36.5	end Dec.	171.8
Invisibles inflows	74.1	No. months of import cover	8.3
Invisibles outflows	-69.2	Official gold holdings, m oz	4.9
Net transfers	6.8	Foreign debt	121.5
Current account balance	48.2	– as % of GDP	29.5
– as % of GDP	11.7	– as % of total exports	41.2
Capital balance	-21.0	Debt service ratio	4.9
Overall balance	12.8		

Health and education

Health spending, % of GDP	3.8	Education spending, % of GDP	4.1
Doctors per 1,000 pop.	0.5	Enrolment, %: primary	101
Hospital beds per 1,000 pop.	2.1	secondary	121
Improved-water source access,		tertiary	46
% of pop.	97.8		

Society

No. of households, m	22.5	Cost of living, Dec. 2017	
Av. no. per household	3.1	New York = 100	79
Marriages per 1,000 pop.	...	Cars per 1,000 pop.	119
Divorces per 1,000 pop.	...	Colour TV households, % with:	
Religion, % of pop.		cable	9.9
Buddhist	93.2	satellite	4.9
Muslim	5.5	Telephone lines per 100 pop.	6.8
Christian	0.9	Mobile telephone subscribers	
Non-religious	0.3	per 100 pop.	173.8
Hindu	0.1	Broadband subs per 100 pop.	10.5
Jewish	<0.1	Internet users, % of pop.	47.5

TURKEY

Area, sq km	785,350	Capital	Ankara
Arable as % of total land	26.8	Currency	Turkish Lira (TRY)

People

Population, m	79.5	Life expectancy: men	72.9 yrs
Pop. per sq km	101.2	women	79.3 yrs
Average annual growth		Adult literacy	95.6
in pop. 2015–20, %	1.4	Fertility rate (per woman)	2.0
Pop. aged 0–19, %	34.1	Urban population, %	74.1
Pop. aged 65 and over, %	7.8		per 1,000 pop.
No. of men per 100 women	96.8	Crude birth rate	15.8
Human Development Index	76.7	Crude death rate	5.8

The economy

GDP	$863bn	GDP per head	$10,860
GDP	YTL2,609bn	GDP per head in purchasing	
Av. ann. growth in real		power parity (USA=100)	43.4
GDP 2011–16	5.5%	Economic freedom index	65.4

Origins of GDP

	% of total
Agriculture	7
Industry, of which:	32
manufacturing	19
Services	61

Components of GDP

	% of total
Private consumption	60
Public consumption	15
Investment	28
Exports	22
Imports	-25

Structure of employment

	% of total		% of labour force
Agriculture	19.5	Unemployed 2016	10.8
Industry	26.8	Av. ann. rate 2006–16	9.7
Services	53.7		

Energy

	m TOE		
Total output	30.8	Net energy imports as %	
Total consumption	144.2	of energy use	75
Consumption per head			
kg oil equivalent	1,657		

Inflation and finance

			% change 2016–17
Consumer price			
inflation 2017	11.1%	Monetary base	12.2
Av. ann. inflation 2012–17	8.6%	Broad money	16.4
Central bank policy rate, Dec. 2017	7.25%		

Exchange rates

	end 2017		December 2017
YTL per $	3.78	Effective rates	2005 = 100
YTL per sdr	5.45	– nominal	...
YTL per €	4.55	– real	...

Trade

Principal exports		Principal imports	
	$bn fob		*$bn cif*
Agricultural products	26.0	Chemicals	29.0
Transport equipment	23.3	Fuels	27.2
Textiles & clothing	15.7	Mechanical equipment	20.9
Iron & steel	12.7	Transport equipment	20.6
Total incl. others	**142.5**	Total incl. others	**198.6**

Main export destinations		Main origins of imports	
	% of total		*% of total*
Germany	9.8	China	12.8
United Kingdom	8.2	Germany	10.8
Iraq	5.4	Russia	7.6
Italy	5.3	United States	5.5
EU28	47.9	EU28	39.0

Balance of payments, reserves and debt, $bn

Visible exports fob	150.2	Change in reserves	-4.5
Visible imports fob	-191.1	Level of reserves	
Trade balance	-40.9	end Dec.	105.9
Invisibles inflows	43.1	No. months of import cover	5.6
Invisibles outflows	-37.0	Official gold holdings, m oz	12.1
Net transfers	1.7	Foreign debt	405.0
Current account balance	-33.1	– as % of GDP	47.0
– as % of GDP	-3.8	– as % of total exports	208.7
Capital balance	23.0	Debt service ratio	32.8
Overall balance	0.8		

Health and education

Health spending, % of GDP	4.1	Education spending, % of GDP	4.4
Doctors per 1,000 pop.	1.7	Enrolment, %: primary	103
Hospital beds per 1,000 pop.	2.7	secondary	103
Improved-water source access,		tertiary	95
% of pop.	100		

Society

No. of households, m	22.4	Cost of living, Dec. 2017	
Av. no. per household	3.5	New York = 100	71
Marriages per 1,000 pop.	7.7	Cars per 1,000 pop.	133
Divorces per 1,000 pop.	1.7	Colour TV households, % with:	
Religion, % of pop.		cable	7.0
Muslim	98.0	satellite	51.0
Non-religious	1.2	Telephone lines per 100 pop.	13.9
Christian	0.4	Mobile telephone subscribers	
Other	0.3	per 100 pop.	94.4
Hindu	<0.1	Broadband subs per 100 pop.	13.2
Jewish	<0.1	Internet users, % of pop.	58.3

UKRAINE

Area, sq km	603,550	Capital	Kiev
Arable as % of total land	56.2	Currency	Hryvnya (UAH)

People

Population, m	44.4	Life expectancy: men	67.0 yrs
Pop. per sq km	73.6	women	76.9 yrs
Average annual growth		Adult literacy	100
in pop. 2015–20, %	-0.5	Fertility rate (per woman)	1.6
Pop. aged 0–19, %	19.8	Urban population, %	69.2
Pop. aged 65 and over, %	15.9		per 1,000 pop.
No. of men per 100 women	85.9	Crude birth rate	10.5
Human Development Index	74.3	Crude death rate	14.9

The economy

GDP	$93bn	GDP per head	$2,101
GDP	UAH2,383bn	GDP per head in purchasing	
Av. ann. growth in real		power parity (USA=100)	13.8
GDP 2011–16	-2.9%	Economic freedom index	51.9

Origins of GDP		**Components of GDP**	
	% of total		% of total
Agriculture	14	Private consumption	65
Industry, of which:	27	Public consumption	19
manufacturing	14	Investment	22
Services	59	Exports	49
		Imports	-56

Structure of employment

	% of total		% of labour force
Agriculture	15.0	Unemployed 2016	9.4
Industry	25.0	Av. ann. rate 2006–16	8.4
Services	60.0		

Energy

	m TOE		
Total output	58.8	Net energy imports as %	
Total consumption	86.7	of energy use	27
Consumption per head			
kg oil equivalent	2,334		

Inflation and finance

Consumer price			% change 2016–17
inflation 2017	14.4%	Monetary base	4.6
Av. ann. inflation 2012–17	16.7%	Broad money	9.6
Deposit rate, Dec. 2017	9.06%		

Exchange rates

	end 2017		December 2017
UAH per $	28.07	Effective rates	2005 = 100
UAH per sdr	38.94	– nominal	40.3
UAH per €	33.82	– real	75.4

Trade

Principal exports		**Principal imports**	
	$bn fob		*$bn cif*
Food & beverages	15.3	Machinery & equipment	10.8
Non-precious metals	8.3	Fuels	8.5
Machinery & equipment	4.2	Chemicals	5.6
Fuels	2.7	Food & beverages	3.9
Total incl. others	**36.4**	Total incl. others	**39.2**

Main export destinations		**Main origins of imports**	
	% of total		*% of total*
Russia	9.9	Russia	12.7
Egypt	6.2	China	11.6
Poland	6.0	Germany	10.7
Turkey	5.6	Belarus	7.1
EU28	34.1	EU28	40.9

Balance of payments, reserves and debt, $bn

Visible exports fob	33.6	Change in reserves	2.2
Visible imports fob	-40.5	Level of reserves	
Trade balance	-6.9	end Dec.	15.5
Invisibles inflows	19.3	No. months of import cover	3.2
Invisibles outflows	-17.4	Official gold holdings, m oz	0.8
Net transfers	3.6	Foreign debt	118.0
Current account balance	-1.3	– as % of GDP	126.5
– as % of GDP	-1.4	– as % of total exports	208.3
Capital balance	3.3	Debt service ratio	36.3
Overall balance	1.4		

Health and education

Health spending, % of GDP	6.1	Education spending, % of GDP	5.9
Doctors per 1,000 pop.	3.0	Enrolment, %: primary	100
Hospital beds per 1,000 pop.	8.8	secondary	97
Improved-water source access,		tertiary	83
% of pop.	96.2		

Society

No. of households, m	17.7	Cost of living, Dec. 2017	
Av. no. per household	2.5	New York = 100	55
Marriages per 1,000 pop.	7.0	Cars per 1,000 pop.	167
Divorces per 1,000 pop.	3.0	Colour TV households, % with:	
Religion, % of pop.		cable	23.2
Christian	83.8	satellite	15.5
Non-religious	14.7	Telephone lines per 100 pop.	20.1
Muslim	1.2	Mobile telephone subscribers	
Jewish	0.1	per 100 pop.	135.2
Other	0.1	Broadband subs per 100 pop.	12.2
Hindu	<0.1	Internet users, % of pop.	52.5

UNITED ARAB EMIRATES

Area, sq km	83,600	Capital	Abu Dhabi
Arable as % of total land	0.5	Currency	Dirham (AED)

People

Population, m	9.3	Life expectancy: men	76.8 yrs
Pop. per sq km	111.2	women	79.0 yrs
Average annual growth		Adult literacy	93.0
in pop. 2015–20, %	1.4	Fertility rate (per woman)	1.7
Pop. aged 0–19, %	17.4	Urban population, %	86.0
Pop. aged 65 and over, %	1.0		per 1,000 pop.
No. of men per 100 women	272.2	Crude birth rate	9.2
Human Development Index	84.0	Crude death rate	1.7

The economy

GDP	$349bn	GDP per head	$37,499
GDP	AED1,281bn	GDP per head in purchasing	
Av. ann. growth in real		power parity (USA=100)	124.8
GDP 2011–16	4.2%	Economic freedom index	77.6

Origins of GDP		**Components of GDP**	
	% of total		% of total
Agriculture	1	Private consumption	58
Industry, of which:	39	Public consumption	14
manufacturing	9	Investment	25
Services	40	Exports	104
		Imports	-101

Structure of employment

	% of total		% of labour force
Agriculture	0.2	Unemployed 2016	1.6
Industry	35.4	Av. ann. rate 2006–16	3.3
Services	64.4		

Energy

	m TOE		
Total output	243.8	Net energy imports as %	
Total consumption	111.2	of energy use	-184
Consumption per head			
kg oil equivalent	7,769		

Inflation and finance

			% change 2016–17
Consumer price			
inflation 2017	2.0%	Monetary base	11.6
Av. ann. inflation 2012–17	2.2%	Broad money	4.1
Treasury bill rate, Dec. 2017	...		

Exchange rates

	end 2017		December 2017
			2005 = 100
AED per $	3.67	Effective rates	2005 = 100
AED per sdr	5.20	– nominal	123.9
AED per €	4.42	– real	...

Trade

Principal exports		Principal imports	
	$bn fob		*$bn cif*
Re-exports	137.2	Precious stones & metals	53.0
Crude oil	25.2	Machinery & electrical equip.	39.4
Gas	6.0	Vehicles & other transport	
		equipment	29.7
		Base metals & related products	11.8
Total incl. others	**295.0**	Total incl. others	**266.5**

Main export destinations		Main origins of imports	
	% of total		*% of total*
India	9.8	China	8.3
Japan	8.8	United States	7.6
Switzerland	8.4	India	6.9
Iran	7.9	Germany	4.6

Balance of payments, reserves and debt, $bn

Visible exports fob	295.0	Change in reserves	-8.5
Visible imports fob	-226.5	Level of reserves	
Trade balance	68.4	end Dec.	85.4
Invisibles inflows	74.1	No. months of import cover	3.2
Invisibles outflows	-90.3	Official gold holdings, m oz	0.2
Net transfers	-39.1	Foreign debt	218.7
Current account balance	13.2	– as % of GDP	62.7
– as % of GDP	3.8	– as % of total exports	57.4
Capital balance	19.3	Debt service ratio	5.2
Overall balance	31.6		

Health and education

Health spending, % of GDP	3.5	Education spending, % of GDP	...
Doctors per 1,000 pop.	1.6	Enrolment, %: primary	111
Hospital beds per 1,000 pop.	1.2	secondary	96
Improved-water source access,		tertiary	37
% of pop.	99.6		

Society

No. of households, m	1.7	Cost of living, Dec. 2017	
Av. no. per household	5.5	New York = 100	73
Marriages per 1,000 pop.	...	Cars per 1,000 pop.	215
Divorces per 1,000 pop.	...	Colour TV households, % with:	
Religion, % of pop.		cable	1.0
Muslim	76.9	satellite	98.4
Christian	12.6	Telephone lines per 100 pop.	24.7
Hindu	6.6	Mobile telephone subscribers	
Other	2.8	per 100 pop.	214.7
Non-religious	1.1	Broadband subs per 100 pop.	14.0
Jewish	<0.1	Internet users, % of pop.	90.6

UNITED KINGDOM

Area, sq km	243,610	Capital	London
Arable as % of total land	24.8	Currency	Pound (£)

People

Population, m	65.8	Life expectancy: men	80.0 yrs
Pop. per sq km	270.1	women	83.5 yrs
Average annual growth		Adult literacy	...
in pop. 2015–20, %	0.6	Fertility rate (per woman)	1.9
Pop. aged 0–19, %	23.4	Urban population, %	82.9
Pop. aged 65 and over, %	18.1		per 1,000 pop.
No. of men per 100 women	97.2	Crude birth rate	12.1
Human Development Index	90.9	Crude death rate	9.0

The economy

GDP	$2,661bn	GDP per head	$40,436
GDP	£1,963bn	GDP per head in purchasing	
Av. ann. growth in real		power parity (USA=100)	73.9
GDP 2011–16	2.1%	Economic freedom index	78.0

Origins of GDP

	% of total
Agriculture	1
Industry, of which:	20
manufacturing	10
Services	79

Components of GDP

	% of total
Private consumption	66
Public consumption	19
Investment	17
Exports	28
Imports	-30

Structure of employment

	% of total		% of labour force
Agriculture	1.1	Unemployed 2016	4.8
Industry	18.5	Av. ann. rate 2006–16	6.5
Services	80.4		

Energy

	m TOE		
Total output	129.1	Net energy imports as %	
Total consumption	204.6	of energy use	35
Consumption per head			
kg oil equivalent	2,764		

Inflation and finance

			% change 2016–17
Consumer price			
inflation 2017	2.7%	Monetary base	4.1
Av. ann. inflation 2012–17	1.5%	Broad money	11.5
Money market rate, Nov. 2017	0.31%		

Exchange rates

	end 2017		December 2017
			2005 = 100
£ per $	0.74	Effective rates	96.6
£ per sdr	1.06	– nominal	96.6
£ per €	0.89	– real	100.8

Trade

Principal exports

	$bn fob
Machinery & transport equip.	161.6
Chemicals & related products	71.3
Food, drink & tobacco	27.4
Mineral fuels & lubricants	26.2
Total incl. others	**407.8**

Principal imports

	$bn cif
Machinery & transport equip.	233.8
Chemicals & related products	73.1
Food, drink & tobacco	56.6
Mineral fuels & lubricants	39.5
Total incl. others	**590.8**

Main export destinations

	% of total
United States	14.9
Germany	10.7
France	6.5
Netherlands	6.3
EU28	47.4

Main origins of imports

	% of total
Germany	14.7
China	10.0
United States	10.0
Netherlands	7.9
EU28	50.5

Balance of payments, reserves and aid, $bn

Visible exports fob	408.1	Overall balance	8.6
Visible imports fob	-591.0	Change in reserves	-13.2
Trade balance	-182.9	Level of reserves	
Invisibles inflows	527.0	end Dec.	134.9
Invisibles outflows	-468.5	No. months of import cover	1.5
Net transfers	-30.4	Official gold holdings, m oz	10.0
Current account balance	-154.9	Aid given	18.1
– as % of GDP	-5.8	– as % of GDP	0.7
Capital balance	152.8		

Health and education

Health spending, % of GDP	9.9	Education spending, % of GDP	5.6
Doctors per 1,000 pop.	2.8	Enrolment, %: primary	102
Hospital beds per 1,000 pop.	2.6	secondary	125
Improved-water source access,		tertiary	57
% of pop.	100		

Society

No. of households, m	28.6	Cost of living, Dec. 2017	
Av. no. per household	2.3	New York = 100	86
Marriages per 1,000 pop.	...	Cars per 1,000 pop.	510
Divorces per 1,000 pop.	1.9	Colour TV households, % with:	
Religion, % of pop.		cable	14.4
Christian	71.1	satellite	41.7
Non-religious	21.3	Telephone lines per 100 pop.	50.9
Muslim	4.4	Mobile telephone subscribers	
Other	1.4	per 100 pop.	120.0
Hindu	1.3	Broadband subs per 100 pop.	38.3
Jewish	0.5	Internet users, % of pop.	94.8

UNITED STATES

Area, sq km	9,831,510	Capital	Washington DC
Arable as % of total land	16.6	Currency	US dollar ($)

People

Population, m	322.2	Life expectancy: men	77.3 yrs
Pop. per sq km	32.8	women	81.9 yrs
Average annual growth		Adult literacy	...
in pop. 2015–20, %	0.7	Fertility rate (per woman)	1.9
Pop. aged 0–19, %	25.9	Urban population, %	81.9
Pop. aged 65 and over, %	14.6		per 1,000 pop.
No. of men per 100 women	97.9	Crude birth rate	12.7
Human Development Index	92.0	Crude death rate	8.4

The economy

GDP	$18,624bn	GDP per head	$57,804
GDP		GDP per head in purchasing	
Av. ann. growth in real		power parity (USA=100)	100
GDP 2011–16	2.2%	Economic freedom index	75.7

Origins of GDP

	% of total
Agriculture	1
Industry, of which:	19
manufacturing	12
Services	80

Components of GDP

	% of total
Private consumption	69
Public consumption	14
Investment	20
Exports	12
Imports	-15

Structure of employment

	% of total		% of labour force
Agriculture	1.7	Unemployed 2016	4.9
Industry	18.8	Av. ann. rate 2006–16	6.8
Services	79.5		

Energy

	m TOE		
Total output	2,106.7	Net energy imports as %	
Total consumption	2,342.7	of energy use	7
Consumption per head			
kg oil equivalent	6,801		

Inflation and finance

			% change 2016–17
Consumer price			
inflation 2017	2.1%	Monetary base	1.3
Av. ann. inflation 2012–17	1.3%	Broad money	10.7
Treasury bill rate, Dec. 2017	1.32%		

Exchange rates

	end 2017		December 2017
$ per sdr	1.42	Effective rates	2005 = 100
$ per €	1.20	– nominal	117.1
		– real	115.0

Trade

Principal exports

	$bn fob
Capital goods, excl. vehicles	519.6
Industrial supplies	396.4
Consumer goods, excl. vehicles	193.8
Vehicles & products	150.3
Total incl. others	**1,451.0**

Principal imports

	$bn fob
Capital goods, excl. vehicles	590.0
Consumer goods, excl. vehicles	583.6
Industrial supplies	443.3
Vehicles & products	350.1
Total incl. others	**2,187.8**

Main export destinations

	% of total
Canada	18.3
Mexico	15.9
China	8.0
Japan	4.4
EU28	18.7

Main origins of imports

	% of total
China	21.2
Mexico	13.4
Canada	12.7
Japan	6.0
EU28	18.9

Balance of payments, reserves and aid, $bn

Visible exports fob	1,455.7	Overall balance	2.1
Visible imports fob	-2,208.2	Change in reserves	22.2
Trade balance	-752.5	Level of reserves	
Invisibles inflows	1,566.3	end Dec.	405.9
Invisibles outflows	-1,145.4	No. months of import cover	1.5
Net transfers	-120.1	Official gold holdings, m oz	261.5
Current account balance	-451.7	Aid given	34.4
– as % of GDP	-2.4	– as % of GDP	0.2
Capital balance	379.7		

Health and education

Health spending, % of GDP	16.8	Education spending, % of GDP	5.0
Doctors per 1,000 pop.	2.6	Enrolment, %: primary	99
Hospital beds per 1,000 pop.	2.9	secondary	97
Improved-water source access,		tertiary	86
% of pop.	99.2		

Society

No. of households, m	124.5	Cost of living, Dec. 2017	
Av. no. per household	2.6	New York = 100	100
Marriages per 1,000 pop.	6.9	Cars per 1,000 pop.	380
Divorces per 1,000 pop.	2.5	Colour TV households, % with:	
Religion, % of pop.		cable	56.6
Christian	78.3	satellite	29.5
Non-religious	16.4	Telephone lines per 100 pop.	37.7
Other	2.0	Mobile telephone subscribers	
Jewish	1.8	per 100 pop.	122.9
Muslim	0.9	Broadband subs per 100 pop.	33.0
Hindu	0.6	Internet users, % of pop.	76.2

VENEZUELA

Area, sq km	912,050	Capital	Caracas
Arable as % of total land	3.1	Currency	Bolivar (Bs)

People

Population, m	31.6	Life expectancy: men	70.9 yrs
Pop. per sq km	34.6	women	79.0 yrs
Average annual growth		Adult literacy	97.1
in pop. 2015–20, %	1.3	Fertility rate (per woman)	2.3
Pop. aged 0–19, %	37.1	Urban population, %	88.2
Pop. aged 65 and over, %	6.3		per 1,000 pop.
No. of men per 100 women	99.2	Crude birth rate	18.6
Human Development Index	76.7	Crude death rate	5.7

The economy

GDP	$236bn	GDP per head	$7,472
GDP	Bs23,752bn	GDP per head in purchasing	
Av. ann. growth in real		power parity (USA=100)	23.8
GDP 2011-14	0.9%	Economic freedom index	25.2

Origins of GDP[a]		Components of GDP[a]	
	% of total		% of total
Agriculture	6	Private consumption	75
Industry, of which:	42	Public consumption	15
manufacturing	14	Investment	25
Services	53	Exports	17
		Imports	-31

Structure of employment

	% of total		% of labour force
Agriculture	9.8	Unemployed 2016	7.9
Industry	23.2	Av. ann. rate 2006–16	8.2
Services	66.9		

Energy

	m TOE		
Total output	191.2	Net energy imports as %	
Total consumption	76.8	of energy use	...
Consumption per head			
kg oil equivalent	...		

Inflation and finance

			% change 2016–17
Consumer price			
inflation 2017	1,087.5%	Monetary base	...
Av. ann. inflation 2012–17	188.9%	Broad money	...
Deposit rate, Mar. 2017	14.56%		

Exchange rates

	end 2017		December 2017
Bs per $	9.98	Effective rates	2005 = 100
Bs per sdr	14.12	– nominal	31.2
Bs per €	12.02	– real	...

Trade

Principal exports[b]		Principal imports[b]	
	$bn fob		$bn cif
Oil	85.6	Intermediate goods	25.9
non-oil	3.2	Capital goods	11.1
		Consumer goods	8.9
Total	**88.8**	Total incl. others	**49.4**

Main export destinations		Main origins of imports	
	% of total		% of total
United States	34.7	United States	32.5
India	17.0	China	21.1
China	13.9	Brazil	10.9
Netherlands Antilles	7.9	Colombia	8.8

Balance of payments, reserves and debt, $bn

Visible exports fob	27.4	Change in reserves	-5.5
Visible imports fob	-16.3	Level of reserves	
Trade balance	11.1	end Dec.	10.1
Invisibles inflows	1.9	No. months of import cover	3.7
Invisibles outflows	-17.0	Official gold holdings, m oz	6.0
Net transfers	0.2	Foreign debt	113.0
Current account balance	-3.9	– as % of GDP	20.0
– as % of GDP	-1.6	– as % of total exports	384.1
Capital balance	0.3	Debt service ratio	59.3
Overall balance	-6.3		

Health and education

Health spending, % of GDP	3.2	Education spending, % of GDP	...
Doctors per 1,000 pop.	...	Enrolment, %: primary	97
Hospital beds per 1,000 pop.	0.8	secondary	86
Improved-water source access,		tertiary	...
% of pop.	93.1		

Society

No. of households, m	7.9	Cost of living, Dec. 2017	
Av. no. per household	4.0	New York = 100	33
Marriages per 1,000 pop.	3.0	Cars per 1,000 pop.	114
Divorces per 1,000 pop.	...	Colour TV households, % with:	
Religion, % of pop.		cable	29.3
Christian	89.3	satellite	5.7
Non-religious	10.0	Telephone lines per 100 pop.	24.3
Muslim	0.3	Mobile telephone subscribers	
Other	0.3	per 100 pop.	87.4
Hindu	<0.1	Broadband subs per 100 pop.	8.3
Jewish	<0.1	Internet users, % of pop.	60.0

a 2014   b 2013

VIETNAM

Area, sq km	330,967	Capital	Hanoi
Arable as % of total land	22.6	Currency	Dong (D)

People

Population, m	94.6	Life expectancy: men	71.9 yrs
Pop. per sq km	285.8	women	81.1 yrs
Average annual growth		Adult literacy	94.5
in pop. 2015–20, %	1.0	Fertility rate (per woman)	2.0
Pop. aged 0–19, %	30.6	Urban population, %	34.5
Pop. aged 65 and over, %	6.7		per 1,000 pop.
No. of men per 100 women	97.9	Crude birth rate	16.2
Human Development Index	68.3	Crude death rate	5.8

The economy

GDP	$201bn	GDP per head	$2,128
GDP	D4,502trn	GDP per head in purchasing	
Av. ann. growth in real		power parity (USA=100)	10.9
GDP 2011–16	5.9%	Economic freedom index	53.1

Origins of GDP		Components of GDP	
	% of total		% of total
Agriculture	18	Private consumption	64
Industry, of which:	36	Public consumption	7
manufacturing	16	Investment	27
Services	45	Exports	94
		Imports	-91

Structure of employment

	% of total		% of labour force
Agriculture	41.9	Unemployed 2016	1.9
Industry	24.8	Av. ann. rate 2006–16	1.5
Services	33.4		

Energy

	m TOE		
Total output	58.1	Net energy imports as %	
Total consumption	61.5	of energy use	...
Consumption per head			
kg oil equivalent	...		

Inflation and finance

			% change 2016–17
Consumer price			
inflation 2017	3.5%	Monetary base	14.3
Av. ann. inflation 2012–17	3.5%	Broad money	14.9
Deposit rate, Oct. 2017	4.86%		

Exchange rates

	end 2017		December 2017
D per $	22,425.00	Effective rates	2005 = 100
D per sdr	31,752.07	– nominal	...
D per €	27,018.07	– real	...

Trade

Principal exports

	$bn fob
Telephones & mobile phones	34.3
Textiles & garments	23.8
Computers & electronic products	19.0
Footwear	13.0
Total incl. others	**176.6**

Principal imports

	$bn cif
Machinery & equipment	28.5
Electronics, computers & parts	28.1
Telephones & mobile phones	11.1
Textiles	10.6
Total incl. others	**175.0**

Main export destinations

	% of total
United States	21.9
China	12.5
Japan	8.4
South Korea	6.5

Main origins of imports

	% of total
China	27.0
South Korea	17.4
Japan	8.1
Taiwan	5.6

Balance of payments, reserves and debt, $bn

Visible exports fob	176.6	Change in reserves	8.3
Visible imports fob	-162.6	Level of reserves	
Trade balance	14.0	end Dec.	36.5
Invisibles inflows	12.8	No. months of import cover	2.3
Invisibles outflows	-26.6	Official gold holdings, m oz	0.0
Net transfers	8.0	Foreign debt	87.0
Current account balance	8.2	– as % of GDP	43.2
– as % of GDP	4.1	– as % of total exports	42.9
Capital balance	11.0	Debt service ratio	3.6
Overall balance	8.4		

Health and education

Health spending, % of GDP	5.7	Education spending, % of GDP	5.7
Doctors per 1,000 pop.	0.8	Enrolment, %: primary	110
Hospital beds per 1,000 pop.	2.6	secondary	...
Improved-water source access,		tertiary	28
% of pop.	97.6		

Society

No. of households, m	27.1	Cost of living, Dec. 2017	
Av. no. per household	3.5	New York = 100	72
Marriages per 1,000 pop.	...	Cars per 1,000 pop.	21
Divorces per 1,000 pop.	...	Colour TV households, % with:	
Religion, % of pop.		cable	17.8
Other	45.6	satellite	19.5
Non-religious	29.6	Telephone lines per 100 pop.	5.9
Buddhist	16.4	Mobile telephone subscribers	
Christian	8.2	per 100 pop.	127.5
Muslim	0.2	Broadband subs per 100 pop.	9.6
Jewish	<0.1	Internet users, % of pop.	46.5

ZIMBABWE

Area, sq km	390,757	Capital	Harare
Arable as % of total land	10.3	Currency	Zimbabwe dollar (Z$)

People

Population, m	16.2	Life expectancy: men	59.9 yrs
Pop. per sq km	41.5	women	63.8 yrs
Average annual growth		Adult literacy	88.7
in pop. 2015–20, %	2.3	Fertility rate (per woman)	3.6
Pop. aged 0–19, %	52.2	Urban population, %	32.3
Pop. aged 65 and over, %	2.8		per 1,000 pop.
No. of men per 100 women	94.8	Crude birth rate	31.7
Human Development Index	51.6	Crude death rate	7.8

The economy

GDP	$16bn	GDP per head	$995
GDP		GDP per head in purchasing	
Av. ann. growth in real		power parity (USA=100)	3.5
GDP 2011–16	4.8%	Economic freedom index	44.0

Origins of GDP

	% of total
Agriculture	11
Industry, of which:	23
manufacturing	10
Services	66

Components of GDP

	% of total
Private consumption	77
Public consumption	25
Investment	12
Exports	25
Imports	-39

Structure of employment

	% of total		% of labour force
Agriculture	67.4	Unemployed 2016	5.2
Industry	7.4	Av. ann. rate 2006–16	5.4
Services	25.2		

Energy

	m TOE		
Total output	3.7	Net energy imports as %	
Total consumption	4.1	of energy use	...
Consumption per head			
kg oil equivalent	...		

Inflation and finance

			% change 2016–17
Consumer price			
inflation 2017	1.3%	Monetary base	...
Av. ann. inflation 2012–17	-0.3%	Broad money	...
Treasury bill rate, Dec. 2017	...		

Exchange rates

	end 2017		December 2017
			2005 = 100
Z$ per $	...	Effective rates	
Z$ per SDR	...	– nominal	...
Z$ per €	...	– real	...

Trade

Principal exports[a]

	$bn fob
Gold	0.7
Platinum	0.7
Tobacco	0.6
Ferro-alloys	0.4
Total incl. others	**3.2**

Principal imports[a]

	$bn cif
Fuels & lubricants	0.4
Machinery & transport equip.	0.4
Manufactures	0.3
Chemicals	0.2
Total incl. others	**4.4**

Main export destinations

	% of total
South Africa	67.8
Mozambique	8.1
United Arab Emirates	3.5
Zambia	2.2

Main origins of imports

	% of total
South Africa	50.0
Zambia	25.7
Botswana	3.8
United States	3.3

Balance of payments, reserves and debt, $bn

Visible exports fob	3.7	Change in reserves	0.0
Visible imports fob	-5.2	Level of reserves	
Trade balance	-1.5	end Dec.	0.4
Invisibles inflows	0.6	No. months of import cover	0.7
Invisibles outflows	-1.7	Official gold holdings, m oz	0.0
Net transfers	2.0	Foreign debt	8.9
Current account balance	-0.6	– as % of GDP	53.5
– as % of GDP	-3.7	– as % of total exports	183.6
Capital balance	0.7	Debt service ratio	25.6
Overall balance	0.1		

Health and education

Health spending, % of GDP	10.3	Education spending, % of GDP	7.5
Doctors per 1,000 pop.	0.1	Enrolment, %: primary	99
Hospital beds per 1,000 pop.	1.7	secondary	47
Improved-water source access,		tertiary	8
% of pop.	76.9		

Society

No. of households, m	3.1	Cost of living, Dec. 2017	
Av. no. per household	5.2	New York = 100	...
Marriages per 1,000 pop.	...	Cars per 1,000 pop.	51
Divorces per 1,000 pop.	...	Colour TV households, % with:	
Religion, % of pop.		cable	...
Christian	87.0	satellite	...
Non-religious	7.9	Telephone lines per 100 pop.	1.9
Other	4.2	Mobile telephone subscribers	
Muslim	0.9	per 100 pop.	79.7
Hindu	<0.1	Broadband subs per 100 pop.	1.1
Jewish	<0.1	Internet users, % of pop.	23.1

a 2015

EURO AREA[a]

Area, sq km	2,759,052	Capital	–
Arable as % of total land	24.2	Currency	Euro (€)

People

Population, m	337.1	Life expectancy: men	79.6 yrs
Pop. per sq km	122.2	women	84.6 yrs
Average annual growth		Adult literacy	...
in pop. 2015–20, %	0.1	Fertility rate (per woman)	1.7
Pop. aged 0–19, %	20.3	Urban population, %	76.5
Pop. aged 65 and over, %	19.9		per 1,000 pop.
No. of men per 100 women	96.0	Crude birth rate	9.5
Human Development Index	89.7	Crude death rate	10.1

The economy

GDP	$12.6trn	GDP per head	$37,250
GDP	€11.1trn	GDP per head in purchasing	
Av. ann. growth in real		power parity (USA=100)	75.3
GDP 2011–16	0.8%	Economic freedom index	67.7

Origins of GDP

	% of total
Agriculture	2
Industry, of which:	25
manufacturing	17
Services	73

Components of GDP

	% of total
Private consumption	55
Public consumption	21
Investment	20
Exports	46
Imports	-41

Structure of employment

	% of total		% of labour force
Agriculture	3.2	Unemployed 2016	10.0
Industry	23.5	Av. ann. rate 2006–16	10.1
Services	73.3		

Energy

	m TOE		
Total output	434.8	Net energy imports as %	
Total consumption	1,236.7	of energy use	58
Consumption per head			
kg oil equivalent	3,329		

Inflation and finance

			% change 2016–17
Consumer price			
inflation 2017	1.5%	Monetary base	24.7
Av. ann. inflation 2012–17	0.7%	Broad money	4.1
Deposit rate, Oct. 2017	0.36%		

Exchange rates

	end 2017		December 2017
€ per $	0.83	Effective rates	2005 = 100
€ per SDR	1.20	– nominal	103.9
		– real	96.2

Trade[b]

Principal exports

	$bn fob
Machinery & transport equip.	673.4
Other manufactured goods	357.6
Chemicals & related products	283.2
Food, drink & tobacco	104.8
Mineral fuels & lubricants	67.7
Total incl. others	**1,577.2**

Principal imports

	$bn cif
Machinery & transport equip.	501.7
Other manufactured goods	406.9
Mineral fuels & lubricants	239.2
Chemicals & related products	167.5
Food, drink & tobacco	98.6
Total incl. others	**1,547.9**

Main export destinations

	% of total
United States	20.8
China	9.7
Switzerland	8.1
Turkey	4.5

Main origins of imports

	% of total
China	20.1
United States	14.6
Russia	6.9
Switzerland	7.1

Balance of payments, reserves and aid, $bn

Visible exports fob	2,356.5	Overall balance	25.7
Visible imports fob	-1,941.0	Change in reserves	40.2
Trade balance	415.6	Level of reserves	
Invisibles inflows	1,572.4	end Dec.	741.8
Invisibles outflows	-1,405.9	No. months of import cover	2.7
Net transfers	-153.3	Official gold holdings, m oz	346.8
Current account balance	428.8	Aid given	57.2
– as % of GDP	3.6	– as % of GDP	0.5
Capital balance	-356.7		

Health and education

Health spending, % of GDP	10.1	Education spending, % of GDP	5.3
Doctors per 1,000 pop.	3.9	Enrolment, %: primary	103
Hospital beds per 1,000 pop.	5.6	secondary	111
Improved-water source access,		tertiary	72
% of pop.	99.9		

Society

No. of households, m, m	149.3	Colour TV households, % with:	
Av. no. per household	2.3	cable	41.0
Marriages per 1,000 pop.	4.0	satellite	25.4
Divorces per 1,000 pop.	1.9	Telephone lines per 100 pop.	37.2
Cost of living, Dec. 2017		Mobile telephone subscribers	
New York = 100	...	per 100 pop.	126.8
Cars per 1,000 pop.	524	Broadband subs per 100 pop.	32.6
		Internet users, % of pop.	81.0

a Data generally refer to the 19 EU members that had adopted the euro as at December 31 2017: Austria, Belgium, Cyprus, Estonia, Finland, France, Germany, Greece, Ireland, Italy, Latvia, Lithuania, Luxembourg, Malta, Netherlands, Portugal, Slovakia, Slovenia and Spain.

b EU28, excluding intra-trade.

WORLD

Area, sq km	134,325,130	Capital	...
Arable as % of total land	11.0	Currency	...

People

Population, m	7,467.0	Life expectancy: men	69.7 yrs
Pop. per sq km	55.6	women	74.3 yrs
Average annual growth		Adult literacy	86.2
in pop. 2015–20	1.1	Fertility rate (per woman)	2.5
Pop. aged 0–19, %	34.2	Urban population, %	54.4
Pop. aged 65 and over, %	8.3		per 1,000 pop.
No. of men per 100 women	101.8	Crude birth rate	18.6
Human Development Index	71.7	Crude death rate	7.7

The economy

GDP	$79.8trn	GDP per head	$10,828
Av. ann. growth in real		GDP per head in purchasing	
GDP 2011–16	3.5%	power parity (USA=100)	29.8
		Economic freedom index	59.1

Origins of GDP

	% of total
Agriculture	4
Industry, of which:	27
manufacturing	17
Services	69

Components of GDP

	% of total
Private consumption	58
Public consumption	17
Investment	24
Exports	29
Imports	-28

Structure of employment

	% of total		% of labour force
Agriculture	26.8	Unemployed 2015	5.5
Industry	22.5	Av. ann. rate 2005–15	5.6
Services	50.7		

Energy

	m TOE		
Total output	13,629.0	Net energy imports as %	
Total consumption	13,508.5	of energy use	-2
Consumption per head			
kg oil equivalent	1,919		

Inflation and finance

			% change 2016–17
Consumer price			
inflation 2017	3.0%	Monetary base	8.3
Av. ann. inflation 2012–17	3.1%	Broad money	5.7
LIBOR $ rate, 3-month, Dec. 2016	1.69%		

Trade

World exports

	$bn fob		$bn fob
Manufactures	11,620	Ores & minerals	691
Food	1,527	Agricultural raw materials	241
Fuels	1,334		
		Total incl. others	**16,072**

Main export destinations

	% of total
United States	13.5
China	9.8
Germany	6.5
United Kingdom	3.9
Japan	3.8

Main origins of imports

	% of total
China	13.5
United States	9.2
Germany	8.4
Japan	4.1
Netherlands	3.6

Balance of payments, reserves and aid, $bn

Visible exports fob	15,619	Overall balance	...
Visible imports fob	-15,164	Change in reserves	-123
Trade balance	455	Level of reserves	
Invisibles inflows	8,497	end Dec.	12,279
Invisibles outflows	-8,456	No. months of import cover	6.2
Net transfers	-197	Official gold holdings, m oz	1,069
Current account balance	298	Aid given	...
– as % of GDP	0.4	– as % of GDP	...
Capital balance	...		

Health and education

Health spending, % of GDP	9.9	Education spending, % of GDP	4.7
Doctors per 1,000 pop.	1.5	Enrolment, %: primary	104
Hospital beds per 1,000 pop.	...	secondary	76
Improved-water source access, % of pop.	91.0	tertiary	37

Society

No. of households, m, m	2,012.2	Cost of living, Dec. 2017	
Av. no. per household	3.7	New York = 100	...
Marriages per 1,000 pop.	...	Cars per 1,000 pop.	129
Divorces per 1,000 pop.	...	Colour TV households, % with:	
Religion, % of pop.		cable	...
Christian	31.5	satellite	...
Muslim	23.2	Telephone lines per 100 pop.	18.1
Non-religious	16.3	Mobile telephone subscribers	
Hindu	15.0	per 100 pop.	106.9
Other	13.8	Broadband subs per 100 pop.	13.9
Jewish	0.2	Internet users, % of pop.	52.1

WORLD RANKINGS QUIZ

Test your knowledge with our new world rankings quiz. Answers can be found on the pages indicated.

Geography and demographics

1. Which country is the largest (by land area)?
   a Brazil **b** China **c** United States **d** Canada *page 12*

2. Which is the world's second-highest mountain?
   a Annapurna I **b** Lhotse **c** K2 (Godwin Austen) *page 13*

3. Which river is longest?
   a Mississippi-Missouri system **b** Amazon **c** Yangtze *page 13*

4. Which is the largest of the Great Lakes?
   a Huron **b** Michigan **c** Superior *page 13*

5. Which of these has the biggest population?
   a Ethiopia **b** Germany **c** Mexico **d** Vietnam *page 14*

6. Which country has the slowest-growing population?
   a Cuba **b** Japan **c** Latvia **d** Serbia *page 15*

7. The top ten countries with the highest rates of teenage births are all in Africa.
   a True **b** False *page 16*

8. Which country has the world's highest fertility rate?
   a Angola **b** Niger **c** South Sudan **d** Timor-Leste *page 17*

9. Greece has a higher percentage of over 65-year-olds than Germany.
   a True **b** False *page 18*

10. Hong Kong has the highest median age in Asia.
    a True **b** False *page 18*

11. Which city has the biggest population?
    a Istanbul **b** Manila **c** Paris **d** Rio de Janeiro *page 19*

12. In which city is the world's tallest building?
    a Chicago **b** Dubai **c** Mecca **d** New York *page 20*

13. Which of these has the biggest foreign-born population?
    a China **b** France **c** Thailand **d** United Kingdom *page 21*

13. Which of these countries has the most refugees?
    a France **b** Germany **c** Iran **d** United States *page 23*

Business and economics

1   Which country has the most equal distribution of
    household income, according to the Gini coefficient
    measure?
    a Ukraine **b** Slovenia **c** Slovakia **d** Canada   *page 28*

2   All of the fastest-growing economies over the past decade
    are in Asia.
    a True **b** False   *page 30*

3   Which country's economy shrank the most over the past
    decade?
    a Libya **b** Syria **c** South Sudan **d** Yemen   *page 30*

4   Which country had both the fastest economic growth and
    growth in services over the past decade?
    a China **b** Ethiopia **c** India **d** Vietnam   *page 31*

5   Which country is the biggest exporter?
    a Russia **b** South Korea **c** France
    d United Kingdom   *page 32*

6   Belgium is more dependent on trade than Taiwan.
    a True **b** False   *page 32*

7   Which country has the largest deficits?
    a France **b** Mexico **c** Australia **d** Argentina   *page 34*

8   Which country receives the highest level of remittances
    from workers in foreign countries?
    a Poland **b** India **c** Philippines **d** Mexico   *page 36*

9   The euro area's official reserves are larger than China's.
    a True **b** False   *page 36*

10 Which country has the most gold reserves?
    a Japan **b** India **c** Germany **d** China   *page 36*

11 Mongolia has the world's highest foreign-debt burden as a
    percentage of GDP.
    a True **b** False   *page 40*

12 Which country has the most foreign debt?
    a Argentina **b** Mexico **c** Poland **d** Turkey   *page 40*

13 Afghanistan gets more foreign aid per person than any
    other country in Asia.
    a True **b** False   *page 42*

14 Which of these donates the most amount of foreign aid?
    a France **b** Italy **c** Japan **d** Saudi Arabia   *page 43*

15 Ethiopia had the highest growth in industrial output
    between 2006 and 2016.
    a True **b** False   *page 44*

16 Which country has the largest services output?
    a China **b** Sweden **c** Japan **d** Brazil   *page 45*

17 Which country depends most on agriculture?
    a Mali **b** Liberia **c** Sierra Leone **d** Kenya   *page 46*

18 Which country produces most tea?
    a Kenya **b** Japan **c** Turkey **d** Myanmar   *page 49*

19 Japan uses more copper than Germany.
    a True **b** False   *page 50*

20 Which country produces the most silver?
    a Peru **b** China **c** Russia **d** Mexico   *page 51*

21 Which country uses most energy?
    a Mexico **b** USA **c** Japan **d** China   *page 54*

22 Hong Kong is the most energy efficient country.
    a True **b** False   *page 54*

23 Which country has the highest rate of unemployment?
    a Spain **b** Namibia **c** Kosovo **d** Lesotho   *page 57*

24 Italy has a lower rate of youth unemployment than Spain.
    a True **b** False   *page 57*

25 Which country has the lowest minimum wage?
    a Ireland **b** France **c** Slovenia **d** United States   *page 58*

26 Longer hours are worked on average in Malaysia than
    Myanmar.
    a True **b** False   *page 58*

Politics and society

1 Education spending is lower in Monaco than Cambodia.
  a True **b** False
  page 69

2 Which country has the highest marriage rate?
  a Afghanistan **b** Kazakhstan **c** Tajikistan
  d Uzbekistan
  page 70

3 Which country has the lowest marriage rate?
  a Iceland **b** Kuwait **c** Netherlands **d** Qatar *page 70*

4 Which country has the highest divorce rate?
  a Cuba **b** Denmark **c** Lithuania **d** Iran *page 71*

5 What is the mean age of marriage in South Sudan?
  a 13.2 **b** 14.6 **c** 15.4 **d** 16.5 *page 71*

6 Which country has the lowest number of households?
  a Thailand **b** Argentina **c** Ethiopia **d** Taiwan *page 72*

7 It costs more to live in Australia than New Zealand.
  a True **b** False
  page 73

8 Which country gives most generously?
  a Singapore **b** United States **c** Kenya **d** Sri Lanka *page 73*

9 Which country has the longest roads relative to its land
  area?
  a Macau **b** Belgium **c** Japan **d** Bahrain *page 74*

10 The most congested city is:
  a London **b** Moscow **c** Paris **d** Mexico City *page 75*

11 Which country has the lowest car ownership?
  a Pakistan **b** Cameroon **c** Ivory Coast **d** Cuba *page 76*

12 Which airport is the busiest?
  a Beijing **b** Amsterdam **c** Atlanta **d** JFK, New York *page 78*

13 Germany has a bigger merchant fleet than the United
  States.
  a True **b** False
  page 80

14 Which country spends most on defence as a percentage
  of GDP?
  a Saudi Arabia **b** Oman **c** Iraq
  page 82

Health and welfare

1 Which of these countries has the highest male life expectancy?
   a Japan **b** Sweden **c** Hong Kong **d** France *page 90*

2 Which country has the lowest life expectancy for women?
   a Nigeria **b** Chad **c** Niger **d** Sierra Leone *page 91*

3 Which country has the highest infant mortality rate?
   a Angola **b** Burundi **c** Chad **d** Mali *page 93*

4 Diabetes prevalence is highest in which country?
   a French Polynesia **b** Kuwait **c** Mauritius **d** Fiji *page 94*

5 Which country has the highest incidence of cardiovascular disease?
   a Serbia **b** Georgia **c** Latvia **d** Ukraine *page 94*

6 Which country has the highest rate of cancer?
   a Italy **b** United Kingdom **c** Estonia **d** Pakistan *page 94*

7 Measles immunisation is lowest in which country?
   a Iraq **b** Mali **c** Angola **d** Ukraine *page 95*

8 AIDS deaths are highest in which country?
   a Botswana **b** Lesotho **c** South Africa
   d Swaziland *page 95*

9 Health spending is lower in South Sudan than in Sri Lanka.
   a True **b** False *page 96*

10 Obesity is highest in which country?
   a Kuwait **b** Qatar **c** Fiji **d** Egypt *page 97*

11 Which country has the greatest food deficit?
   a Haiti **b** North Korea **c** Zimbabwe **d** Ethiopia *page 97*

12 Germany has more landline telephones per person than France.
   a True **b** False *page 98*

Culture and entertainment

1   Which country publishes the most new books per person?
    a China **b** France **c** Japan **e** Italy   *page 100*

2   More people visit the cinema in France than in Russia.
    a True **b** False   *page 101*

3   Which country has the most expensive cinema tickets?
    a Denmark **b** Hong Kong **c** Qatar **d** Switzerland   *page 101*

4   Which country has the most press freedoms?
    a Iceland **b** Ireland **c** New Zealand **d** Norway   *page 102*

5   Which of these has imprisoned the most journalists?
    a China **b** Egypt **c** Iran **d** Turkey   *page 102*

6   Which country has produced the most Nobel prize winners?
    a Canada **b** Russia **c** Sweden **d** France   *page 103*

7   Tennis's Davis Cup has been won most often by:
    a Germany **b** Argentina **c** France **d** Sweden   *page 104*

8   Which country has won the most gold medals at Winter Olympics?
    a United States **b** China **c** Canada **d** Norway   *page 105*

9   More beer is drunk in Germany per person than in any other country.
    a True **b** False   *page 106*

10 Where do people smoke the most per day?
    a Belarus **b** Bulgaria **c** Lebanon **d** Russia   *page 106*

11 Which of these lost the most on gambling?
    a Australia **b** Canada **c** France **d** Germany   *page 106*

12 Americans are bigger tourist spenders than the Chinese.
    a True **b** False   *page 107*

Glossary

Balance of payments The record of a country's transactions with the rest of the world. The **current account** of the balance of payments consists of: visible trade (goods); "invisible" trade (services and income); private transfer payments (eg, remittances from those working abroad); official transfers (eg, payments to international organisations, famine relief). Visible imports and exports are normally compiled on rather different definitions to those used in the trade statistics (shown in principal imports and exports) and therefore the statistics do not match. The **capital account** consists of long- and short-term transactions relating to a country's assets and liabilities (eg, loans and borrowings). The **current and capital accounts**, plus an errors and omissions item, make up the **overall balance**. **Changes in reserves** include gold at market prices and are shown without the practice often followed in balance of payments presentations of reversing the sign.

Big Mac index A light-hearted way of looking at exchange rates. If the dollar price of a burger at McDonald's in any country is higher than the price in the United States, converting at market exchange rates, then that country's currency could be thought to be over-valued against the dollar and vice versa.

Body-mass index A measure for assessing obesity – weight in kilograms divided by height in metres squared. An index of 30 or more is regarded as an indicator of obesity; 25 to 29.9 as over-weight. Guidelines vary for men and for women and may be adjusted for age.

CFA Communauté Financière Africaine. Its members, most of the francophone African nations, share a common currency, the CFA franc, pegged to the euro.

Cif/fob Measures of the value of merchandise trade. Imports include the cost of "carriage, insurance and freight" (cif) from the exporting country to the importing. The value of exports does not include these elements and is recorded "free on board" (fob). Balance of payments statistics are generally adjusted so that both exports and imports are shown fob; the cif elements are included in invisibles.

CIS is the Commonwealth of Independent States, including Georgia, Turkmenistan and Ukraine.

Crude birth rate The number of live births in a year per 1,000 population. The crude rate will automatically be relatively high if a large proportion of the population is of childbearing age.

Crude death rate The number of deaths in a year per 1,000 population. Also affected by the population's age structure.

Debt, foreign Financial obligations owed by a country to the rest of the world and repayable in foreign currency. The **debt service ratio** is debt service (principal repayments plus interest payments) expressed as a percentage of the country's earnings from exports of goods and services.

Debt, household All liabilities that require payment of interest or principal in the future.

Economic Freedom Index The ranking includes data on labour and business freedom as well as trade policy, taxation, monetary policy, the banking system, foreign-investment rules, property rights, government spending, regulation policy, the level of corruption and the extent of wage and price controls.

Effective exchange rate The nominal index measures a currency's depreciation (figures below 100) or appreciation (figures over 100) from a base date against a trade-weighted basket of the currencies of the country's main trading partners. The real effective exchange rate reflects adjustments for relative movements in prices or costs.

EU European Union. Members are: Austria, Belgium, Bulgaria, Croatia, Cyprus, Czech Republic, Denmark, Estonia, Finland, France, Germany, Greece, Hungary, Ireland, Italy, Latvia, Lithuania, Luxembourg, Malta, Netherlands, Poland,

Portugal, Romania, Slovakia, Slovenia, Spain, Sweden and the United Kingdom.

Euro area The 19 euro area members of the EU are Austria, Belgium, Cyprus, Estonia, Finland, France, Germany, Greece, Ireland, Italy, Latvia, Lithuania, Luxembourg, Malta, Netherlands, Portugal, Slovakia, Slovenia and Spain. Their common currency is the euro.

Fertility rate The average number of children born to a woman who completes her childbearing years.

G7 Group of seven countries: United States, Japan, Germany, United Kingdom, France, Italy and Canada.

GDP Gross domestic product. The sum of all output produced by economic activity within a country. GNP (gross national product) and GNI (gross national income) include net income from abroad, eg, rent, profits.

Import cover The number of months of imports covered by reserves, ie, reserves ÷ $\frac{1}{12}$ annual imports (visibles and invisibles).

Inflation The annual rate at which prices are increasing. The most common measure and the one shown here is the increase in the consumer price index.

Life expectancy The average length of time a baby born today can expect to live.

Literacy is defined by UNESCO as the ability to read and write a simple sentence, but definitions can vary from country to country.

Median age Divides the age distribution into two halves. Half of the population is above and half below the median age.

Money supply A measure of the "money" available to buy goods and services. Various definitions exist. The measures shown here are based on definitions used by the IMF and may differ from measures used nationally. Narrow money (M1) consists of cash in circulation and demand deposits (bank deposits that can be withdrawn on demand). "Quasi-money" (time, savings and foreign currency

deposits) is added to this to create broad money.

OECD Organisation for Economic Co-operation and Development. The "rich countries" club was established in 1961 to promote economic growth and the expansion of world trade. It is based in Paris and now has 35 members from July 1st 2016, when Latvia joined.

Official reserves The stock of gold and foreign currency held by a country to finance any calls that may be made for the settlement of foreign debt.

Opec Set up in 1960 and based in Vienna, Opec is mainly concerned with oil pricing and production issues. The current members (2017) are: Algeria, Angola, Ecuador, Equatorial Guinea, Gabon, Iran, Iraq, Kuwait, Libya, Nigeria, Qatar, Saudi Arabia, United Arab Emirates and Venezuela.

PPP Purchasing power parity. PPP statistics adjust for cost of living differences by replacing normal exchange rates with rates designed to equalise the prices of a standard "basket" of goods and services. These are used to obtain PPP estimates of GDP per head. PPP estimates are shown on an index, taking the United States as 100.

Real terms Figures adjusted to exclude the effect of inflation.

SDR Special drawing right. The reserve currency, introduced by the IMF in 1970, was intended to replace gold and national currencies in settling international transactions. The IMF uses SDRs for book-keeping purposes and issues them to member countries. Their value is based on a basket of the US dollar (with a weight of 41.73%), the euro (30.93%), the Chinese renminbi (10.92%), the Japanese yen (8.33%), and the pound sterling (8.09%).

List of countries

	Population	GDP	GDP per head	Area	Median age
	m, 2016	$bn, 2016	$PPP, 2016	'000 sq km	yrs, 2016
Afghanistan	34.7	19.5	1,921	653	17.6
Albania	2.9	11.9	11,723	29	36.6
Algeria	40.6	159.0	15,015	2,382	27.8
Andorra	0.08	2.9	33,270	0.5	42.0
Angola	28.8	95.3	6,444	1,247	16.5
Argentina	43.8	554.1	20,064	2,780	31.0
Armenia	2.9	10.6	8,913	30	34.3
Australia	24.1	1,264.9	49,678	7,741	37.5
Austria	8.7	391.0	48,233	84	43.4
Azerbaijan	9.7	37.8	17,388	87	30.7
Bahamas	0.4	11.3	28,113	14	32.9
Bahrain	1.4	32.2	47,913	1	31.4
Bangladesh	163.0	235.6	3,865	148	26.0
Barbados	0.3	4.8	17,020	0.4	38.8
Belarus	9.5	47.7	18,070	208	39.7
Belgium	11.4	468.1	44,772	31	41.4
Benin	10.9	8.6	2,162	115	18.3
Bermuda	0.06	6.1	34,084	0.1	42.0
Bolivia	10.9	34.1	7,226	1,099	24.4
Bosnia & Herz.	3.5	16.9	12,195	51	41.3
Botswana	2.3	15.7	16,244	582	24.7
Brazil	207.7	1,793.1	15,177	8,516	31.7
Brunei	0.4	11.4	81,910	6	30.5
Bulgaria	7.1	53.2	20,459	111	43.7
Burkina Faso	18.6	11.3	1,775	274	17.1
Burundi	10.5	3.1	748	28	17.6
Cambodia	15.8	20.2	3,735	181	24.3
Cameroon	23.4	32.2	3,615	475	18.4
Canada	36.3	1,535.8	46,484	9,985	40.7
Central African Rep.	4.6	1.8	692	623	17.9
Chad	14.5	10.1	1,997	1,284	16.2
Channel Islands	0.2	9.0	46785ᵃ	0.2	43.0
Chile	17.9	250.0	24,397	756	34.0
China	1,403.5	11,221.8	15,169	9,563	37.3
Colombia	48.7	280.0	14,152	1,142	30.4
Congo-Brazzaville	5.1	7.8	5,830	342	18.8
Congo-Kinshasa	78.7	39.3	826	2,345	16.8
Costa Rica	4.9	57.8	16,289	51	31.8
Croatia	4.2	51.4	23,062	57	42.9
Cuba	11.5	89.7	11,557	110	41.5
Cyprus	1.2	20.1	24,898	9	35.4
Czech Republic	10.6	195.3	33,383	79	41.8
Denmark	5.7	306.9	48,400	43	41.7
Dominican Rep.	10.6	71.7	15,275	49	26.4
Ecuador	16.4	98.6	11,232	256	26.9
Egypt	95.7	332.5	11,829	1,001	24.8
El Salvador	6.3	26.8	8,678	21	26.2

	Population	GDP	GDP per head	Area 'ooo sq	Median age
	m, 2016	$bn, 2016	$PPP, 2016	km	yrs, 2016
Equatorial Guinea	1.2	10.2	25,986	28	22.2
Eritrea	5.0	5.0	1,755	118	19.0
Estonia	1.3	23.3	29,953	45	41.8
Ethiopia	102.4	73.2	1,732	1,104	18.8
Fiji	0.9	4.7	9,098	18	27.8
Finland	5.5	238.8	42,310	338	42.6
France	64.7	2,466.5	42,274[b]	549	41.4
French Guiana	0.3	5.0	16,667[a]	84	24.7
French Polynesia	0.3	5.4	18,300	4	31.3
Gabon	2.0	14.0	17,889	268	22.7
Gambia, The	2.0	1.0	1,709	11	17.1
Georgia	3.9	14.3	9,541	70	38.1
Germany	81.9	3,479.2	48,799	357	46.0
Ghana	28.2	42.8	4,296	239	20.5
Greece	11.2	192.8	25,847	132	43.7
Guadeloupe	0.4	12.0	27,515[a]	2	41.9
Guam	0.2	5.8	24,410	1	30.4
Guatemala	16.6	68.8	7,936	109	21.6
Guinea	12.4	8.5	1,966	246	18.5
Guinea-Bissau	1.8	1.2	1,623	36	19.0
Guyana	0.8	3.5	7,560	215	24.9
Haiti	10.8	8.2	1,792	28	23.3
Honduras	9.1	21.6	4,759	112	23.4
Hong Kong	7.3	320.9	58,961	1	43.5
Hungary	9.8	129.1	27,856	93	42.0
Iceland	0.3	20.3	55,680	103	36.3
India	1,324.2	2,273.6	6,574	3,287	27.0
Indonesia	261.1	932.4	11,612	1,911	28.3
Iran	80.3	404.4	19,294	1,745	30.1
Iraq	37.2	171.7	17,536	435	19.5
Ireland	4.7	304.5	69,242	70	37.3
Israel	8.2	317.7	36,695	22	30.3
Italy	59.4	1,860.2	37,663	301	46.3
Ivory Coast	23.7	36.4	3,727	322	18.4
Jamaica	2.9	14.0	8,744	11	29.8
Japan	127.7	4,949.3	41,058	378	46.7
Jordan	9.5	38.7	9,006	89	22.3
Kazakhstan	18.0	133.7	25,065	2,725	29.6
Kenya	48.5	70.5	3,153	580	19.2
Kosovo	1.9	6.0	3,158[a]	11	27.3
Kuwait	4.1	110.9	71,649	18	33.5
Kyrgyzstan	6.0	6.6	3,599	200	25.5
Laos	6.8	15.9	6,654	237	23.0
Latvia	2.0	27.6	25,326	64	42.8
Lebanon	6.0	49.6	14,184	10	29.0
Lesotho	2.2	2.4	3,013	30	21.5
Liberia	4.6	3.3	1,271	111	18.7

	Population	GDP	GDP per head	Area	Median age
	m, 2016	$bn, 2016	$PPP, 2016	'000 sq km	yrs, 2016
Libya	6.3	18.5	5,879	1,760	27.6
Liechtenstein	0.04	6.2	165,933	0.2	41.3
Lithuania	2.9	42.8	29,768	65	42.9
Luxembourg	0.6	58.7	99,190	3	39.4
Macau	0.6	45.3	107,558	0	37.9
Macedonia	2.1	10.8	14,481	26	37.7
Madagascar	24.9	10.0	1,506	587	18.9
Malawi	18.1	5.5	1,168	118	17.5
Malaysia	31.2	296.5	27,671	331	28.1
Maldives	0.4	4.5	19,131	0.3	28.4
Mali	18.0	14.0	2,125	1,240	16.1
Malta	0.4	11.3	44,490	0.3	41.2
Martinique	0.4	12.0	28,770[a]	1	44.1
Mauritania	4.3	4.8	3,818	1,031	19.8
Mauritius	1.3	12.2	19,970	2	36.0
Mexico	127.5	1,076.9	18,562	1,964	27.9
Moldova	4.1	6.8	4,625	34	36.0
Monaco	0.04	6.5	191,800	0	51.0
Mongolia	3.0	11.1	12,364	1,564	27.4
Montenegro	0.6	4.4	17,362	14	38.0
Morocco	35.3	103.6	7,972	447	28.2
Mozambique	28.8	11.3	1,217	799	17.3
Myanmar	52.9	63.3	5,720	677	28.0
Namibia	2.5	10.9	10,539	824	21.2
Nepal	29.0	21.1	2,476	147	23.6
Netherlands	17.0	777.5	51,339	42	42.3
New Caledonia	0.3	9.4	35,900	19	32.9
New Zealand	4.7	185.4	38,258	268	37.4
Nicaragua	6.1	13.2	5,585	130	25.6
Niger	20.7	7.5	985	1,267	14.9
Nigeria	186.0	405.4	5,861	924	17.9
North Korea	25.4	16.8	1,575	121	34.3
Norway	5.3	371.1	69,177	385	39.3
Oman	4.4	66.8	41,776	310	29.3
Pakistan	193.2	278.9	5,105	796	22.7
Panama	4.0	57.8	24,217	75	28.7
Papua New Guinea	8.1	22.6	3,590	463	21.9
Paraguay	6.7	27.4	9,603	407	25.2
Peru	31.8	195.4	12,789	1,285	27.8
Philippines	103.3	304.9	7,806	300	24.3
Poland	38.2	471.2	27,572	313	40.1
Portugal	10.4	205.3	28,834	92	44.4
Puerto Rico	3.7	105.0	34,796	9	36.8
Qatar	2.6	152.5	126,009	12	31.4
Réunion	0.9	22.0	24,444[a]	3	34.8
Romania	19.8	187.8	22,324	238	41.6
Russia	144.0	1,281.3	26,924	17,098	38.9

	Population	GDP	GDP per head	Area	Median age
	m, 2016	$bn, 2016	$PPP, 2016	'000 sq km	yrs, 2016
Rwanda	11.9	8.5	1,916	26	19.6
Saudi Arabia	32.3	644.9	54,338	2,150	30.2
Senegal	15.4	14.7	2,574	197	18.4
Serbia	8.8	38.3	11,562	88	40.2
Sierra Leone	7.4	3.8	1,475	72	18.5
Singapore	5.6	309.8	89,219	1	40.5
Slovakia	5.4	89.8	31,556	49	39.6
Slovenia	2.1	44.7	31,666	20	43.3
Somalia	14.3	6.2	1,222	638	16.6
South Africa	56.0	295.7	13,254	1,219	26.3
South Korea	50.8	1,411.0	38,062	100	41.3
South Sudan	12.2	3.1	1,697	644	18.7
Spain	46.3	1,237.8	36,522	506	43.7
Sri Lanka	20.8	81.0	12,583	66	32.7
Sudan	39.6	57.6	4,496	1,879	19.1
Suriname	0.6	3.3	13,928	164	28.6
Swaziland	1.3	3.8	8,548	17	20.6
Sweden	9.8	514.5	50,992	447	40.9
Switzerland	8.4	668.7	59,841	41	42.4
Syria	18.4	22.2	2,733	185	20.5
Taiwan	23.6	530.6	48,005	36	40.1
Tajikistan	8.7	7.0	2,991	141	22.6
Tanzania	55.6	47.7	2,703	947	17.4
Thailand	68.9	411.8	16,929	513	38.3
Timor-Leste	1.3	2.5	5,582	15	17.5
Togo	7.6	4.5	1,603	57	19.0
Trinidad & Tobago	1.4	22.3	30,975	5	34.3
Tunisia	11.4	42.1	11,451	164	31.4
Turkey	79.5	863.4	25,085	785	30.2
Turkmenistan	5.7	36.2	16,752	488	25.9
Uganda	41.5	25.3	2,009	242	15.9
Ukraine	44.4	93.3	7,958	604	40.5
United Arab Emirates	9.3	348.7	72,163	84	33.5
United Kingdom	65.8	2,660.7	42,740	244	40.3
United States	322.2	18,624.5	57,804	9,832	37.7
Uruguay	3.4	52.4	21,899	176	35.0
Uzbekistan	31.4	66.7	6,612	447	26.7
Venezuela	31.6	236.1	13,763	912	27.7
Vietnam	94.6	201.3	6,294	331	30.8
Virgin Islands (US)	0.1	4.0	37,920	0	41.4
West Bank & Gaza	4.8	13.0	2,708[a]	6	19.5
Yemen	27.6	20.9	1,594	528	19.4
Zambia	16.6	20.9	3,935	753	17.2
Zimbabwe	16.2	16.1	1,999	391	19.1
Euro area (19)	337.1	12,608.0	43,547	2,759	43.9
World	7,467.0	79,865.0	17,225	134,325	29.9

a Latest available year.
b Including French Guiana, Guadeloupe, Martinique and Réunion.

Sources

AFM Research

Airports Council International, *Worldwide Airport Traffic Report*

Bank of East Asia

Bloomberg

BP, *Statistical Review of World Energy*

CAF, *The World Giving Index*

CBRE, *Global Prime Office Occupancy Costs*

Central banks

Central Intelligence Agency, *The World Factbook*

Company reports

Cornell University

Council of Tall Buildings and Urban Habitat

Credit Suisse

The Economist, www.economist.com

Economist Intelligence Unit, *Cost of Living Survey; Country Forecasts; Country Reports; Liveability Index*

Encyclopaedia Britannica

Euromonitor International

Eurostat, *Statistics in Focus*

FIFA

Finance ministries

Food and Agriculture Organisation

Global Democracy Ranking

Global Entrepreneurship Monitor

Global Internal Displacement Database

Global Terrorism Database, University of Maryland

Government statistics

H2 Gambling Capital

The Heritage Foundation, *Index of Economic Freedom*

Holman Fenwick Willan

IFPI

IMD, *World Competitiveness Yearbook*

IMF, *International Financial Statistics; World Economic Outlook*

INRIX

INSEAD

Institute for Criminal Policy Research

International Civil Aviation Organisation

International Cocoa Organisation, *Quarterly Bulletin of Cocoa Statistics*

International Coffee Organisation

International Cotton Advisory Committee, *March Bulletin*

International Cricket Council

International Diabetes Federation, *Diabetes Atlas*

International Grains Council

International Institute for Strategic Studies, *Military Balance*

International Labour Organisation

International Olympic Committee

International Organisation of Motor Vehicle Manufacturers

International Publishers Association

International Rubber Study Group, *Rubber Statistical Bulletin*

International Sugar Organisation, *Statistical Bulletin*

International Telecommunication Union, *ITU Indicators*

International Union of Railways

Inter-Parliamentary Union

Johnson Matthey

McDonald's

National Institute of Statistics and Economic Studies
National statistics offices
Nobel Foundation

OECD, *Development Assistance Committee Report; Economic Outlook; Government at a Glance; OECD.Stat; Revenue Statistics*

Pew Research Centre, *The Global Religious Landscape*
Population Reference Bureau
Progressive Media

Reporters Without Borders, *Press Freedom Index*

Sovereign Wealth Fund Institute
Stockholm International Peace Research Institute
Swiss Re

Taiwan Statistical Data Book
The Times, *Atlas of the World*
Thomson Reuters

UN, *Demographic Yearbook; National Accounts; State of World Population Report; World Fertility Report*
UNAIDS
UNCTAD, *Review of Maritime Transport; World Investment Report*
UNCTAD/WTO International Trade Centre
UN Development Programme, *Human Development Report*

UNESCO Institute for Statistics
UN High Commissioner for Refugees
UN Office on Drugs and Crime
UN, Population Division
US Department of Agriculture
US Energy Information Administration
US Federal Aviation Administration

Visionofhumanity.org

WHO, *Global Health Observatory; Global Immunisation Data; World Health Statistics*
World Anti-Doping Agency
World Bank, *Doing Business; Global Development Finance; Migration and Remittances Data; World Development Indicators; World Development Report*
World Bureau of Metal Statistics, *World Metal Statistics*
World Economic Forum, *Global Competitiveness Report*
World Federation of Exchanges
World Health Organisation
World Intellectual Property Organization
World Tourism Organisation, *Yearbook of Tourism Statistics*
World Trade Organisation, *Annual Report*

Yale University

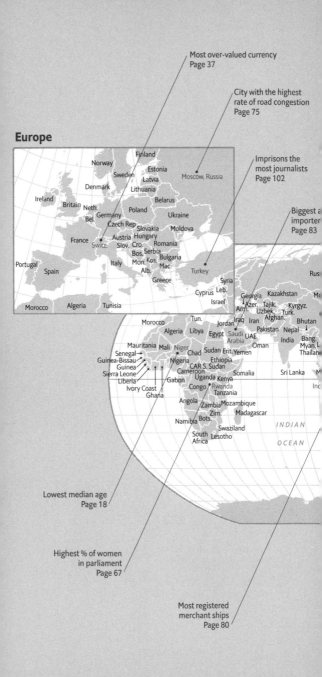

Most over-valued currency
Page 37

City with the highest
rate of road congestion
Page 75

Europe

Imprisons the
most journalists
Page 102

Biggest a
importer
Page 83

Moscow, Russia

Finland
Norway
Sweden
Estonia
Latvia
Denmark
Lithuania
Ireland
Britain
Neth.
Belarus
Bel
Germany
Poland
Czech Rep
Ukraine
Austria
Slovakia
Moldova
France
Switz.
Hungary
Slov.
Cro.
Romania
Italy
Bos.
Serbia
Bulgaria
Mon. Kos.
Portugal
Spain
Alb.
Mac.
Greece
Turkey
Cyprus
Leb.
Israel
Syria

Morocco
Algeria
Tunisia

Georgia
Kazakhstan
Mo
Arm.
Azer.
Tajik.
Kyrgyz.
Uzbek.
Turk.
Afghan.
Morocco
Tun.
Jordan
Iraq
Iran
Pakistan
Nepal
Bhutan
Algeria
Libya
Egypt
Saudi
UAE
India
Bang
Arabia
Oman
Myan.
Mauritania
Mali
Niger
Chad
Sudan
Erit.
Yemen
Thailan
Senegal
Guinea-Bissau
Nigeria
Ethiopia
Guinea
CAR
S. Sudan
Cameroon
Somalia
Sri Lanka
Sierra Leone
Gabon
Uganda
Kenya
Liberia
Congo
Rwanda
Ivory Coast
Tanzania
Inc
Ghana
Angola
Zambia
Mozambique
Zim.
Madagascar
Namibia
Bots.
INDIAN
Swaziland
South
Lesotho
OCEAN
Africa

Rus

Lowest median age
Page 18

Highest % of women
in parliament
Page 67

Most registered
merchant ships
Page 80